POWER ON THE PRECIPICE

POWER ON THE PRECIPICE

The Six Choices America Faces in a Turbulent World

ANDREW IMBRIE

Yale

UNIVERSITY PRESS

New Haven and London

Published with assistance from the foundation established in memory of Calvin Chapin of the Class of 1788, Yale College.

Yale University Press books may be purchased in quantity for educational, business, or promotional use. For information, please e-mail sales.press@yale.edu (U.S. office) or sales@yaleup.co.uk (U.K. office).

Set in Janson type by IDS Infotech Ltd., Chandigarh, India.
Printed in the United States of America.

Library of Congress Control Number: 2020935014
ISBN 978-0-300-24350-5 (hardcover : alk. paper)

A catalogue record for this book is available from the British Library.

This paper meets the requirements of ANSI/NISO Z39.48-1992 (Permanence of Paper).

10 9 8 7 6 5 4 3 2 1

To my family,

L'essentiel est invisible pour les yeux.

—Antoine de Saint-Exupéry, *The Little Prince*

Those who can will not and those who will cannot.

—MARTÍN GONZÁLEZ DE CELLORIGO, Spanish economist and reformer of the sixteenth and seventeenth centuries

At what point then is the approach of danger to be expected? I answer, if it ever reach us, it must spring up amongst us. It cannot come from abroad. If destruction be our lot, we must ourselves be its author and finisher. As a nation of freemen, we must live through all time, or die by suicide.

—ABRAHAM LINCOLN, "The Perpetuation of Our Political Institutions," Address Before the Young Men's Lyceum of Springfield, Illinois, January 27, 1838

Contents

Acknowledgments

THE PHILOSOPHER MARTIN BUBER wrote, "All real living is meeting." This book has benefited enormously from meetings over the years with teachers, colleagues, students, friends, and loved ones. I am grateful to each and owe special thanks to all.

I begin by thanking my teachers. David Edelstein encouraged me to take up this topic when I was a graduate student at Georgetown University. David approaches great power politics with a theorist's gift for clarity and a historian's eye for detail. I am grateful for his years of mentorship and for always pushing me to question my assumptions. Andy Bennett is a scholar's scholar of qualitative methods and a brilliant theorist of international relations. Charlie Kupchan combines terrific policy insight with prodigious scholarly output. I admired his work long before I profited from his advice as a student.

One of the great blessings of serving in the United States Senate and the US Department of State is the chance to work with extraordinarily talented colleagues who've made public service their lifework. I will always be grateful to Secretary John Kerry for the opportunity to benefit from his knowledge and experience. I'll never forget walking into his office in the Russell Senate Office Building for the first time and seeing a picture of him with John Lennon at an anti–Vietnam War rally in the 1970s. Before I could ask about the photograph, he put his big arm around me and said, "You look just like your Dad!" We talked at length about everything from the latest polls to our shared love of Cicero. I was hooked. Thank you, JK. And thanks to my entire Senate family on the Foreign Relations Committee.

As the son of a US Foreign Service officer, I grew up with a special reverence for the State Department. The acronyms seemed forbidding from the outside, but after nearly four years on the inside I became intimately familiar with OBE, FYSA, PC, "The Line," P, D, and S. More than the nomenclature of foreign policy, I am grateful for the opportunity to have taken a master class from America's diplomatic all-star team. It goes without saying that the opinions and characterizations in this book are those of the author and do not necessarily represent those of the US government.

Writing your way around the world as a speechwriter for a secretary of state makes you appreciate the gift of good colleagues even more. In particular, I am grateful to the small team of writers who encouraged, inspired, and challenged me to do my best work. Thanks to Ariana Berengaut, Matan Chorev, Steph Epner, Chris Haugh, Steve Krupin, Shana Mansbach, Jonny Powell, and Bill Woodward. I am also grateful to Jon Finer, David McKean, David Wade, and Secretary Kerry's intellectually formidable, yet always approachable policy planners. I could not have done my job or learned half as much as I did without their guidance, friendship, and support.

After leaving the State Department, I found a remarkable home at the Carnegie Endowment for International Peace. Carnegie stands out not only for the breadth and depth of its analysis but also for the global perspective it brings to bear on major policy issues. In particular, I want to thank Ambassador William J. Burns and Carnegie's management team, including Tom Carothers, Matan Chorev, Liz Dibble, and Jen Psaki. Secretary Kerry and his team at Carnegie offered critical support and encouragement as I finished this book. Special thanks to Steph, Matt Summers, David Wade, and Julie Wirkkala—for everything.

I am grateful for the insights and feedback I received on this book during a research-in-progress workshop at Carnegie and from colleagues at Carnegie, Georgetown University, and other institutions who provided excellent feedback on this project at various stages, including Salman Ahmed, Alexander Bick, Jarrett Blanc, Erik

Brattberg, Ben Buchanan, Perry Cammack, John Campbell, Maureen Campbell, Charles Edel, Steve Feldstein, Yukon Huang, David Livingston, Tim Maurer, Larry Meyer, Moisés Naím, Kimberly G. Olson, Scott Olson, James Schwemlein, F. Shannon Sweeney, Varun Sivaram, Ashley Tellis, and Milan Vaishnav. Special thanks to Len Hawley, a wonderful friend and mentor who read the manuscript with great care and offered tremendously helpful suggestions.

My deep appreciation to Dan Berschinski, Nicholas Burns, Sarah Chayes, Robert Gallucci, John Kerry, and Arati Prabhakar for letting me tell their powerful stories. Many thanks to the Carnegie librarians Kathleen Higgs and Lisa Lindle for their expert assistance in tracking down research materials and to Carnegie's creative director, Jocelyn Soly, for producing the excellent graphics.

I am grateful to my brilliant editor at Yale University Press, Jaya Chatterjee, for believing in this project from the start and for her thoughtful, incisive feedback. I also want to thank the anonymous reviewers of my manuscript for their valuable comments. Special thanks to Eva Skewes, Jeffrey Schier, Lawrence Kenney, and the design and production teams at Yale for bringing this book to fruition. I could not imagine a more creative or talented agent than Bridget Matzie. Many will say that she's a rising star in the literary world. By my lights, she's already in the firmament. Thanks to Fred Wehrey for the kind introduction to her.

For several years now I've had the good fortune of teaching foreign policy speech writing and rhetoric to graduate and undergraduate students at Georgetown and American Universities. To my students: your willingness to see all sides of the issues, disagree agreeably, and reach for the common ground gives me hope for the next generation. Thank you for indulging my fondness of Mr. Rogers and Abraham Lincoln and for teaching me so much about the craft I love.

In the process of completing this book I got married to the love of my life. The English poet John Donne wrote that love "makes one little room an everywhere." Teresa, you are my intellectual partner, my rock, my everywhere. Thank you for your endless faith in me and in this book.

Finally, I want to thank my family. Mom, Dad, Chris, Patty—you enrich my life beyond measure. I could not imagine undertaking a project of this scope without your abiding love, intellectual nourishment, and tender care. We've moved from place to place, but no matter where we go, you are my home. IPOY. This book is dedicated to you.

POWER ON THE PRECIPICE

Introduction

"I F YOU REALLY WANT to know what's going on in another country, make sure you look at it not only through your own lens, but through the lens of the people who live there." When John Kerry said those words to me during his final year as US secretary of state I made a point of writing them down. My reality was the always fascinating and sometimes frenetic task of shaping his words into speeches. Traveling the globe with Secretary Kerry taught me to pay attention to the stories of others. Above all, I learned to respect a fundamental truth about diplomacy. Seeing an issue from different perspectives may not seem like an urgent task for a secretary of state, but rare is the foreign policy problem that can be solved without it. As I reflect on my time in government, I have come to appreciate how relevant that lesson is, not only for Americans seeking to understand a changing world but also for the world seeking to understand a changing America. The Cold War debate over America's decline was about two superpowers locked in a global struggle, from waging proxy wars in Central America, the Middle East, and Asia to being the first to put a man on the moon. When the Berlin Wall fell in 1989, US money and might were unrivaled. Now the geopolitical picture has changed. America's decline today is about one superpower at war with itself, even as other states are rising and gaining in stature.

The list of challenges facing America is long and growing. Rivals seek to outmaneuver it abroad amid troubling signs at home. Bitter partisanship and legislative gridlock prevent the United States from governing effectively or adapting its institutions to changing political, security, and economic conditions. Widening income inequality and stagnant wages, declining social mobility and life expectancy, racial tensions, and environmental stress are creating new fissures and dampening optimism about the future. On top of these problems, innovation in America is stalling thanks to diminishing investments in education and basic research, crumbling infrastructure, and the diversion of federal dollars from productive areas to interest payments on the growing national debt and a looming entitlements crisis.

Arrayed against these internal weaknesses are some enduring strengths. US capital markets are deep and flexible, undergirding its continued leadership of the global financial system. America's commitment to political and economic freedom still inspires immigrants to flock to its shores. The United States enjoys abundant energy resources, a large, youthful population, world-class colleges and universities, and a superior military and defense industrial base. Despite slowing federal investments in basic research, its capacity for scientific inquiry and technological innovation is unique among great powers. America maintains a privileged position in the world, but even the most optimistic analysts concede that the foundations of US power are not as sturdy as they once were.

This is a book about bolstering American leadership in an era of turbulence abroad and deepening polarization at home. It is a book about choices, the tough policy trade-offs that US political leaders need to make to reinvigorate American money, might, and clout. In the conventional telling, the United States is either destined for continued dominance or doomed to irreversible decline. The reality is that it must adapt to the changing global dynamics in new ways and compete more wisely.

Hardly a decade has gone by in US politics when the public mood is not swept by the fear that America may be in decline. The soothsayers of yesterday are often proved wrong tomorrow, rendering linear projections based on the recent past a tempting yet tangled proposition. So what's different this time? Is the United States in terminal decline? Can it recover? These are the questions that this book seeks to answer.

To begin, I argue that US power and influence are in decline and that the causes of this decline are structural as much as they are contingent on any particular US administration or set of policies. Recent books on the future of American power offer important and timely perspectives on different aspects of this question.[1] What's missing is a narrative account of US decline that brings together the broad policy choices confronting American leadership with a framework for navigating the trade-offs among them. The challenges facing the United States are many, but the waning of American power and influence underlies them all. If there is a central theme of this book, it is that policy makers and analysts need to focus squarely on America's decline and the major policy choices that will define its course in a turbulent world.

Just as we cannot ignore the profound shifts in US power and influence, so we cannot fully understand America's prospects by focusing on rising rivals or the warning signs at home.[2] Scholars and practitioners need to integrate two levels of analysis: US domestic political gridlock and polarization coupled with its loss of international standing and competitiveness. Economic resources matter, but the wise and effective use of those resources matters even more. Partisan politics and institutional decay can frustrate the conversion of resources into global influence. That is why this book draws on the concepts of relative and absolute decline from international relations theory as a way to bridge the two analytical perspectives, namely, America's declining power and influence in the world and its increasingly dysfunctional political, economic, and social institutions.[3]

By emphasizing the connections between the domestic and international levels of analysis this book reveals another perspective: the creative possibilities of American statecraft. National decline is not an abstract phenomenon. It is lived and felt by people who make real choices every day. To frame the stakes and bring them to life, I introduce six conscientious leaders in the United States who have wrestled with these choices firsthand: a soldier, an innovator, a diplomat, a negotiator, a scholar, and a statesman. My hope is that readers will come to see a part of their story in the stories I tell in these pages and perhaps ask similar questions about the choices facing America today.

After nearly two decades of war, a great recession, and wither-
ing blows to its prestige as an exemplar and advocate of democratic
values, can the United States arrest its decline? We were wrong to
underestimate America's strengths during the stagflation and oil
crises of the 1970s, and we should not overestimate its weaknesses
today.[4] The United States has a window of opportunity to accomplish critical tasks: shore up its domestic foundations and shape a
modern, rules-based international order that reflects US interests
and values, thereby constraining rising powers before they create
new or parallel orders. If America manages its resources responsibly and makes the right choices, it will continue to exercise leadership abroad as it strengthens its fundamentals and deals with more
troubling signs at home.

Lessons from History

President Harry Truman said, "The only thing new in the world is
the history you don't know."[5] Every age is unique, and the twenty-
first century will be distinct from the preceding ones. To acknowledge this fact is not to argue that history is irrelevant—far from it.
What it suggests is the need for humility in drawing cookie-cutter
parallels between past historical cases and the present.[6] We should
think of history as a guide and companion, revealing patterns and
warnings that America's political leaders of today would do well
to heed.

This book contains illustrative examples from history, including the decay and reform of the Ottoman Empire in the seventeenth century, the decline and adaptation of Spain in the
seventeenth and eighteenth centuries, the alliance strategies of
Austria–Hungary in the eighteenth century, the erosion and transformation of British power in the nineteenth century, and the collapse of the Soviet Union in the twentieth century.[7] In sketching
the contours of these histories, I aim not to break new ground on
the facts and circumstances of each case but instead to extract insights for present times. I will probe the historical record to un-
cover lessons about how and why great powers decline, what policy
decisions were most important in changing the pace or character

of decline, and the conditions for successful strategies. The decline of great powers past is living history for a simple reason: the lessons learned speak to America's predicament today and offer clues about the choices at stake and how America can make the best decisions going forward.

As the historian Paul Kennedy shows in his seminal work on the rise and fall of great powers, it is the interaction of military and economic capabilities that determines the relative standing of nations.[8] Economies surge, cities thrive, incomes rise, and countries industrialize. Over time, assuming technological change remains constant, economic growth sputters and productivity declines. Larger, more populous states assert their interests. Costly wars drain the national treasury.[9] Step back from the booms and busts that characterize any nation's ascent and one pattern holds: what rises, falls; what surges, stagnates; who rules is ruled in return.

Will America in the early twenty-first century follow this age-old pattern? The answer turns on whether US decline is a *secular reality*, inevitable over the long run; a *transient reality*, likely to prove short-lived irrespective of US actions and decisions; or a *contingent reality*, fundamentally dependent on US choices.[10] I argue that American decline is a contingent reality. The United States is not fated to remain a superpower indefinitely. At the same time, it is reasonable to assume that US might and influence will decline over the next three decades and then come back as demographic pressures, debt, and diminishing resources constrain China's economic growth by midcentury. This scenario represents what I call the post-dominant world. It is a world of transition in which power is more contested, the rules of the road are less fixed, and influence is harder to wield. The post-dominant world is here to stay, at least for the policy-relevant time horizons about which this book is concerned. What the United States should seek is a stable post-dominant order that favors its interests and values. What it must prevent is the erosion of American power that underpins this order. Given the fundamental uncertainties of the future, much will depend on the choices the United States makes today. America's decline is not inevitable, but the demand for wise US leadership is inescapable.

The Road Ahead

In this book I explore six broad policy choices that America faces if it is to revitalize US leadership in a post-dominant world. These choices are not unique to declining nations: both emerging and established powers have a stake in navigating the policy options detailed here. When economic growth slows and rising rivals contend for supremacy, however, the challenge of managing trade-offs becomes critical. The task for America's leaders today is to approach these choices with an awareness of the limits of US power and influence. If America makes the right decisions at this moment of decline, it can bolster its leadership and, in fact, secure its interests and values well into the future. The six choices are as follows:

- *Core or Periphery?* Should a declining great power limit its
  military commitments in the periphery so as to concentrate its
  forces in core areas in order to protect the homeland against
  dangerous proximate threats; or should it undertake more
  substantial military commitments in the periphery to neutralize
  transnational threats, acquire new resources, and deter rising
  competitors?
- *Butter or Guns?* Should a declining power invest more in the
  sources of its economic and productive capacity, including
  increased spending on research and development, science and
  technology, education, and infrastructure; or should it invest
  more in the sources of its military might, including increased
  defense spending on modern hardware and software, new
  systems and platforms, and larger force structures?
- *Allies or Autonomy?* Should a declining power defend its interests
  and project influence through alliances, security guarantees, and
  forward deployments of troops and equipment; or should it
  maximize flexibility and conserve resources by cutting loose
  allies and partners, asserting unilateral advantage, and using a
  heavy hand to advance its political and security interests over
  compliant neighbors?
- *Persuasion or Coercion?* Should a declining power deal with assertive
  challengers through diplomatic tradecraft, commercial
  engagement for profit and contacts, and multilateral institutions

to ensure compliance with international agreements; or should it seek to avoid trading with the enemy and weaken rivals by pursuing a range of preventive military actions before it's too late?

- *People Power or Pinstripe Rule?* Should a declining power remain committed to good governance, the rule of law, and transparent, accountable institutions that reflect the collective will of the people; or should it permit the growth of a system that allows leaders to target resources to wealthy elites, corporate executives, and special interest groups with the means to manipulate the political process?

- *Open or Closed?* Should a declining power modernize the rules-based, liberal international order on the basis of democratic principles, strengthened multilateral cooperation, and free trade; or should it disengage from today's liberal order and allow it to be replaced by closed trading systems and protectionism, greater freedom of maneuver for national ambitions, bilateral arrangements, and competing spheres of influence, led by the United States, China, and Russia?

These choices should not be viewed in binary terms, although some may see them as simply "either do this or do that." Indeed, within each choice the various strategic approaches are complex, and there are no easy answers or silver bullets about America's way ahead. Some choices inspire bitter public debate today, such as the choice of butter or guns, where the final decision is never binary. Other choices might appear obvious or easy to some but nonetheless ensnare great powers in decline, such as the choice of people power or pinstripe rule. While few leaders would choose to be corrupt, the tragic reality is that too often and in too many cases leaders of great powers succumb to the forces of corruption and, wittingly or unwittingly, enable a system of rule that privileges self-enrichment over the public good. This pattern recurs frequently in the historical record and therefore deserves special treatment in any analysis of the decline of great powers. Still other choices are a matter of degree, such as persuasion or coercion. For example, a declining power can employ the strategic approach of coercive diplomacy, which combines military might, targeted sanctions, and diplomatic persuasion to advance its interests and values. In the concluding chapter, the reader will witness a future US president wrestling with these same choices in an attempt to craft an integrated, balanced strategy that navigates the thorny power dynamics America is likely to face in the coming years.

My purpose in writing this book is to evaluate the trade-offs of each policy choice, consider the lessons of history, and offer a perspective on where the United States needs to go. No doubt some will disagree with my perspective. That debate is the conversation to which I hope this book contributes. In the twenty-first century America's greatest challenges fester on the home front, but there are also serious threats pressing from abroad.

The United States can arrest its decline through skillful leadership and the judicious management of resources. History shows that declining nations can adapt to growing competitors.[11] Today, America must contend with multiple rising powers at continental distances, each developing separately and yet all bound together economically.[12] Navigating this complex environment will require farsighted US leadership. The question posed in this book is, What shape will American leadership take in a post-dominant world?

CHAPTER ONE

A Post-dominant World

THE FOURTEENTH-CENTURY ARAB historian Ibn Khaldun was a keen observer of decline. He believed that
dynasties rise and fall over three generations.[1] The first
generation builds, the second manages, and the third
neglects. Nations decay and then decline until a new generation
awakens from its slumber and forges a new order from the old.

In the United States today it's timely to ask: Is this the generation that builds, manages, or neglects? Presidents Franklin Roosevelt and Harry Truman and former US secretary of state Dean
Acheson were builders: they forged new alliances and created institutions to preserve and extend American power in the wake of
World War II. President Richard Nixon and former US secretary
of state Henry Kissinger were managers: they sought to lower the
costs of global competition with the Soviet Union and strengthen
the economic foundations of American power. Will future generations remember today's America as the age of neglect? Political
leadership matters, and wise policies can slow America's descent,
steer it away from longer-term decline, and enable it to adapt to
changing political and economic conditions.

My Decline, Your Rise

The decline in American power and leadership does not imply that other powers will pick up the slack. In fact, the opposite is happening. Other countries are pressing their advantage and free-riding on an international system that requires the active, sustained, and constructive engagement of the major powers. In the coming years, the result will not be a Chinese- or a Russian-led international order. Instead, it will probably be global *disorder* in which the constraints on American power grow more extensive, not less.

Welcome to America's situation today: a post-dominant world. It is a world best characterized as the interlude between unrivaled American supremacy in the decade following the collapse of the Soviet Union in 1991 and the future rise of a different international order, perhaps at worst coming after major conflict among the great powers. During this interlude China, Russia, and other authoritarian states will seek to modify today's global system in ways that advantage them more than the United States. How long this post-dominant world will last and how skillfully US political leaders will navigate its currents is uncertain. What is certain is that the choices America makes now will bear decisively on its future power and position.

Understanding the dynamics of this post-dominant landscape entails knowing who's going up, who's going down, and who's stuck in the messy middle. That requires some definitions and distinctions. I begin with a central distinction: for a great power, relative decline is manageable but absolute decline is fatal.

The difference between relative and absolute decline is straightforward. Suppose that America has ten warplanes in 2020 and builds five more by 2025; meanwhile, China has five warplanes in 2020 and builds five more by 2025. In absolute terms, America's airpower increased: it went from having ten warplanes in 2020 to fifteen warplanes by 2025. In relative terms, however, America's airpower declined: it went from having 50 percent more warplanes than China in 2020 to having only 33 percent more warplanes than China by 2025. In this scenario, if one takes a snapshot of the current year, America's absolute advantages in airpower look pretty good. But if one considers relative trends for the coming years, America's strength in airpower is declining compared with China's.

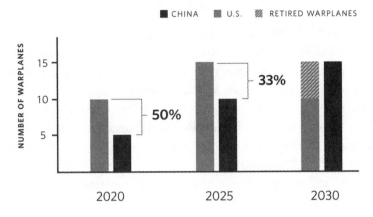

Figure 1.1. Relative versus absolute decline.

What about absolute decline? Well, suppose America stops producing warplanes altogether and retires five planes from its arsenal by 2030, giving it only ten warplanes total. During the same period, China increases its production of warplanes and adds five more to its arsenal by 2030, giving it fifteen total. In this scenario, American airpower would be in absolute and relative decline. The United States would have five fewer warplanes by 2030 than it did in 2025 (absolute decline), and China would have reversed the trends in relative airpower, from America having 33 percent more warplanes in 2025 to China having 33 percent more warplanes by 2030 (relative decline).

In short, when it comes to the rise and fall of nations, one question matters above all: Is it my decline or your rise? Pressures mount and options narrow when both happen at the same time. Take the declining Soviet Union in the 1980s: its overall power trajectory was on a downward slope relative to the United States, but the Soviets failed to adapt their economic system, which crashed absolutely. By contrast, Britain wisely sought to arrest its decline in the late nineteenth century, allowing it to retain sufficient power in the face of the growing clout of the United States and Germany.

Is the United States declining as a great power by eroding from within? By losing to a rival? Or both? Answering these questions requires one to appreciate the extent of American power and its limits.

Power and Its Limits

Few understand the limits of power better than America's diplomats, who advance US interests and values through persuasion, negotiation, and often-acceptable compromise. I grew up the son of a US Foreign Service officer. While experiencing all of our family's moves and transitions, from Amman to Paris, from Washington, D.C., to London, Brussels, and Rome, I learned a valuable lesson: American influence is a subtle and stubborn quality to measure with precision. "You know when you have it, and you know when it's gone," my father told me after a tough meeting on US Middle East policy at the Belgian Foreign Ministry in 2006.

What does it mean to say that America today is a great power in decline? The balance sheet of countable assets is a good place to start. This balance sheet is measured in terms of such indicators as gross domestic product (GDP), industrial production, numbers of soldiers and warplanes, naval tonnage, and stockpiles of nuclear weapons. GDP is an imperfect measure, but it enables comparisons of power across time and space with relative clarity and fidelity.[2] It also tracks with a range of indicators that measure economic performance, such as industrial production and high-technology exports. While acknowledging its problems as a measure of power, the political scientists Paul MacDonald and Joseph Parent argue that "no other measure offers the historical reach, analytical objectivity, and scientific comparability of GDP."[3]

The limitation of gross indicators like GDP is that they favor populous countries by failing to subtract the costs of producing wealth and power.[4] In his study of US–China relations, the political scientist Michael Beckley goes beyond gross indicators to look at the net costs associated with welfare, that is, the costs of feeding, housing, and caring for a country's citizens; economic production, the costs of depleting raw materials and fueling pollution; and security, the costs of policing a country's people and protecting its borders.[5] By focusing on net stocks as opposed to gross indicators, Beckley finds that "the United States is several times wealthier than China, and the absolute gap is growing by trillions of dollars each year."[6] He also finds that the United States has "five to ten times the military capabilities of China."[7] Beckley's analysis marks an important advance in the literature on power and improves our understanding of the utility and limits of gross indicators of national military and economic capabilities.

Beckley tells a story of absolute trends in time, but it is just as important to look at the relative trends over time. Getting a fuller picture of America's power and position, in other words, requires moving beyond snapshots of the current moment to what one analyst has described as "moving frames."[8] Relative to China over time, America's trend lines are not as favorable. Consider this: in 1993 household income in China was one thirty-fourth that of the United States; today, it's one-seventh.[9] Changing ratios of economic power tell a similar story. Between 1990 and 2018 the ratio of GDP per capita between the United States and China fell from 75:1 to 6:1.[10] In 2000 China's economy was 11.7 percent of America's economy at market prices; today, it has risen to 66 percent of America's economy.[11] In terms of purchasing power parity China has already surpassed America as the world's largest economy: in 2018 America held a 15 percent share of global GDP, while China held a nearly 20 percent share.[12]

Some will argue that China has a long way to go before it overtakes America. We need to take these arguments seriously without dismissing the overall picture of America's decline relative to a rising China. Disruptive as its growth in political and economic power may be, China's ascendancy is not foreordained. Economists predict that, on average, growth will slow once a country reaches a certain income level. This problem is called the middle-income trap, and it looms large for China.[13] Its population is aging. An already weak social security system could deplete its savings. Labor costs continue to rise, blunting its low-cost manufacturing edge. China's model of investment-led, export-driven growth may prove unsustainable.[14] And its debt levels exceeded 300 percent of GDP in the first quarter of 2019, which will force difficult trade-offs as Beijing seeks to rebalance demand.[15] This task will prove harder if China's increasingly authoritarian model of governance runs aground in the coming years. Much will depend on how Chinese leaders adapt to setbacks and unexpected turns.

Skeptics of China's rise today point reassuringly to the case of Japan in the 1980s: a rising rival that appeared to contest US

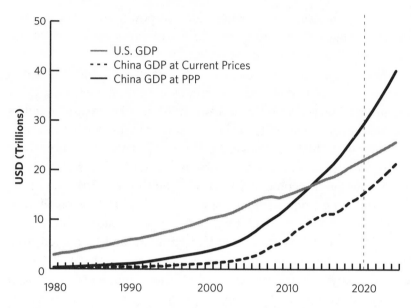

Figure 1.2. US GDP and China GDP at current prices and PPP dollars (estimates for 2019 onward). Sources: International Monetary Fund and the World Bank.

leadership, yet through a mix of good policy and good fortune the United States rebounded while Japan entered a prolonged slump. This analogy is misplaced. China is larger, more populous, and less developed than Japan; therefore, its dynamic potential for growth is much greater. China may be confronting new economic headwinds, but its dominance of global trade far exceeds that of Japan at its peak. In 1989 Japanese exports were dominant in 69 countries, whereas US exports were dominant in 108 jurisdictions; today, China leads the United States in exports to more than 174 countries, and America leads in only 8 countries.[16] The differences extend beyond trade. Japan did not pose any kind of military challenge to America in the 1980s. In fact, Japan fell under America's security umbrella and benefited from the positioning of US forces on its homeland. China's rapid military modernization will constrain the United States, particularly in the Western Pacific. America also confronts a rising China from a weaker position today compared with its position relative to a rising Japan in the 1980s.

The US debt burden is higher, its entitlement crisis is greater, and its indebtedness to foreign nations is far more significant.[17]

China's rise is evident not just in the economic realm but also in the areas of science and technology, research, and innovation. Chinese investments in research and development (R&D) increased from 34 percent of US spending on R&D in 2012 to 45 percent of US spending in 2016 in current prices, or 88 percent of US spending in terms of purchasing power.[18] Since 2000 China has boosted its R&D spending on average by 18 percent annually. The US National Science Board estimates that China may have already eclipsed the United States in R&D spending in 2018.[19] Add to these trends China's increasing cooperation with other countries on science and technology through its Belt and Road Initiative, an ambitious plan to transform regional and global connectivity through a vast network of roads, railways, bridges, ports, fiber-optic cables, and other infrastructure projects.[20] Just as America is pulling up the drawbridge to international collaboration in scientific research, China is making a concerted pitch to attract the best talent from around the world.

It's true that China lags behind America in innovation, but it is closing the gap. According to the World Intellectual Property Organization, China's share of patent applications increased from 10.5 percent of global totals in 2008 to 40 percent in 2017; by contrast, the US global share of patent applications fell from 22 percent in 2008 to 16.2 percent in 2017.[21] One measure of innovation is the number of patents a country registers in the United States, Europe, and Japan, or triadic patents. In 2005 China filed just 2 percent of US triadic patent totals; in 2018 China filed nearly 20 percent of US totals.[22] A similar measure of America's relative decline and China's rise in technological prowess is the share of global venture capital investments. In 1992 the US share of global venture capital was 97 percent; today, it has declined to just over 50 percent. And China? Its share of global venture capital spending increased from $5.6 billion in 2010 to $105 billion in 2018, just $6 billion shy of US totals.[23] These developments are notable markers of China's growing technological might.

As for military capabilities, America maintains an edge in high-end technology and the advanced systems that enable it to project

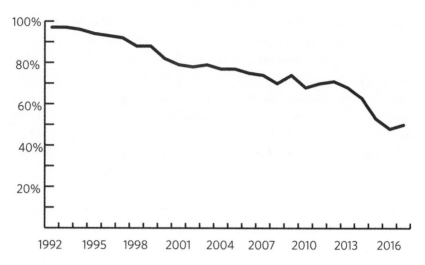

Figure 1.3. US share of global venture capital invested. Source: Richard Florida and Ian Hathaway, "Rise of the Global Start-up City: The New Map of Entrepreneurship and Venture Capital," Center for American Entrepreneurship, 2018.

power across the land, sea, air, and space domains. The United States accounts for nearly 40 percent of global defense outlays and spends as much on defense as the next eight powers combined, giving America an absolute lead in military power.[24]

Notwithstanding these advantages, America's relative military edge is slipping.[25] This trend was already visible at the peak of US power in the immediate post-9/11 period, when it struggled to impose its will against insurgents in Afghanistan and Iraq.

Now, American military power confronts even more treacherous terrain. New technologies are spreading rapidly and remain untested in battle, complicating assessments of the balance of power among nations.[26] The challenge of recruiting and retaining the best talent will necessitate continued reforms, broader outreach, and greater attention to technical skillsets. Compounding these problems, US military personnel and procurement costs are rising, which will constrain its power projection.[27] Much of America's military spending suffers from investments in outdated legacy systems for political purposes. The United States enjoys superior technological capabilities, but a free-rider problem arises when US investments in R&D produce new technologies that China and others copy or steal.[28] To be sure, China faces hurdles in adopting and deploying complex, capital-intensive military systems.[29] That is why it seeks to pivot to asymmetric strategies and emerging technologies that may provide a decisive advantage in the future, including the use of advanced simulations and war-gaming to overcome a deficit in combat experience.[30]

The scope and scale of Chinese defense investments will further constrain American military power.[31] China has expanded its island building and patrols in the South China Sea. It has also engaged in a rapid military buildup, investing in anti-ship ballistic missiles, integrated air defense systems, and other asymmetric capabilities that will limit American force projection in critical theaters, such as the Indian Ocean and Western Pacific. The Chinese People's Liberation Army (PLA) saw its budget increase by 83 percent over the past decade.[32] As the US Department of Defense concluded in its 2019 annual report to Congress on Chinese military power, "The PLA . . . continues to implement the most comprehensive restructure in its history to become a force capable of conducting complex joint operations," and its "military modernization also targets capabilities with the potential to degrade core US operational and technological advantages."[33] President Xi Jinping of China has made military modernization a top priority, including restructuring the PLA, demobilizing personnel, reforming procurement, and organizing the armed forces into five theaters on the model of US combatant commands.[34] China has also created a Strategic Support Force to integrate emerging technologies into the domains of space and cyber.

The rise of other non-Western powers will complicate this picture. The global professional services network Pricewaterhouse Coopers estimates that by 2050 non-Western countries will account for six of the seven largest economies.[35] In 2018 India captured 16 percent of global GDP growth, up three percentage points from the previous year. The research firm Capital Economics predicts that India will grow on average between 5 and 7 percent a year through 2040, outpacing the United States, Japan, China, and the Eurozone.[36] The "Global Trends 2025" report of the US National Intelligence Council (NIC) concludes with a stark prediction: "Although the United States is likely to remain the single most powerful actor, the United States' relative strength—even in the military realm—will decline and US leverage will become more constrained."[37] The NIC estimates that by 2030 the US share of the combined output of the G-20 economies will drop from a third to a quarter.

The Intangibles of Power

Until recently, anxiety over falling behind triggered investments in America's future. The more Americans worried about decline, the more they invested in building America's strength and the faster the country rebounded. In the 1960s the Soviets leaped ahead of the United States in the space race, launching the world's first satellite, Sputnik, in 1957. Pundits dubbed it the Sputnik Moment. Fearing decline, Americans doubled down on investments in education, scientific research, and infrastructure, eventually growing their way back to US leadership in technological innovation. Similarly, President Ronald Reagan's spurring of the nation to believe it was "Morning in America" after the malaise of the 1970s and President Bill Clinton's refrain of "Don't stop thinking about tomorrow" after the recession of the early 1990s served dual purposes: to remind Americans about their storied past and reorient them toward a shared future. The Harvard economist and former US treasury secretary Larry Summers calls this tendency America's "self-denying prophecy."[38]

Today, we are witnessing the opposite. As is the case with most complex historical developments, America's decline is the result of many forces of change. Some of these forces lend themselves to quantitative analysis of gross indicators and net costs; others require more qualitative forms of diagnosis. Looking only at the tangible elements of power, that is, the assets that can be empirically measured and counted, one misses some important and concerning trends. Writing this book led me to four insights about power and how it relates to the rise and fall of nations.

First, the flows of power matter as much as the stockpiles of power. When assessing the prospects of a great power's decline, one must look not simply at gross indicators or net costs but also at the direction of change, the rate of change, and the context within which that change takes place. Power varies according to the scope and domain of its use: nuclear weapons can serve as a formidable deterrent, but they cannot mobilize a coalition to confront a disease outbreak, contain a financial crisis, or advance international action on climate change.[39] The upshot is that we need to pay attention to the changing ratios of relative economic, military, and technological power in specific areas, not just to shifts in the size and significance of gaps in aggregate capability between rising and falling powers.[40] Equally important, we need to understand relative changes in the ability of great powers to convert their resources into economic, military, and political advantage.[41]

Powerful states in the twenty-first century combine the ability to adapt to new circumstances with what the historian Jeremi Suri calls the "effective internal political capacity" to mobilize capital and manage revenue and credit in service of national power.[42] Even if one agrees with Beckley that there is an absolute gap between the United States and China in terms of military and economic resources today, the ability of the United States to convert those resources into desired outcomes is not guaranteed. In fact, as I argue in this book, America's ability to transform its endowments into political and military advantage is at greater risk today than it has been since the end of the Cold War.

The second insight is that there are intangible elements of power that cannot be neatly tallied up or empirically calculated.[43] These elements of power are vital and should not be dismissed. The effects of a great power's social and political cohesion, entrepreneurial drive, commitment to achieving successful policy outcomes, public trust in government, respect for the rule of law, and national identity are not easily counted, but they count nonetheless. Further, indicators of countable assets may lag behind the actual balance of power, thereby skewing assessments of the current situation. The question of intangible power goes beyond the difficulty of measuring wealth among nations and the relative merits of selecting data based on GDP at market prices or purchasing power parity, or tradeable versus non-tradeable goods. Different metrics point to different conclusions about the rise and fall of great powers. And measures of power that seem vitally important today may prove less so in the future.

The third insight adds more nuance: the impact of power is mediated through perceptions, expectations, and time. Perceptions convert power into policy. If the trends are unfavorable, but a leader believes otherwise, he or she may adopt different policies than the raw data prescribe. In the fifteenth century, for example, China's navy was vastly superior to those of its European counterparts. By the sixteenth century, however, China had destroyed its Treasure Fleet and turned inward, setting the stage for a centuries-long contraction in power and influence.[44] Expectations about the future also shape decisions about power: if leaders believe that decline is reversible, they will behave differently and pursue different policies than if they believe that decline is inevitable.[45] Furthermore, it is often impossible to know whether there is a gap between resources and commitments without the benefit of hindsight, hence the importance of time as a variable in assessing power.[46]

Finally, leadership, institutions, and resolve are crucial enablers. In the absence of skillful leadership, a great power can be led astray and fail to make the right choices. Lacking competent institutions, a nation will be unable to convert its power resources into constructive action. And without resolve to achieve long-term goals, an otherwise capable nation can get trapped in needless, costly controversies. The scholar David Baldwin coined the phrase "the paradox of unrealized power" to account for the disparity between a nation's resources and the influence it wields on the world stage.[47] The paradox of American power today is this: even as the United States faces serious threats from the ambitions of a rising China and the dangers of an aggressive Russia, it may fail to confront these threats or shore up its power at home because of misguided policies, political paralysis, and a public weary of bearing the burdens of global leadership.

These four insights about power encourage a shift in the way we think about big trends in international politics. We need to appreciate that America's strength is not just about a numerical accounting of diverse components of power. It is also about the intangibles of power, the ironies of history, and the role of chance, uncertainty, and indeterminacy.[48] Put differently, there's the science of thinking about power and then there's the art of doing so. The science crunches the numbers and the data associated with power; the art looks to history as a guide and assesses the skill of leaders, the balance of resolve, and the pathologies of decision making.[49] Both are important when making the broad policy choices outlined in this book. It would be foolish to ignore the science, but it would be equally unwise to dismiss the art. Although one must consider the science of decline, the focus of this book is on the art of decline: the lessons of the past, the choices US political leaders face in the present, and the strategies that will arrest America's decline in the future.

The Waning of American Hegemony

One of the intangibles of American power is what political scientists call hegemony. This concept should be distinguished from brute displays of power or the desire merely to dominate other states. As the scholar John Ruggie defines it, hegemony is the blending of power with legitimacy.[50] It entails a bargain between a dominant state and a subordinate one whereby the latter cedes some influence to the former in exchange for security or the provision of economic and social benefits. This form of "relational authority" differs from legal conceptions by grounding authority not in law but in a relationship between two or more states.[51] The relationship is a social bargain in that the dominant state exercises influence over its subordinates in a way that is mutually advantageous. Consider the case of US hegemony over Europe since 1945, or what the scholar Geir Lundestad has termed America's "empire by invitation."[52] According to Lundestad, "US efforts to control and dominate were, of course, based on American values. . . . [But] these values left wide scope for European self-organization."[53] In other words, the way in which the United States exercised its power was different from the modus operandi of traditional great powers in history. As a consequence of this transatlantic social bargain, both the Americans and Europeans achieved economic and social benefits within a "hierarchical system of political relationships, radiating from a center."[54] Hegemonies vary across time and space, as do the social bargains underpinning them. The thicker the bargain, the more durable the system.[55]

The degree to which the United States should assume a leadership role in the world has long been a debate in the country's foreign policy. What makes the post-1945 trajectory in US foreign policy unique by historical standards, as the scholar Hal Brands notes, is that America "exercised its power in a comparatively consensual and benevolent fashion."[56] The post-1945 bargain the United States struck with its European partners was actually two bargains: one based on the realities of the new distribution of power, which meant that the United States at times sacrificed values in the name of containing the Soviet Union; and another based on the principles of a new political settlement with Europe, which saw the United States agree to binding restraints on its power in exchange for European assent to US leadership of its postwar design.[57] What came to be known as the liberal international order of common agreements, standards, and institutions constituted the foundation for US hegemony and its principled engagement in the world.

To appreciate the value of the postwar order America made, consider another definition of hegemony as "the mobilization of leadership."[58] As the political scientist Daniel Nexon observes, the foundation of US power in the post–World War II period, and certainly since the end of the Cold War, rests not only on its military and economic resources but also on the legitimacy of its social purpose. Traditionally, Canada, European nations, and allies in Asia consented to a US-led international order because they perceived the United States as acting both in its own interest and in the enlightened interests of other nations. The practical result of this hegemonic order was that the United States could rely on the cooperation—and, when necessary, the commitments—of the advanced, industrialized democracies. These countries contributed vital resources to the United States and in addition underbuilt their militaries and refrained from balancing against US interests because they accepted the social bargains underpinning US leadership in the liberal international order.

Since 2000 the geopolitical picture has become more complicated. The rise of China and a series of self-inflicted wounds made by misguided US policies have eroded the foundational bargains of American power and influence.[59] According to Gallup, the percentage of global publics who hold a favorable view of the United States plunged from 48 percent during the final year of the administration of President Barack Obama to a new low of 31 percent in 2018.[60] By contrast, China's leadership increased its approval from 29 percent in 2012 to 34 percent in 2018.[61] Majorities in Japan and South Korea and nearly 50 percent in Germany, France, Canada, and Greece see US power and influence as a threat. Strikingly, more people globally view America as a threat than they do Russia or China. And more than a third of publics around the world say the United States is less involved in international affairs than in the past.[62]

Meanwhile, the appeal of the American model is waning. This model rests on a core assumption: free markets, democratic politics, and a liberal order that protects fundamental rights are essential for growth and prosperity. The American model isn't moribund, but it's fraying and in need of repair. The leading democracy scholar Larry Diamond estimates that in the first fifteen years of this century democracy failed in twenty-seven countries. The Economist Intelligence Unit assesses that in 2017 democracy advanced in twenty-seven countries and retrenched in eighty-nine. One need only look at the decline of democracy in Brazil, Hungary, Kenya, Myanmar, Pakistan, Poland, and Thailand to grasp a disquieting trend.[63] Combining free market economics with heavy state control, the so-called Beijing consensus looks ever more appealing to emerging powers that were once Western-oriented and democratic. This contest of alternative models is escalating as great powers compete for influence in proxy conflicts from Syria to Venezuela and vie for scarce resources, new markets, and control of mobile network technologies and platforms.[64]

Nexon rightly points out that the question today isn't whether America should lead, but how and to what end? Or, to recast the question, what vision of international order should the United States promote to secure its interests and those of its allies in the current era of decline?

The End of the American Century?

Politicians and analysts debate the origins of America's rise to global leadership. Some date its beginnings to the late nineteenth century, with the growth of America as an industrial power. Others trace its roots to the immediate post–World War II period, when the United States emerged from the wreckage with upward of 50 percent of global GDP.[65] My reference points for assessing America's power and influence in the world are at once more personal and immediate. I remember I was living in London in the 1990s, when President Bill Clinton embarked on his grand project of democratic enlargement, expanding NATO to Eastern Europe, negotiating peace in Northern Ireland, and dispatching American forces to end the brutal and destabilizing ethnic conflicts in the Balkans. I was a high school senior in Maryland when the World Trade Center in New York City collapsed, tragically puncturing the aura of invincibility of the world's sole superpower. I lived in Brussels during the years when America's financial prowess reached its gauzy heights and then crashed on the shoals of subprime mortgages and credit default swaps.

When I returned to Washington at the end of 2007 the atmosphere and politics reflected the perilous state of the US economy. America felt smaller as a nation, more consumed by partisan infighting and tribal scapegoating than by taking responsibility for governing. The anger and disaffection of some voters found its voice in the Tea Party movement, which put the question of debt and deficits on the front burner of the national conversation; then in the Occupy Wall Street protests, which called attention to the corrosive effects of social and economic inequality and the growing perception that Wall Street fixed the rules of the game, favoring insiders. As lenders foreclosed on people's homes and savings dried up, the anger swelled, divisions multiplied, and a palpable sense of indignity and injustice festered.

Two years later I landed a job working for then Senator John Kerry on the US Senate Foreign Relations Committee. My portfolio included human rights and South and Central Asia; but nearly every week, often by mistake, sometimes by design, I'd get a call from a worried constituent or anxious citizen about health care (the costs were too high or government spending was too much), education (the debt was crippling or the gap between report cards and paychecks was growing), or immigration (the senator should vote for our common humanity and devise a path to citizenship, or uphold our common security and do more to lock down the border). I thought of what my father had told me about the difficulties of measuring and deploying American influence and how we would feel the effects when it's gone. I wondered whether America's broken politics and fragile markets at home diminished its leverage and staying power abroad.

In the summer of 2013 I leapt at the chance to find out. President Obama appointed Senator Kerry to be secretary of state during the president's second term. I joined Secretary Kerry at the State Department as one of his speechwriters, flying around the world in what he joked was our "human petri dish" of a Boeing 757. We flew to Geneva in 2013 to negotiate with the Russians on removing Syria's declared chemical weapons and struggled to find a path forward that would end the bloodletting of the Syrian civil war. We flew to Beijing to inject new momentum into global climate change negotiations and ratchet up pressure on a North Korean regime that was racing ahead to develop nuclear weapons. We flew to Kabul in 2014 to manage the fallout from disputed elections and preserve the fragile gains for which so many American and allied troops had given their lives. We flew to Myanmar in 2014 and again in 2015 to encourage political and economic reforms. We flew to Havana in 2015 to reopen America's embassy there, after more than half a century of isolation and estrangement between the United States and Cuba. We flew to Muscat, Vienna, and Geneva on countless occasions to meet with representatives from the United Kingdom, France, Germany, China, and Russia to negotiate a rollback and strict verification and monitoring of Iran's nuclear program. We flew to Hanoi and Ho Chi Minh City in 2016 with President Obama to cement his "rebalance to Asia" and deepen ties with a former hostile enemy. Secretary Kerry would always say that America was engaged in more places and with more players than ever before. He was right.

On each trip and in every meeting I enjoyed a front-row seat to how senior decision makers from across the US government worked mightily to preserve American influence. Some trips underscored the extent of that influence. Without American leadership and resolve, it's hard to imagine the containment of the 2014 Ebola epidemic in West Africa, a global climate change accord in Paris in 2015, or the successful conclusion of nuclear negotiations with Iran in 2016.

There were also trips that underscored credibility lost. I'll never forget the frustration on Secretary Kerry's face after a meeting with one of his counterparts in the Middle East. He pushed, prodded, and cajoled this minister to do more on good governance, enact transparent budgets, and promote investments in infrastructure. He got a quizzical look and then the retort: "Mr. Secretary, with great respect, your government shut down because Congress couldn't pass a budget, and you're telling me that we have to get *our* affairs in order?" The efficacy of American diplomacy in the twenty-first century starts at home.[66]

In a post-dominant world the United States confronts a window of opportunity and risk. The opportunity is that America can shape the international rules of the road in ways that will favor its interests and values. China and other rising powers face domestic hurdles and may decline by midcentury. The risk is that the United States becomes complacent, acts rashly, or fails to make the domestic investments needed to sustain its power and influence over the long term. America's decline relative to a rising China and other non-Western powers is a fact; whether the United States falls into absolute decline at home because of its internal dysfunction is a choice. Since it is the combination of relative and absolute decline that proves fatal to a great power, the paramount task for US political leaders is clear: adapt to relative decline compared with rising competitors and take all practical steps now to avert America's absolute decline at home.

The First Choice

This task must start with a clear-eyed appraisal of when and where the United States should use force. Deploying military force is one of the most consequential decisions a leader can make. When future historians look back on the early twenty-first century and contemplate US military interventions in faraway lands, will they say that America's leaders made the choices that preserved the nation's power and influence? Somewhere on the dusty plains of Afghanistan, one American soldier was already finding out the answer, the hard way.

CHAPTER TWO

Core or Periphery?

F OR LT. DAN BERSCHINSKI, time is the enemy. Eight years, two months, and a split second mark the choices that defined his military service: the eight years between the US invasion of Afghanistan and the start of his tour of duty, the two months he deployed in the Afghan theater, and the final step that would change his life. Dan grew up in a small town in Georgia. He was a Boy Scout and relished the outdoors. He watched war movies and read history. His older brother Rob completed Air Force ROTC, so it was only natural that Dan dreamed of joining the military and becoming an officer. It all made sense: he'd go to college, get an education, and then get paid to jump out of airplanes. At least he'd have a guaranteed job for a few years. What was not to like? What could go wrong?

Then the twin towers of the World Trade Center fell. On TV Dan watched the first scenes of America's first twenty-first-century war. It would be its longest war. The terrorist attacks of 9/11 never shook Dan's intent to join the military. His mind was made up from an early age. "I figured the military would play some role in the response to 9/11," Dan told me from his home in Georgia. "It was horrific, and I knew I'd be impacted directly in some way, but I had four years of college to get through first." When Dan entered West Point as a cadet, he had a hunch he'd end up in the infantry.

He didn't want an office job. He wanted to get his hands dirty and lead troops in action. "The infantry goes where the fighting is," he would tell his friends.

After 9/11 the United States went into Afghanistan to topple the Taliban government, which had sheltered Osama bin Laden and his foot soldiers in al-Qaeda. Dan and his buddies were well aware of the stakes for America in Afghanistan. They debated the ever-grimmer death tolls and the mounting controversies at home. They knew young guys like them would probably be deployed into the Afghan fight after they graduated. They knew that many might be coming back wounded or in body bags.

When Dan graduated from West Point in 2007 he harbored doubts about America's continuing war in Afghanistan. One part of his brain resolved to follow through on the mission. America was at war, and his government had declared it justified. Like a lot of soldiers his age he wanted to see combat up close and personal. He was drawn to the fight. He'd joined the infantry and felt ready to honor his commitment despite the risks.

The other part of his brain weighed his concerns and the costs. As a student of history, he grew increasingly skeptical about the merits of military intervention. He didn't think a prolonged occupation of another country was a prudent use of manpower, resources, or international goodwill. But as the world's sole superpower America could afford to prosecute the war despite the costs. I asked Dan whether he opposed the war from the start. "I didn't personally find our pursuit of the war to be so immoral or unethical that I couldn't serve," Dan said when I pressed him on his reasons for volunteering. "There was no hard science about the war. I had my doubts, but I was reserving judgment. I wanted to lead soldiers and do the right thing. And if we were going to continue to fight, I wanted to fight side by side with them."

By 2009 Dan would finally get his chance two years after he was commissioned as a second lieutenant. The first thing that struck him when he landed in southern Afghanistan was the heat. "It was like walking into an oven," he recalls of that sweltering day in July 2009. Dan's unit arrived from Fort Lewis, Washington. He met the soldiers of his platoon. His commanding officer, or CO, told them they'd be able to "get things done" in Afghanistan. Dan suppressed his concerns. The platoon mulled over the area of operations and then their mission. Dan learned that his unit would be the pointed end of the spear for the brigade based out of Kandahar Airfield in the south of Afghanistan. In a letter home he wrestled with his doubts about the war: "I wish you guys could see this place because it really blows my mind to think that all of this has been constructed for the sake of killing some ridiculously poor people."

On August 18 Dan's CO ordered him to conduct a joint patrol in the town of Shuyene Sufla. The Arghandab River cuts across the area from southwest to northeast and feeds the farmland and orchards that surround the village. Dan and his men took a road they called Route Red Dog. They headed into the patrol with eyes wide open. The area was known as a hornet's nest of insurgents and improvised explosive devices (IEDs). Friendly vehicles had taken incoming enemy fire. Just a week before, Dan and his platoon had beaten back an ambush there. When they got to Shuyene Sufla Dan and his men patrolled through town. They stayed alert and braced for enemy fire. As they worked their way through the dense orchards they came to a small, hand-built footbridge that crossed an irrigation canal. Dan clenched his rifle. The village was empty—a bad sign.

Dan and his soldiers crossed the bridge of the irrigation canal. With half of his platoon behind him on the near side of the canal, Dan, his radio operator, Specialist Roger Garcia, and his forward observer, Private First Class Jonathan Yanney, walked across the small bridge. As Dan's soldiers closed ranks, a bomb exploded. Blown down into the ground, Dan was still gripping his rifle. All he could see was dust. All he could hear was the sound of his forward team firing into the orchard. Blood was leaking out of his radio operator's ears. Garcia had been a few steps closer to the explosion than Dan. The squad leaders took a head count; everyone was there except Yanney. The last they remembered, Yanney was on the bridge. When the dust cleared and they turned around to look, all they saw was a crater. The water dammed up. There was no sign of Yanney.

Soldiers practice taking casualties and saving the wounded. They call for a medevac helo and follow the protocol. But nothing prepares them for the gut-wrenching image of seeing a buddy blown to bits. Dan radioed his CO and said, "I have a presumed KIA, but I don't have any remains." The sister platoon was still pinned down in a firefight. Dan and his soldiers spent the remainder of the afternoon searching around the crater for Yanney's remains.

Specialist Garcia was badly injured and needed rapid evacuation. One of his men volunteered to take over radio duties. As a forward observer, Yanney carried a radio that he or Dan could use to call in artillery and airstrikes. Garcia carried the same kind of radio, and his was used for communication with other units. Yanney and Garcia had been closest to the explosion when it was triggered. Dan suspected the enemy was targeting soldiers with radios, so he denied the soldier's offer to assume radio duties. Dan made room in his backpack and carried it himself.

As darkness fell, the CO ordered Dan to bring his platoon to the sister platoon's location. Dan and his soldiers moved on foot about a kilometer across the orchards. It was risky. Dan didn't have an interpreter or metal detectors or bomb-sniffing dogs or counter-IED personnel. Some days they patrolled with the Afghan army. On this day the platoon was alone, keeping clear of the trails and advancing knee-deep through water and mud. "That was the scariest part of my tour," Dan recalls. With IEDs potentially everywhere, he never knew whether his next step would be his last.

When Dan's platoon finally arrived at the rendezvous they felt a sense of relief. They moved into a hamlet abutting the orchard. Several hours later, around midnight, Dan got a call from his CO, who wanted to meet with all the platoon leaders. The conversation with the CO was brief; they were to continue the search for Yanney in the morning. Dan started back toward his platoon's location, carefully tracing the same path he'd taken an hour before. Two or three seconds later he took the one step that would change his life forever.

When the IED exploded, Dan didn't feel like he got blown up. It felt like he got hammered down into the ground: "It was like I got punched in the head by Mike Tyson." He had no visual memories, just a feeling of tremendous pressure and a burning sensation near his lower limbs. He reached down to touch his legs and felt only dirt. The explosion had thrown him to his left into a wall, and he landed upside down in a crater, his head resting below his body at the center of the crater. He remembers calling out to his men, who were on the other side of the wall. He screamed for help. His left arm suffered a compound fracture. The force of the blast ripped off his finger and broke his jaw. Both of his legs were gone.

Less than a minute later his soldiers dragged their lieutenant out of the hole. For the next hour Dan slipped in and out of consciousness, his men yelling at him to keep his eyes open. The medics got tourniquets on both legs and put the wounded lieutenant on a medevac helo to Kandahar, where he remained in the emergency room for five days. When he stabilized, he was put on a US Air Force medevac plane and flown first to Bagram and then to the major hospital in Landstuhl, Germany. Ten days later Dan woke up in the intensive care unit at Walter Reed Army Medical Center in Washington, DC. He looked up, and his dad's eyes greeted him. Dan's father asked him, "Do you know what happened?" There was no simple answer to that question.

For all America's strengths, Dan sees a paradox. The US military is formidable. It enjoys all of the advantages of a fully networked battlefield. And yet, after the wear and tear of nearly two decades of grinding war the United States is still fighting the Taliban to a stalemate at the cost of more than twenty-three hundred lives and over $1 trillion. In 2018 the United States spent more on the war than twice Afghanistan's GDP, giving a new and quite literal meaning to the Pottery Barn rule, "You break it, you own it."

Many have tried to assign blame for America's mission creep in Afghanistan. Successive administrations of both parties have struggled to answer fundamental questions: Is remaining in Afghanistan in the vital national interest of the United States? Does America need tens of thousands of boots on the ground to secure those interests? To what extent does Afghanistan pose a threat to the US homeland? Given the uncertain future of Afghan democracy, will America's longest war truly become a forever war? Afghanistan is not South Korea or Germany, where the United States has kept troops and bases for decades. It is a landlocked country with an active insurgency. American voters do not want to deploy military forces in Afghanistan indefinitely, but can the Afghan government protect US interests there without US troops?

Strategic Choice: Core or Periphery?

Dan's story underscores the stakes of American military intervention in a distant land that suffers from pervasive poverty, failed institutions, and brutal internal conflicts. Since 1989, when the Soviet Union lost control over Eastern Europe, the United States has deployed its armed combat forces abroad more than two hundred times.[1] These US military interventions have taken place in largely weak, undeveloped, and war-torn states, such as Somalia, Yemen, and Libya. While more than two hundred interventions over thirty plus years represents a high annual rate, only nine have entailed major US commitments of long duration, including Iraq (1990–91), Haiti (1994–96), Bosnia (1992–96), Afghanistan (since 2001), and Iraq again (2003–11; 2014–onward).

This record of US military deployments abroad demonstrates that as a nation's power grows, so do its responsibilities and aspirations. Threats accumulate. Commitments multiply. When a great power declines, it faces growing pressure to make good on those commitments. New dangers emerge and old threats linger. At the same time, rising rivals test the resolve of an established power to defend its many interests in far-flung corners of the globe. The question isn't simply whether to intervene in the periphery. Instead, if a foreign country hosts threats to America and its allies—such as al-Qaeda hiding in Afghanistan leading up to 9/11—advocates for military intervention must answer the following key policy questions: To what ends, with what strategy, at what cost, and for how long?

Those questions have stalked the numerous US military interventions throughout the post–Cold War period, from Bosnia and Kosovo to Afghanistan, Iraq, and Libya. In deciding on the right approach, leaders of a declining power face a strategic choice: defend their homeland and allies of the core, while dealing with threats in the periphery through diplomacy and development, or pursue military intervention in fragile states. This choice engages both aspects of decline: absolute and relative. Relative decline to a rising power can tempt the established power to intervene in the periphery. This action, in turn, can bog down the declining power, consume its resources, and exacerbate economic conditions in the core, thereby leading to absolute decline.

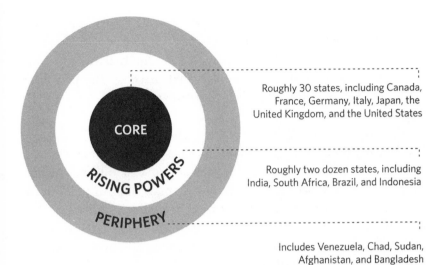

Figure 2.1. Core–periphery.

The core–periphery model is a common framework that maps the distribution of political, military, and economic power in the world. It shows the relationship between a few dominant, fully developed core states, rising powers that make up the near-core, and less developed peripheral states.[2]

Today, the G-7 nations of Canada, France, Germany, Italy, Japan, the United Kingdom, and the United States comprise the heart of the core. In addition to the G-7 countries, core states include NATO and EU member states, Australia, Israel, New Zealand, and South Korea. Many of these countries are militarily advanced, free-market, industrial democracies that enjoy rule of law and high levels of per capita income, economic development, and integration with global supply chains and networks of communication, infrastructure, energy, and commercial logistics. While the determination of which states meet these criteria rests in part on subjective judgments, the core refers to those states that are democratic, economically advanced, and highly connected to the major political and economic systems of the liberal international order. Roughly thirty countries in Europe, North America, and Asia may be considered core states.

States of the periphery, such as Russia, Venezuela, Chad, Sudan, Afghanistan, and Bangladesh, are less developed economically and often plagued by organized crime, internal violence, and poor governance. Many of the states that make up the periphery are located in Central America, Sub-Saharan Africa, the Middle East, and Eurasia.

Russia fits uncomfortably in this categorization. On the one hand, it possesses a large nuclear arsenal, holds a permanent seat on the UN Security Council, lays claim to vast oil and gas resources, and stretches across eleven time zones, abutting the strategic regions of the Arctic, the Black Sea, the South Caucasus, Central Asia, and Northeast Asia. By dint of its size, nuclear weapons status, diplomatic influence, and geopolitical ambition, Russia demands the attention of core states.

On the other hand, Russia runs on a single-engine economy, having failed to diversify away from hydrocarbons. Corruption is pervasive, and organized crime dominates its corporate political and economic structures.[3] Its system of governance is at once authoritarian and brittle, historically subject to periods of upheaval and transformation.[4] Its citizens are highly educated, but they suffer from a variety of public health ills. And its longer-term demographic outlook is dire. The demographer Nicholas Eberstadt calls this combination of high education and low innovation the "Russian paradox": "Russia (with a population of 145 million) earns fewer patents each year from the US Patent and Trademark Office than the state of Alabama (population: five million). Russia earns less from service exports than Denmark, with its population of six million, and has less privately held wealth than Sweden, with a population of ten million."[5] In short, Russia is a declining great power with a revisionist agenda and a penchant for tactical opportunism. Core states must guard against the dangers of an aggressive Russia while soliciting its cooperation on issues of mutual interest, such as the regulation of global financial imbalances, counterterrorism, and nonproliferation.

Lying in the middle of the core–periphery model are about two dozen or so rising powers, such as China, India, South Africa, Brazil, and Indonesia. Some observers refer to these countries as near-core states: while they are less developed than core states and have weaker systems of governance and the rule of law, some are growing in political, military, and economic clout and becoming more integrated with global networks and supply chains.

China presents an enigma in this categorization. As one scholar notes, China is best characterized as an "upper-middle-income country" that fuses elements of market economics with heavy state control.[6] China has integrated economically with many nations of the core and has surpassed the United States as the largest economy in purchasing power terms. By one estimate China is now the top trading partner of more than two-thirds of the world's states, and trade between China and Europe now surpasses trade between the United States and Europe.[7] China has demonstrated a capacity for sustained growth and technological innovation. Yet it is not a constitutional democracy and lacks many of the aspects of rule of law that other core states adhere to emphatically in principle, if not always in practice.

The strategic choice between core and periphery represents an often-daily policy debate for a great power. Since the end of the Cold War it is common to see brutal conflicts perpetrated by armed groups in more than thirty troubled or failing states on any given day of the week. A few of these horrible situations in the periphery, such as those in Afghanistan in 1996–2001, give safe harbor to threats against America and its allies of the core. In a globalized world the United States is connected to everyone else, and bad neighborhoods abroad can easily project dreadful outcomes on the American people and their homeland. Dealing with this serious challenge of the twenty-first century requires a great power to be vigilant, rigorous in its policy deliberations, steadfast with its allies of the core, and wise in making commitments to deter or derail threats from the periphery as they arise. Nothing about this strategic choice is simple for a great power, especially in the highly interconnected, fast-paced, globalized world of today.

A country's standing in the core–periphery model depends on the domestic and international decisions it makes. Over time, uneven growth rates among nations reshuffle the deck of core–periphery relations. Core states can fall into near-core or peripheral status through bad leadership, strategic blunders, prolonged wars, mismanagement of finances, and economic stagnation. Similarly, peripheral and near-core states can rise to core state status through skillful leadership, sound policies, and prudent management of resources. Many rising powers in Asia, for example, are integrating economically and forging new political and military ties. Core states can enlarge their number through effective diplomacy and development policies. The core can also diminish in number when its leading members get bogged down in conflicts in the periphery.

When a great power faces challenges from outside its core, it may be tempted to intervene to impose order in a troubled state. Leaders face difficult trade-offs: Should a declining great power limit its military commitments in the periphery so as to concentrate its forces in core areas for close protection of the homeland against dangerous proximate threats? Or should it undertake more substantial military commitments in the periphery to neutralize transnational threats, deter rising rivals, and enable the further economic, political, and social development of its partner nations?

The challenge of managing dynamics between the core and the periphery is compounded when power shifts and rising rivals threaten the interests of established core states. The most prudent option in that case is to protect a resilient core while promoting targeted, cooperative, and multilateral strategies for building the capacity of fragile states in the periphery. As history shows and as Dan's harrowing experiences remind us, pursuing wars in peripheral states may bring disastrous consequences. Interventions beyond vital interests are more likely to entangle great powers in quagmires, consume finances, deplete military capabilities, and sap political legitimacy. Such actions hasten, rather than arrest, national decline.[8]

Given the long shadow of uncertainty in international politics, it's not surprising that policy missteps and ill-considered, costly, and extended commitments in the periphery have played a role in the decline of great powers. Few cases exemplify the risks more dramatically than the British and Soviet interventions in Afghanistan. This history carries lessons for America today. An understanding of the policy decisions that change the pace and character of decline can be gained by taking a closer look at how leaders of these great powers managed dynamics in the core and periphery.

Whistling Past the Graveyard of Empires

Afghanistan is known as the graveyard of empires for a reason. It ensnared the British Empire for seventy years, from 1839 to 1919. In the eyes of British strategists, protecting India justified the Anglo–Afghan Wars. The central question, however, is whether Britain should have maintained its rule in India. From the late nineteenth century on India drained British finances, and yet British leaders insisted on preserving it. They waged three Anglo–Afghan wars over the nineteenth and early twentieth centuries to check Russian influence and maintain their control over the passageways to India, costing the British army some fifteen thousand lives.

The British misadventures in Afghanistan served as a backdrop to interventions by the Soviet Union in 1979 and then by the United States in 2001. Were the Soviet and American military occupations of Afghanistan a reprise of Britain's imperial overreach? With respect to the American intervention Dan would surely say yes. And he's not the only one.

In an intelligence assessment the US Central Intelligence Agency (CIA) notes that, years after the invasion of Afghanistan, counterinsurgency forces are "bogged down in a guerilla war of increasing intensity." They have had "little success in reducing the insurgency or winning acceptance by the Afghan people, and the Afghan resistance continues to grow stronger and to command widespread popular support. Fighting has gradually spread to all parts of Afghanistan." They control "less territory" than they did when they launched the operation, and "airfields, garrisons, and lines of communication are increasingly subject to insurgent attack." The CIA assessment notes the "serious shortcomings of the Afghan Army" and judges "unlikely" the prospect of "[making] real progress toward quelling the insurgency in the next two years." It cautions against the view that more aggressive tactics will "over the long term, grind down the will of the insurgents to resist and allow the Kabul government to consolidate" its rule.[9] That CIA assessment was produced in 1985 in regard to the Soviet presence in Afghanistan. Substitute "America" for the "USSR" and troubling parallels emerge.[10]

Why did the Soviets invade Afghanistan? The causes are as varied as they are complex. Some argue that the intervention reflected the application of the Brezhnev Doctrine, named after the Soviet premier Leonid Brezhnev. Under this doctrine the Soviet Union asserted its right to intervene in the domestic affairs of socialist countries to prevent their slide into the democratic–capitalist camp. Others attribute the Soviet move to economic motives, including its search for oil and its long-standing ambition to dominate energy resources in and around the Persian Gulf. Still others see it as a classic case of a prevailing northern power seeking access to warm-water ports.[11] More recent work, however, calls into question the notion that the Soviets desired to gain access to the Indian Ocean. Newly declassified documents show that fears of American gains in the Third World were uppermost in the minds of Soviet leaders.[12] In particular, the Soviet leadership worried that the United States would seek a beachhead in Afghanistan as compensation for its loss of influence in Iran following the Iranian revolution in 1979.

In addition to fears of growing American influence along its southern flank, the Soviets were in the grip of some dangerous lessons they had learned, above all from their intervention in Angola in 1975 and their loss of client states in Egypt and Somalia. These troubled military adventures in the periphery encouraged the Soviet leadership to believe that force was effective in achieving political outcomes; that developing countries would fall under Soviet influence; that intervention in support of liberation movements would not jeopardize US–Soviet relations; and that nationalist movements presaged a rising tide of socialism in the Third World, from Vietnam and Angola to Laos, Ethiopia, Mozambique, Zimbabwe, Cambodia, Nicaragua, and Iran.[13] More than any other reason, the Soviet belief in the incompatibility of American and Soviet interests and the inevitability of conflict drove their early decisions on when to intervene and how.[14]

The simmering tensions in Afghanistan came to a boil in 1979. The previous year, amid internal strife and political infighting, pro-Soviet forces mounted a coup d'état under the leadership of Nur Mohammad Taraki. His new regime initiated a program of large-scale economic development and reform. Many Afghans resisted top-down efforts to modernize the country. By the spring of 1979 the Soviet-backed Afghan government faced a growing insurgency and had lost control of much of the countryside. The Soviet leadership initially proved reluctant to get involved. That hesitation changed after Prime Minister Hafizullah Amin overthrew Taraki on his return from a trip to the Soviet Union. Taraki's overthrow in September and Amin's outreach to the United States deepened fears in Moscow that Afghanistan would slip into the US orbit.[15]

The Soviet leadership increased support for the Afghan army incrementally and pressured its newly installed president, Hafizullah Amin, to step down. Fearing an anti-Soviet countercoup, Moscow prepared to intervene. Closed decision making, limited information and expertise, conflicting goals, and narrow ideological constructs hampered the Soviet intervention from the start.[16]

In December Soviet forces swept into the capital by land and by air. President Amin was killed, and Babrak Karmal assumed office as the new Afghan president and chairman of the Revolutionary Council. Many Afghans viewed Karmal as nothing more than a Soviet stooge. The insurgency spread as the sides settled into a bloody stalemate. By the end of 1984 the Soviets had deployed upward of 130,000 troops in Afghanistan, but its escalation was insufficient to quell the violence.

The Soviet occupation of Afghanistan prompted a firm response from the United States.[17] America ramped up its assistance to anti-Soviet insurgent forces. President Jimmy Carter increased defense spending and announced the Carter Doctrine, which defined the Persian Gulf as a region of vital interest to the United States, and pledged to back up that commitment with force. The United States and China deepened their cooperation, further cementing the Sino–Soviet split.

The costs of the Soviet intervention were apparent as early as 1984. In a report on October 25 of that year the CIA assessed the domestic costs to the Soviet Union in stark terms: "In addition to the economic burden, the internal costs to the Soviets of their nearly five-year war in Afghanistan include the aggravation of an array of pre-existing societal problems. The war has worsened morale among Soviet conscripts, led more citizens to avoid the draft, and introduced Soviet youths to new forms of drug abuse. It has fed ethnic tensions, increased working class resentment of intelligentsia privileges, and strained regime credibility among a population increasingly cynical about Soviet propaganda claims. In addition, it has been a source of frustration and friction within the military, the KGB and the party, enhancing the potential for serious political conflict within the Soviet elite that could damage regime cohesion."[18] The war claimed as many as fifteen thousand Soviet lives and cost between $4 and $5 billion in 1985 and upward of $50 billion over seven years of war.[19]

While not insurmountable, the financial strains made the complex political situation in the Soviet Republics even more volatile.[20] The war sapped the legitimacy of the Red Army and deepened public doubts about the wisdom of the Soviet government's expansive, interventionist foreign policy. As one account of the Soviet debacle concluded, "No other step in the Brezhnev years did more to weaken Communist power in Russia and hasten its eventual collapse."[21]

When Mikhail Gorbachev took over the reins as general secretary of the Communist Party of the Soviet Union in 1985, he faced a growing economic crisis. Budget deficits and inflation were on the rise. He led the Soviet Union, in the estimation of one scholar, "closer to real democracy than it had ever been in its centuries-long history."[22] But entrenched interests and bureaucratic resistance to reform limited Gorbachev's room for maneuver. Soviet leaders sought to learn from the past and even from China's experiences under the leadership of Deng Xiaoping. As recent evidence shows, however, China's path of greater authoritarian control and military dictatorship would not have worked in the Soviet Union.[23]

The causes of the Soviet Union's decline are many, but the ill-fated intervention in Afghanistan surely ranks among them. From the British and Soviet campaigns to America's lengthy involvement today, the conclusion is inescapable: leaders stumble when they assume that large-scale military interventions in the periphery are essential for protecting vital interests and retaining prestige as a great power. Instead of acquiring new resources, bolstering legitimacy, or deterring rivals, military intervention in the periphery risks squandering resources, eroding legitimacy, and leaving the declining power exposed to challenges from adversaries. Dan is right to plead that "America's troops don't need to be thanked; they need to know that they are being used wisely and judiciously."[24]

Since 2001 the US role in Afghanistan has suffered from unrealistic policy decisions and miscalculations about desired goals, appropriate strategies, and the capabilities of the forces needed. The initial intervention quickly drove the Taliban and al-Qaeda from their sanctuary, but the window of opportunity for Afghanistan's postwar revival closed when American money and might were diverted to another state in the periphery, the US intervention in Iraq in 2003. This action strained US civilian and military capabilities, which undermined the opportunity for progress in Afghanistan.

Despite the lost opportunity in the early years of the intervention in Afghanistan, successive administrations from both parties surged forces or scaled them back based on a tangle of unsupportable strategic aims. What could not be accomplished with 140,000 troops was attempted with 14,000 troops. Both parties recognized that there was no military solution to this war.[25] And yet US policy makers failed to articulate a theory of victory beyond the imperative of not losing militarily. While leaders focused almost exclusively on Iraq, the United States lost sight of basic questions on Afghanistan: What are the interests that justify keeping American forces in Afghanistan? Are there more sustainable ways to prosecute US counterterrorism policy and prevent the conflict in Afghanistan from destabilizing neighboring Pakistan? If there is no military victory at hand, would a political settlement within Afghanistan allow for a graceful withdrawal that protects US interests?

It is easy to have conditions-based success when policy makers leave those conditions undefined and try to muddle through. The United States carried the water in Afghanistan, but China, Russia, Iran, and other countries reaped the benefits of lucrative energy, mining, and transportation deals. By spending $46 billion a year on the war, the United States diverted resources away from winning the peace. The opportunity costs are significant. As the journalist and author Robert Kaplan notes, "A small fraction of that money could be better spent on smarter infrastructure investments in Asia ... to compete with China's maritime Belt and Road Initiative."[26] Indeed, what would the geopolitical picture look like today if America had invested the resources it spent in Afghanistan in its own Belt and Road Initiative for the region?

Dan would be the first to point out that the lengthy US intervention in Afghanistan weakened America in the core by depleting
resources and diverting attention from other challenges and
threats on the horizon. US policy in Afghanistan is a case study in
the dangers of intervening militarily in the periphery when objectives, risks, and investments are misaligned. Like the British Empire, America failed to ask the first-order question of whether
Afghanistan is central to US security interests. From a strategic
perspective, this is a dubious proposition. The United States has a
real interest in preventing al-Qaeda and other terrorist networks
from using Afghanistan as a base from which to strike the US
homeland. The question is whether there are more limited and
sustainable ways to accomplish that objective. By insufficiently addressing this second-order question at the outset, US political
leaders set the stage for America's longest war.

A more tailored and sustainable policy for Afghanistan would
have done several things differently. It would have vetted, trained,
and fielded Afghan military and police forces earlier. It would have
avoided the diversion of troops and resources to Iraq and leveraged
initial gains on the battlefield to achieve a political settlement with
the Taliban. And it would have brought greater focus and clarity to
the task of helping the Afghan government create legitimate, effective institutions that enable Afghans to govern themselves responsibly and ensure their security. Bombs and bullets alone will not
wipe away the terrorist threat or bring the Taliban to heel. Credible governance is a prerequisite for defanging the insurgency, integrating the Taliban into Afghan politics and society, securing US
interests in denying terrorist groups safe haven, and maintaining
stability in Pakistan.

Lessons for Statecraft

The United States need not choose to engage in sustained military
conflicts in the periphery to secure its vital interests in the core.
There are no easy solutions for Afghanistan, but there are lessons
from the history of British and Soviet military interventions that
speak to the choices America faces today.

First, large-scale military interventions in the periphery trap great powers in prolonged, costly occupations. The cases of the Anglo–Afghan Wars and the Soviets in Afghanistan offer a cautionary lesson: always ask the first-order strategic questions. The outer edges of empire and the farthest reaches of a hegemon's perimeter are rarely of vital interest to the core. A great power in pursuit of a quick win against a weaker foe in the periphery risks overreaching in a lengthy effort that depletes resources.

Leaders of great powers get trapped by wishful thinking if sound judgment and careful planning are lacking. To apply the counsel of the former US diplomat and United Nations official Jock Covey, the former senior State Department and Pentagon official Len Hawley, and retired colonel Michael Dziedzic, in any crisis in the periphery "it is likely that the local situation will be poorly understood, adversaries and difficult actors misjudged, ill-defined threats dismissed as unlikely, potent economic incentives overlooked, operational needs underestimated, partner commitments misread, and hopeful projections of indigenous popular support simply wrong."[27] The prevalence of miscalculation requires great-power decision makers to practice restraint and manage risks with foresight, creativity, and persistence.

History is replete with examples of how interventions in the periphery bring ruinous consequences to a great power.[28] In the twenty-first century, large-scale military interventions of long duration function not as a mark of a great power's prestige but as an anchor around that state's neck. Invading and occupying countries yields fewer dividends in knowledge-based economies, where centralization and control frustrate efforts to attract foreign investment and stimulate innovation in a world of globalized production.[29] What's more, rising nationalism, nuclear deterrence, and cyber weapons render great-power landgrabs a costly proposition. Military occupations require time, but as Dan learned and the historical record makes clear, time is the one commodity in short supply: the longer the occupation, the more likely it is to inspire nationalist resentment among the occupied population and the more impatient the occupying power's domestic populace becomes.[30]

Second, maintain balance by strengthening the core and avoiding overcommitments in the periphery. Declining great powers preserve their strength and influence by pursuing shared interests, collective responsibility, and burden sharing within the core while avoiding overcommitments in the periphery. Unforeseen global problems require the prevailing power within the core to be actively vigilant, adapt its strategic approach, and employ skillful statecraft.

Focusing attention on the core can avert costly uses of armed force in the periphery, reduce incentives for aggression, and afford the declining power a crucial advantage in deciding where and how to concentrate its forces.[31] In a post-dominant world this advantage should not be underestimated or dismissed on the grounds of amoralism, for it is precisely the husbanding of resources in the core that enables a great power to intervene decisively when strategic or humanitarian imperatives demand it. Consider that Ukraine lies on the frontiers of the core in Europe. The decision of the United States to sanction Russia for its invasion of eastern Ukraine in 2014 was a necessary course to deter further aggression against its NATO core. Similarly, the European Union's (EU) diplomatic and financial engagement in Ukraine is critical to improving the prospects of Ukraine's long-term stability and democratic political development. Both the United States and its European allies wisely chose not to intervene militarily in Ukraine, thereby avoiding overcommitment in the periphery.

Strengthening a resilient core also requires an established power to formulate strategies to prevent or, if necessary, reverse the erosion of democratic norms and institutions in core states. The decline of democracy in Hungary and Poland today, for example, demands the focus of the United States and its European partners. Hungary and Poland are NATO allies, EU member states, and bellwethers of the fate of democracy in Central and Eastern Europe. Since democratic allies make for stronger and more reliable economic and security partners, the United States should take active steps to prevent further backsliding in these countries. Western democracies can accomplish this goal through a blend of positive incentives, such as bolstering civil society and formulating comprehensive policies for democratic reform in Hungary and Poland, and more punitive measures, including diplomatic pressure, disciplinary sanctions, and reductions in economic assistance.[32]

Third, set realistic goals and stay strategically solvent. Adapting to relative decline requires setting clear goals and balancing ends and means. Britain faltered in setting achievable goals in the Anglo–Afghan Wars. Similarly, the Soviets invaded Afghanistan on the basis of a welter of conflicting priorities and policy pressures. The more complex the war and the more contradictory a great power's rationale for intervention, the higher the odds that it will lose control of events. The proliferating rationales put forward to justify the American presence in Iraq and Afghanistan are cases in point.

From time immemorial leaders of great powers stumble when the impulse to act outweighs the imperative to act wisely. The journalist Walter Lippmann famously wrote that foreign policy "consists in bringing into balance, with a comfortable surplus of power in reserve, the nation's commitments and the nation's power."[33] Scholars use the term "strategic solvency" to describe a situation in which a great power matches ends to means and sets realistic goals.[34] Just as no household or company stays afloat if it accumulates debts it cannot pay, no great power can remain solvent when it incurs obligations it cannot meet. Britain's intervention in the Anglo–Afghan Wars exacerbated its unsound fiscal situation and exposed vulnerabilities in its imperial defense; the Soviet Union's intervention in Afghanistan imposed weighty internal costs, fueled a budget crisis and inflation, and rendered the task of balancing its resources and commitments even more fraught. Today, the United States must recognize that its resources are not unlimited. If policy makers fail to attend to the sources of insolvency, Washington runs the risk that rising powers will expose as hollow its foreign policy and security commitments.[35]

When a great power declines, the imperative to restore solvency is all the more urgent. After all, it is possible to overreach in the core itself. NATO can expand too quickly and admit members that are difficult to defend or host intractable conflicts, thereby weakening the credibility of NATO's commitment to mutual defense. Similarly, the EU can pursue enlargement rounds without sufficient deepening and reform of its institutions, thereby undermining public support and effective policy making.

To avoid getting stuck in quicksand outside the perimeter, leaders of a declining great power must set realistic goals and balance ends and means judiciously: Will military intervention dangerously erode a great power's fiscal standing? Will it ensnare the great power in abuses that tarnish its brand or risk greater loss of life than lives saved? A substantial military intervention carries the risk of unintended consequences—both on a national level and, as Dan's story reminds us, on a deeply personal level. Managing those consequences requires a declining power to tether leverage to strategy and strategy to resources.[36] Policy makers must assess whether a particular threat on the periphery requires a major commitment or a smaller, long-term investment in stabilization, training, advising, and institution building. As many wise military leaders have warned, if a great power enters a conflict, it can never know the full range of potential costs, outcomes, or unintended consequences. It's easy to get in; hard to get out. Following the US invasion of Iraq in 2003, the former commander of US Central Command general David Petraeus asked the right question: "Tell me how this ends?"[37]

The historical lesson of the British military commitment to three Anglo–Afghan Wars and the Soviet occupation of Afghanistan is not simply that these interventions were misguided from the start; it is that London and Moscow started these wars without thinking about how to end them.[38] The journalist Gregory Feifer calls the Soviet intervention in Afghanistan "the great gamble." It is a gamble that the United States repeated, in a different key, when it diverted resources from Afghanistan to intervene in Iraq. "Twenty-four years after the Politburo's contemplation of a 'quick' invasion of Afghanistan in 1979," Feifer laments, "the Bush administration believed it could withdraw within months of invading Iraq."[39] Great gambles do not a responsible strategy make.

Finally, if military intervention in the periphery is absolutely necessary, "do it wisely and do it well." The rise of al-Qaeda following US disengagement from Afghanistan in the 1990s and the resurgence of the terrorist group Islamic State of Iraq and Syria (ISIS) in the wake of America's withdrawal from Iraq in 2011 underscore the need to plan for all contingencies. The same can be said of financial contagion, radioactive materials, greenhouse gas emissions, and deadly pathogens, which cross borders with impunity. To deal with these transnational challenges effectively, core states should give priority to tailored, cooperative, and nonmilitary engagements in the periphery. Strategic investments in civil society and democratic governance, security sector reform, climate mitigation and adaptation, public health capacity, and basic education are more likely to address the root causes of instability and provide a foundation for resilient societies.

There are cases in which military intervention in the periphery may be compelling in the extreme, such as genocides and civil wars that endanger vital US interests or terrorist safe havens that threaten the US homeland. In these instances a declining great power should heed former US national security advisor Brent Scowcroft's advice to "do it wisely and do it well."[40] This task calls for leaders of a great power to set clear priorities, mobilize and sustain public support and bipartisan backing, mitigate risks, and constantly evaluate the costs and benefits of intervention. Early action and joint planning are critical for integrating military and intelligence tools with political, diplomatic, and humanitarian objectives, combining strengths with allies from the core and partners in the region, and developing realistic exit strategies.

In defining the extent of its involvement in the periphery, a declining great power should steer clear of the credibility trap and draw red lines with great caution or not at all. The temptation for a declining power to put fences around its interests and overseas possessions is ever present. Striking the right balance between reassurance and deterrence is especially challenging during moments of decline.

Rising powers threaten the established order and limit the options of the declining power. All the more reason to avoid drawing lines that a great power would be unable or unwilling to enforce down the road. Circumstances can change after leaders draw red lines.[41] Red lines also generate unforeseen, unintended consequences. To draw a red line is to give the rising power a green light to test the declining power. If the rising power crosses that line, leaders of the declining power need to be prepared to enforce it, which raises a host of vexing issues.[42]

The credibility trap lies in the assumption that use of force is the only way to demonstrate seriousness of purpose and commitment.

Like power, credibility is a matter of perception. There are myriad ways to influence perceptions of resolve, including through the use of alliances, application of economic and diplomatic pressure, raising of local readiness and alert levels, and increases in air and missile defense.[43] Surely a declining great power's threats and promises are more credible if it conserves enough power to make good on them. The insight of the political scientists Paul MacDonald and Joseph Parent is worth underlining: "Commitments are checks: they only cash when there is something behind them."[44] The United States today would be wise to conserve its strength, avoid drawing red lines, invest in assertive diplomacy and prudent alliance management, and explore all options short of war before committing to force.[45]

In the fall of 2018 America marked a grim milestone: the US military could enlist recruits to fight in Afghanistan who were born after the war started there in 2001. How does the United States weigh the costs of what the journalist C. J. Chivers calls the "War Without End"? For a generation of soldiers like Dan Berschinski, the costs are measured in personal terms. Dan's trauma puts a human face on the more than $1 trillion spent, the more than twenty-three hundred US military personnel who gave their lives for this cause, and the more than twenty thousand US service members who bear the scars on their bodies and in their minds.[46] The costs of war today fall overwhelmingly on the shoulders of the ¾ of 1 percent of Americans who have served in Afghanistan and Iraq since 2001. This lopsided distribution of responsibility widens an already troubling gap in civil–military relations.

The Next Choice

Then there are the economic and social costs. Rosella Cappella Zielinski of Boston University argues that the toll of the Afghan war includes not just the estimated $5.6 trillion that the United States has spent on its post–9/11 military campaigns. The costs are also felt in how America funds its wars. To pay for World Wars I and II and the Korean War the United States relied on direct taxes and bond campaigns, which reduced income inequality; to pay for today's wars it cuts taxes and relies on deficit financing and borrowing from abroad, which fuels inequality at home.[47] For great powers in decline the stakes go beyond core or periphery. Leaders need to manage the trade-offs between butter or guns: How do policy makers allocate scarce resources among competing ends and avoid strategic insolvency?

CHAPTER THREE

Butter or Guns?

"We're not here to do small things—we're here to do the big things that will change the world." Innovation doesn't usually happen at bus stops. But when Arati Prabhakar heard those words on her evening commute, she knew that she made the right choice.

Arati immigrated from India to Texas as a child. By the age of six she was already musing to her mom about whether she should become a scientist or an engineer. Perhaps more than most people, Arati is keenly aware that life is a series of choices that may create promising futures. It was a curiosity that would serve her well. By the time she entered college at Texas Tech University, Arati had refined a theory about what scientists and engineers value. "The scientist," she tells me, "wants to know and understand." The engineer responds, "That's a good starting point, now what are we going to build?" Arati's mind was made up: she was a builder.

She navigated the following years, in her modest telling, "by the seat of her pants." She became the first woman to earn a doctoral degree in applied physics at the California Institute of Technology. The thought of staying up until 2 a.m. in a laboratory didn't sound very appealing. So she applied "on a lark" for a congressional fellowship and went to work in the Office of Technology Assessment in Washington, DC, a legislative branch office that advised members of Congress on the major science and technology issues of the day. It didn't take long for Arati's talents to get noticed. By 1986 she had joined the Defense Advanced Research Projects Agency, or DARPA, rising in short order to lead its Microelectronics Technology Office.

DARPA pushes beyond the frontiers of discovery. Its mission is to anticipate, prevent, and create technological surprise. When the Soviets launched the Sputnik satellite into orbit, President Dwight Eisenhower resolved that America would never again fall behind in the space race—or any technological race. If there's a motto at DARPA, it's Change the World. And change the world it has. From developing the Internet's precursor, ARPANET, to the miniaturized Global Positioning System (GPS) that we use in our cars and phones, to the user-friendly interfaces that define today's computers, DARPA has played a seminal role in creating the technologies that power the information revolution. One of DARPA's program managers, Matt Hepburn, puts it more starkly: "If you don't invent the internet, you get a B."[1]

Arati thought about this storied history when she became the head of DARPA on July 30, 2012. After being away from the agency for nineteen years, she was coming back as its director, a job that includes responsibility not only for identifying the next technological revolution but also for getting there first. Arati was driven by a sense of purpose. She was also brimming over with questions. The last time she had worked at DARPA, memories of the Cold War were still fresh. I asked her about the differences between then and now. "The Internet hadn't taken off yet," she recounted. "Business cards didn't even have an email address!" No one imagined the iPhone, let alone a map of the human genome. As Arati explains,

> When DARPA was founded, the center of gravity and all the work was within the United States. American companies and manufacturers would build their products in the United States and gear them to US markets. Universities focused on communities at home, because that's where the students came from. Today, companies at the forefront of commercializing new technologies are not always in the

United States; the first market they serve is not always the
US market. And universities welcome students from
around the world. Now there's a global market for generating research and turning it into commercial output. One
visible example is research in clean energy technologies.
Our country is struggling to figure out how we play our
role in this new environment. Over and over, you see Chinese or Singaporean investors coming in and saying, "Not
only will I invest—I will provide the land and the infrastructure." They make it easy for innovation to happen
somewhere else. This was inconceivable in prior decades.

All of these challenges swirled around in Arati's head when she
took up the mantle of leading DARPA. The culture of an organization is essential to its purpose. How could DARPA's culture adapt
to this new era? Would the organization live up to its achievements? What level of commitment would be required to drive
groundbreaking research in a world where more players were
shaping the technological map with greater intensity and at more
levels than ever before? Arati recalled the words she heard at the
bus stop on her evening commute, when one of DARPA's program
managers paused to offer his congratulations on her appointment
as director. His commitment to "do the big things that will change
the world" confirmed to her that DARPA's culture was ready for its
next challenge.

Arati and her team called the new program Safe Genes, one of
a number of programs DARPA developed to advance its mission in
this new environment. Scanning the horizon, they realized that the
revolutions now occurring in biology and the physical sciences
contain all the elements of a technological surprise: the same technologies that allow us to eradicate infectious diseases could also be
used by terrorists to spread diseases. The risks of "bio-error" and
"bio-terror" are very real. The challenge is to harness the best possibilities of the biological revolution and tame the worst. After all,
it's not hard to imagine what could go wrong. Start with the lack of
controls and countermeasures.[2] DARPA Program Manager Renee
Wegrzyn draws a helpful comparison: "If you want to pursue
new genomic therapies for cancer or blindness, what if there are

'off-target' effects. If you're taking a drug, you can stop taking it and eventually it leaves your system. But if it's changing your genome, you need to think creatively."[3] There is no off switch yet for a gene editor that sets out to make a change in a genome.

That is where DARPA's Safe Genes program comes in. It seeks to accelerate gene-editing capabilities while making them more controlled and reversible. Wegrzyn puts it this way: "What do the surprises look like—what's the Sputnik of this type of work?"[4] It's a good question, and one that could lead to all sorts of strange and wondrous things, from reviving long-extinct creatures like woolly mammoths to creating new data storage systems at the level of DNA. The question is not whether improbable, unforeseen events will confront America in the future; the question for Arati is whether such events "might come in the form of a terrible surprise from a radical actor or from visionary leadership that decides a strategic change is necessary. The challenge is that when those moments present themselves, are you ready with concepts that prove something new is possible? That's why we invest in research and development."

The work Arati and her colleagues at DARPA do takes intense thought and vision. Breakthrough leaps in innovation require more than a village. They are the product of a research ecosystem that connects the federal government with private industry, foundations, national laboratories, and research universities. Innovation results from long-term, persistent investments in R&D, science and technology, education, and infrastructure. It relies on teamwork across the public and private sectors and the sharing of knowledge from one generation to the next.[5] Above all, it requires leaders to cultivate an innovator's mind-set that embraces long-term thinking, anticipates change, creates and seizes opportunities, and promotes national productivity.

Strategic Choice: Butter or Guns?

All societies face a choice between butter and guns. Since countries have limited resources and potentially unlimited national goals, it is the responsibility of political leaders to negotiate the trade-offs.[6] This strategic choice boils down to two basic goods: "butter" refers to investments in those goods that promote economic well-being and productivity, such as R&D, science and technology, education, and infrastructure; "guns" refer to investments in goods that promote the security and defense of the nation, such as military weaponry and personnel.[7]

Deciding between butter and guns is not an either/or choice; it is about setting the right balance between them. It is also an annual choice. Nations must continually reassess the balance of investments in light of changing political, economic, and security conditions at home and abroad. Getting the balance wrong can reduce a great power's competitiveness relative to other nations. Getting the balance wrong repeatedly can lead a great power to absolute decline.

America's capacity for innovation is the wellspring of its economic might; its economic might, in turn, underpins its military power. As Paul Kennedy observes, "The history of the rise and later fall of the leading countries in the Great Power system since the advance of western Europe in the sixteenth century . . . shows a very significant correlation over the longer term between productive and revenue raising capacities on the one hand and military strength on the other."[8] Trace the decline of great powers and one sees the symptoms not only of imperial overstretch and military exhaustion but also of underinvestment, declining productivity, and rising inflation. By overspending on the military in the short term declining great powers draw resources away from investments that bolster economic competitiveness and military advantage over the long term.[9]

For a declining America today, the choice is clear: Should the United States invest more in the sources of its productive capacity, including increased spending on R&D, science and technology, education, and infrastructure? Or should it invest more in the sources of its military capacity, including increased defense spending on hardware, new platforms, and bigger force structures?

In his "Chance for Peace" speech in 1953 President Eisenhower highlighted the trade-offs between butter and guns in vivid terms: "The cost of one modern heavy bomber is this: a modern brick school in more than 30 cities. It is two electric power plants, each serving a town of 60,000 population. It is two fine, fully equipped hospitals. It is some 50 miles of concrete highway. We pay for a single fighter plane with a half million bushels of wheat. We pay for a single destroyer with new homes that could have housed more than 8,000 people."[10] The trade-offs President Eisenhower describes are aptly illustrated in the production possibilities frontier, a common graph in economic analysis. The closer one moves to one end of the frontier (guns), the higher the opportunity cost in terms of production at the other end (butter). As the political scientist Paul Poast observes, "As an economy allocates more and more resources toward the production of a particular input, those resources are less and less efficient at producing a given output. As the economy allocates more resources to gun production, eventually the best butter producers . . . are drawn into gun production."[11]

Setting the balance between butter and guns requires careful management and a broader definition of national security. DARPA shows the potential for synergy when investments in defense agencies are geared toward the long-term goal of "expand[ing] the frontiers of technology and science far beyond immediate military requirements."[12] The US defense budget supports employment for those who serve in the military, civilian employees at the Pentagon, and the many government contractors, scientists, and technicians who comprise the defense industrial base.[13] Research shows, however, that large military budgets come with opportunity costs. Defense spending in peacetime is associated with rising income inequality.[14] It produces fewer jobs and technological breakthroughs than alternative forms of government expenditure, such as investments in basic research and infrastructure.[15] Excessive defense spending also has a negative, indirect relationship with economic growth.[16] The challenge is to find the optimal balance between spending on economic productive capacity and spending on military capacity and to ensure that national security is construed broadly to include flexible, creative investments in overlapping diplomatic and development areas.

This classic tension between investing in the sources of a nation's economic might and allocating funds to military operations and modern weaponry stalks American power today. Arati's story compels us to think of this choice in terms of three broad goals: national innovation, national security, and national finance.

America's edge is eroding on all three of these goals. Instead of promoting national productivity and innovation, the United States is setting itself up for a period of prolonged stagnation by its lack of adequate investment in R&D, science and technology, infrastructure, and human capital development.[17] Instead of adapting its national security investments to twenty-first-century challenges, America is stuck with legacy military hardware, a bloated bureaucracy, and bumper sticker solutions to complex problems.[18] And instead of balancing its finances for the long term the United States is trapped in short-term thinking that runs up deficits and debt without generating additional productive capacity. Absent serious changes in how it sets priorities the United States risks diminishing its national wealth in the long term, thereby undermining its military power.

National Innovation

Arati's pioneering work at DARPA demonstrates that innovation happens with the right mix of principles, people, product, and process.[19] Successfully weaving these elements together is the mark of what one assessment of national power called "ideational capacity," or the ability to make the right production choices with the right resources, given a country's stage in the innovation cycle and the level of global economic competition.[20] In an age of 5G telecommunications networks and almost breathless advances in robotics and artificial intelligence, striking the right balance between butter and guns isn't an option; it's a strategic necessity for American leadership.

Instead of speeding up the wheels of innovation, however, the United States is pumping the brakes. The rate of new starts-ups in America is slowing, and more and more companies are reaching maturity (sixteen years or older).[21] The United States benefits from an open and competitive marketplace, but consolidation is increasing across industries. China's economic model is hampered by weak rule of law and inefficient allocation of investment. Despite these constraints, its commercial ecosystem is dynamic and has produced nearly half of the world's top performing technology companies.[22] US federal spending on R&D as a percentage of

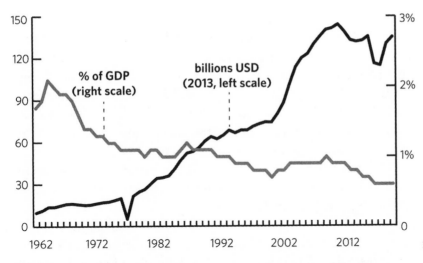

Figure 3.1. US federal outlays for the conduct of research and development.
Source: Congressional Budget Office.

GDP declined by more than half between 1964 and 2013. Since the early 1990s China's R&D spending has increased thirtyfold. Today, China is poised to outspend the United States in R&D, out-innovate the United States in quantum computing, biotechnology, and artificial intelligence, and outpace the United States and its allies in turning innovations into commercial applications.

An innovation ecosystem requires patient, long-term investments in R&D, science and technology, education, and infrastructure. America needs to reinvigorate its purpose on all fronts. I have already mentioned the declining share of US federal investments in basic research and science and technology. Uneven access and socioeconomic inequities limit the reach and effectiveness of the US education system. Since the 1970s education spending per capita in the United States has gone up relative to other economies in the Organization for Economic Cooperation and Development, but its average scores in math and science lag behind those of many developed nations.[23] By contrast, China produces more than double the number of science and engineering bachelor degrees as the United States, and it rivals the United States in terms of the number of science and engineering doctoral degrees.[24] Publications and citations in science, technology, engineering, and math papers are imperfect measures. Still, it's notable that China's share of such papers increased from 4 percent of world totals in 2000 to 19 percent in 2016, topping America's. China produces more published artificial intelligence papers than the United States and may overtake it in the top 1 percent of most-cited AI papers by 2025.[25] Tsinghua University in China ranks first in the number of highly cited papers in mathematics and computing, and China is home to six of the top fifteen universities in these subjects.[26]

As for infrastructure, a key driver of economic development, the United States faces a looming investment gap that will cost upward of $3.9 trillion in GDP by 2025.[27] Fixing crumbling roads, bridges, and other support systems makes the economy more efficient in taking advantage of the results of basic research. President Eisenhower recognized this fact when he pushed for the Interstate Highway System. Today, the United States has failed to build the underlying infrastructure to meet current needs, let alone next-generation advances in the digital economy. China, by contrast, has made investments in infrastructure a strategic priority through its Belt and Road Initiative, including through its Digital Silk Road and investments in Southeast Asia.[28] The Belt and Road Initiative is more than an economic vision. It is the opening salvo in China's efforts to extend its influence, develop client states, and secure new markets, raw materials, and trading routes over land and sea.[29] Current trends indicate that the disparities in US and Chinese investments in basic research, education, and infrastructure will not be changing anytime soon: America needs to restart its innovation engines.

Innovation requires determined focus and steady investments from government in several disciplines, both civilian and military. The economist Mariana Mazzucato challenges the notion of government as the long arm of an administrative state that corrects market failures. She argues instead that we need to think of government as the "entrepreneurial state." The US government helped to create and shape its domestic aerospace and consumer electronics industries in the post–World War II period; it can apply that same energy and vision to shaping the clean energy market today.[30] There are many reasons for government to invest in basic research. Investments in the military alone will not enable the

United States to build a future workforce of trained scientists and engineers or compete effectively with other nations. And while companies focus on strategic investments in their respective markets, R&D spending in the private sector tends to leave gaps in areas that require large collaborations over time without immediate market incentives, such as research in pure mathematics, the physical sciences, and other fields that push the boundaries of scientific discovery. To understand the role of government in stimulating innovation, consistent with market principles, consider the effort to sequence the human genome. This project cost the US federal government $3 billion, but the return on that investment produced more than a quarter of a million jobs and $19 billion in personal income.[31] In fact, as researchers from the Massachusetts Institute of Technology show, for every $10 million in additional funding for the National Institutes of Health, private companies generate 2.7 additional patents and gain $30.2 million in added value on the stock market.[32] These success stories are not isolated cases. Recall the history of government investments in science and technology: the role of DARPA in creating the precursor to the Internet; the military's early investments in Navstar, which lay the groundwork for GPS; and NASA's Apollo missions, which drove the invention of the microchip. In each case, teamwork between government, industry, and academia proved critical.

National Security

Given the possibilities of greater investments in national innovation, it is troubling that the United States continues to spend enormous sums on outdated defense facilities, high-maintenance military platforms, and legacy hardware and systems at the expense of the capabilities it needs to advance its security at home and around the world. The commercial sector increasingly drives the innovation of technologies that are critical to warfighting, such as applications of artificial intelligence and machine learning. America's free and open economic model is a strength, but the federal government's ability to harness emerging technologies is limited by antiquated bureaucratic practices and a complicated relationship with technology companies.

By comparison, China seeks to leverage commercial developments through a top-down, whole-of-nation approach to innovation, known as military–civil fusion. Beijing pursues asymmetric strategies and capabilities to offset US advantages and deny it access to critical theaters of operation. Instead of investing in the capabilities and operational concepts necessary to adapt to this new strategic environment, America continues to invest in organizations, facilities, and weapons systems that are of little value to its security today or in the near future.[33] The National Defense Strategy of 2018 recognizes the changing security environment. Its strategic focus on China and Russia is a step in the right direction, but critical questions remain about its implementation, resource allocations, prioritization, and operational requirements.[34]

Equally concerning with regard to expenditures on national security, the United States is allowing its diplomatic and development capacity to wither on the vine. The International Affairs budget, which funds the State Department and the US Agency for International Development (USAID), makes up only 7 percent of discretionary spending on national security.[35] Whereas China has doubled its budget for foreign affairs in recent years and now boasts more diplomatic posts than any other country, the United States is moving in the opposite direction.[36] The administration of Donald Trump requested a 10 percent increase to the defense budget for fiscal year 2018, while proposing to slash the budget for the State Department and USAID by 30 percent. Defenders in the administration called it "a security budget."[37] This is dangerous folly.

Diplomacy and development are indispensable complements to hard-power assets. US diplomats and development experts keep Americans safe and secure, promote human rights and democracy, solve conflicts without firing a shot, and create new markets for US goods and services. Force and diplomacy are mutually reinforcing. During the Obama administration the reversal of the tide of Ebola in West Africa, the resolution of Afghanistan's political crisis in 2014, and the negotiation of the Iran nuclear deal are prime examples of the need for close and continuing cooperation between the State Department and the Pentagon. The former US defense secretary James Mattis spoke from experience when he said, "If you don't fund the State Department fully, then I need to buy more ammunition."[38]

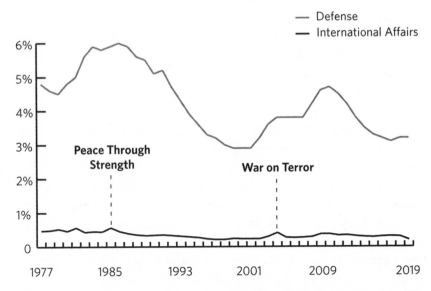

Figure 3.2. US defense and international affairs spending (percentage of GDP).
Source: US Global Leadership Coalition.

The American Academy of Diplomacy issued a report on the pitiful state of investment in diplomacy and development. The report put it starkly:

> Since the fall of the Berlin Wall, the diplomatic capacity of the United States has been hollowed out. A combination of reduced personnel, program cuts and sharply increased responsibilities has put maximum pressure on the capacity of agencies responsible for the missions of core diplomacy, public diplomacy, foreign assistance, and stabilization and reconstruction. ... During the 1990s—as the peace dividend was cashed—overseas staffing for these functions was significantly reduced in the context of the roughly 30 percent real-dollar reduction in US international affairs spending. In addition, the implosions of the Soviet Union and Yugoslavia resulted in the need to staff 20 new embassies in the new countries created as a result, and to expand staff based in other Eastern European nations without an overall increase in Department personnel.[39]

Those words were written in 2008. Sadly, they are even more relevant today. The State Department and USAID face major personnel shortfalls. Resources for language skills and functional training in emerging technologies, climate change, and anticorruption policies are sorely lacking. Following the end of the Cold War the United States slashed funding and staffing for public diplomacy and deprived US diplomats of the resources they needed to contest the information space globally. This shortfall is glaring at a time of rapid acceleration in social media and smartphone usage worldwide. The 2008 report also notes the "militarization of diplomacy."⁴⁰ These trends have only worsened as the Defense Department and regional combatant commanders increase their role and influence in political and diplomatic activities traditionally under the purview of the State Department and USAID, including support for foreign forces, counterterrorism, counternarcotics, police training, and economic capacity building.⁴¹

This imbalance in America's national security investments is not surprising. The growing prominence of the military in US national security policy is the product of decisions stretching back to the early years of the Cold War.⁴² Successive reforms of US national security institutions, from the National Security Act of 1947 to the Patriot Act of 2001, have privileged the military over diplomacy and development initiatives. Periodic crises focus the minds of policy makers and the public on the need for investments in defense. The consensus in favor of US military power over American political, diplomatic, and economic power also reflects a consensus between liberals and conservatives. The political scientist and national security expert Richard Betts points out that since Pearl Harbor "faith in the American mission and fear of enemies' power have united liberals and conservatives in a consensus for activism abroad and muscular military strategies, even when they argued about whether economic or military programs should be the focus of that activism. Only a bloody nose suppresses the impulse to military activism, and then not for long."⁴³

Since 9/11, budgetary gimmicks, supplemental appropriations, and the creation of an overseas contingency operations account to fund the wars in Iraq, Afghanistan, and other operations outside the regular appropriations process have combined to put oversight and accountability for military deployments abroad on the back burner. As a result, America's national security is heavily weighted toward defense while our diplomats and development experts scramble for meager resources to meet an ever-growing number of threats and responsibilities.

It's not surprising that America lacks the resources and expertise to deal with Russian propaganda, political interference, and disinformation campaigns after years of cuts to training in the Russian language and shortages of regional experts on countries in Eurasia. Diplomacy and development go hand in hand with defense. To pretend otherwise, as America's sixth president, John Quincy Adams, might say, is to strike out blindly in pursuit of monsters to destroy.

National Finances

To manage the trade-offs between butter and guns the United States needs to make farsighted decisions about how to allocate scarce resources among competing ends. Unfortunately, gross mismanagement of the US federal budget threatens to crowd out productive investments.

A crucial area is mandatory entitlement programs, which include Social Security, Medicare, and Medicaid, along with such domestic programs as Temporary Assistance for Needy Families, veterans' benefits, food stamps, child tax credits, and housing assistance. The scale of the challenge is daunting. At $2.5 trillion, mandatory entitlement spending comprises about 60 percent of federal spending and 12.7 percent of GDP.[44] Social Security spending makes up the biggest slice of that pie at roughly $1 trillion per year. Before the 2008 financial crisis Social Security took in more in taxes than it delivered in benefits, with more than three workers contributing for every one collecting. In 2018 the rising tide of baby boomer retirees forced Social Security to draw down on its principal for the first time. By 2034, absent a tax increase, Social Security will hit insolvency and be forced to cut back on benefits by 21 percent.[45]

The outlook for Medicare is even more precarious. Each year the United States spends about $625 billion on Medicare, which provides health care for seniors and persons with disabilities as well as prescription drug benefits. As health care costs rise the proportion of Medicare funded through general tax revenues increases. By 2048 general revenues will account for some 50 percent of Medicare costs, up from 43 percent today.[46] Trust Fund accounting obscures the fact that Medicare has been in the red for decades. Unless Congress acts, the Medicare Hospital Insurance Trust Fund will become insolvent by 2026. Depending on the fate of the Affordable Care Act, the costs of treatments, and the extent of coverage, unfunded liabilities for Social Security and Medicare over the next seventy-five years could top $50 trillion.[47] The fiscal cliff is a lot closer than we think.

Reining in the costs of federal entitlement programs is not a hypothetical challenge or the sole preserve of green eyeshade wearers. Behind the cost curves and budget justifications are worthy programs, needy families, and real lives at stake. Increasing the eligibility age, reforming benefits structures, and making prudent adjustments to spending and revenue would restore solvency to mandatory entitlement programs.

The solutions aren't the issue. There are more task forces and blue ribbon commissions working on reform of entitlement programs than just about any other topic in Washington, DC. The challenge is to summon the resolve to put entitlements on a sustainable footing for the good of ordinary American citizens. That task will require more than simple slogans. Entitlement costs are rising largely because of an aging population, declining birthrates, widening inequality, and rising costs in health care, education, and other basic services.[48] Addressing these fundamental challenges demands innovative approaches to resolving the political deadlock. Most important, America's political leaders need the courage to decide on both revenue and spending adjustments in entitlement programs.

This raises the question of debt and deficits. America's federal debt now exceeds $21 trillion. According to a report from the Congressional Budget Office, US public debt is forecast to rise to 144 percent of GDP by 2049.[49] Public debt in the United States over the past half century, by comparison, averaged 42 percent of GDP. Entitlements are not the only culprit. Two wars, tax cuts in

2001, 2003, and 2017, and the Great Recession helped turn a $100 billion surplus in 2001 into annual deficits that are forecast to exceed $1 trillion.

One thinks of economics and great-power politics as separate realms. But there's no denying that rising annual deficits and the national debt pose a problem for American power. The more a government borrows, the higher the interest rate it pays on its debt. The United States shelled out about $363 billion in interest on the national debt in 2018, or 6 percent of federal spending. That's about ten times what the next major power spends in serving the interests on its debt.[50] As a share of GDP, US interest payments on the debt are forecast to increase from 1.6 percent today to 3.1 percent in 2028.[51] Higher interest rates will slow economic growth and limit the capacity of government to respond to downturns.

The opportunity costs don't end there. Excessive debt creates the illusion of growth and introduces uncertainty about the distribution of debt-serving costs, which distorts the economy and hampers productive investments.[52] Every dollar the federal government spends on paying down the interest on debt is a dollar not spent on R&D, science and technology, education, and infrastructure. To be sure, nations can accumulate debt to stimulate demand in hard times or invest in productivity-boosting capabilities for the next generation. But large tax cuts that benefit the rich when the economy is booming and unemployment is low will only exacerbate America's serious fiscal challenges, not solve them.

Growing US debt and deficits pose a longer-term geopolitical challenge to American power, for two reasons. First, financial imbalances render declining powers vulnerable to what the former US defense official Andrew Marshall termed "competitive strategies," which seek to exploit and worsen inefficiencies in how countries mobilize resources for war. In peacetime competition, the great power that uses its resources most efficiently will gain a crucial advantage over the long term.[53] The ability of the United States to raise the costs of long-term competition for the Soviet Union and exploit inefficiencies in its economic planning were paving stones on the road to its collapse in 1991.

The second geopolitical challenge of rising US debt and deficits relates to the benefits America enjoys from the hegemony of

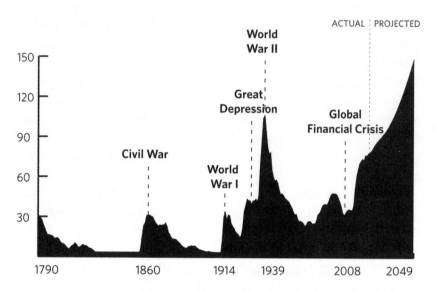

Figure 3.3. US federal debt held by the public (percentage of GDP).
Source: Congressional Budget Office.

the greenback, which accounts for more than 60 percent of global
reserves. The dollar's reserve status affords the United States key
advantages, including financial power over cross-border payments
and the ability to finance its external deficits by, in effect, "printing
money and lending it abroad."[54] In the scholar Michael Mastanduno's words, the United States is a "system maker and privilege
taker."[55] America's macroeconomic autonomy comes at a price:
global reserve currencies tend to appreciate relative to other currencies, which makes it harder for the issuer to boost exports.[56]
The benefits to the United States of having the dollar as the
world's reserve currency are manifold. That is why China pressures
African nations to denominate their debt in yuan, lobbies nations
to cut deals on bilateral currency swaps, and pursues workarounds
to the Society for Worldwide Interbank Financial Telecommunica-
tion, a global financial clearinghouse in Brussels.

After the Trump administration walked away from the Iran
deal in 2018 and threatened secondary sanctions on European
companies, the EU forged ahead with a "special purpose vehicle,"
and Turkey and India moved to trade in local currencies.[57] The

renminbi and euro don't hold a candle to the dollar today. The greenback remains preeminent, the US Federal Reserve remains the global lender of last resort, and the US dollar enjoys advantages in global financial transactions.[58] But, again, the snapshots of today should not be mistaken for the signposts of tomorrow, particularly if the United States continues on a path toward fiscal profligacy and wields its international financial power with abandon.[59] Rising debts and deficits are matches to the kindling. Investors flock to the dollar because of America's deep capital markets, commitment to the rule of law, global leadership, and competent monetary authorities.[60] If the US debt-to-GDP ratio climbs staggeringly higher, it will damage the country's reputation as a safe haven for global capital and make borrowing harder.

Challenging Trade-offs

National innovation, national security, and national finances are tightly linked. America cannot solve one without addressing the others. Adequately funding discretionary programs over the long term depends on getting US debt and deficits under control. An imbalanced national security toolkit could accelerate the militarization of foreign policy and increase the likelihood of America getting bogged down in foreign wars, which would further strain US finances and the solvency of mandatory federal programs. Funding entitlement programs and increasing spending without boosting revenues will mean more debt, which could slow growth, raise interest rates, and widen the trade deficit.[61]

The difference between productive, or self-liquidating, debt and unproductive debt is important in making this strategic choice. Productive debt supports investments in R&D, science and technology, education, and infrastructure. As the financial expert Michael Pettis notes, this form of debt "adds to the total debt in the economy, but rather than heighten the economy's debt burden it usually reduces the burden by increasing the wealth or productive capacity created by the project by more than the costs of the project. . . . [Self-liquidating debt] is ultimately sustainable because it allows economic actors to service the rise in debt by more than the associated debt-servicing costs."[62] Low interest rates offer some flexibility for deficit spending in the near term, but prudence dictates that the United States heed practical limits on its fiscal policy.[63] Interest rates and deficits could rise faster than projected, and the national debt cannot be allowed to grow in perpetuity. Exploding debt would entail a worsening fiscal picture, thereby putting additional pressure on defense spending. It's no coincidence that former chairman of the Joint Chiefs of Staff admiral Michael Mullen warned that "our national debt is our biggest national security threat."[64] The defense analyst Michael O'Hanlon and the former US under secretary of defense for policy Jim Miller agree. In their assessment, "There is a real threat to long-term economic power and thus national security when publicly held debt approaches the size of GDP, as will likely happen in the 2020s."[65]

With China and Russia combined approaching three-quarters of US GDP, the United States cannot simply wish away the trade-offs or substitute more spending for responsible financial management. If America fails to pay the tab on its leadership bill in Europe or the Asia-Pacific, its allies may look elsewhere to meet their security needs. The United States hardly benefits from a world in which its closest partners accommodate themselves to Moscow and Beijing, practice self-help and trigger arms races, or discover the benefits of neutrality along the major fault lines of geopolitics.[66]

To continue funding its entitlement commitments, the United States can increase revenue or decrease benefits. The Simpson–Bowles and Domenici–Rivlin commissions, not to mention a blizzard of think tank and nonpartisan reports, all recommend sensible options for the way forward. Such options include raising marginal tax rates on the highest earners, adjusting rates for capital gains and dividends, simplifying the tax code and closing loopholes, and raising corporate tax rates while allowing for deductions on new investments.[67] To repeat, the solutions are not the problem. The problem is whether US leaders can muster the political will to implement them before the country veers off the fiscal cliff.

As the economist Martín González de Cellorigo warned the leaders of a declining Spain in the seventeenth century, "Those who can will not and those who will cannot."[68] Cellorigo was part of a group of reformers in Spain known as the *arbitristas*. Think of them as modern-day opinion columnists with direct access to the president. But instead of opinion pieces in the *New York Times*, they wrote memorials to the king on such topics as monetary inflation, economic planning, and the costs and benefits of importing precious metals from the New World. As this history shows, the United States is not the first great power to face the consequences of decadence or to grapple with economic challenges that threaten its global position. Jeremi Suri rightly notes the centrality of economic power to long-term geopolitical heft. The reason Britain surged ahead in the eighteenth century was not because of its superior military capability. British leaders unleashed a revolution in prudent financial management that enabled the island nation to mobilize credit and raise revenue more efficiently and at greater scale than the Spanish or the Dutch.[69] Indeed, one way to interpret the rise and fall of great powers after the abdication of Charles V in 1556 is to consider these cycles as a prolonged competition in managing revenue and burnishing credentials in global capital markets.

Spain's Stagnation and Reform

Spain emerged as the strongest power in Europe through conquest and unification, the discovery of America and New World silver, the union of the Portuguese and Spanish crowns, and the management of a vast empire. Its decline in the seventeenth century stands as an object lesson in the close coupling of butter and guns for any nation's long-term fiscal health and security. The scholar Earl J. Hamilton put it this way: "Economics and politics were clearly interrelated, but a loss of economic strength appears to have been more largely a cause than a result of the political decline."[70]

The history of Spain's decline reveals its own twists and surprising turns. Recent historiography on early modern Spain emphasizes the importance of defeats on the battlefield in understanding its ultimate demise.[71] But Spain's military decisions were not taken in a vacuum. They shaped and were shaped by its fiscal and financial decisions, including multiple bankruptcies that stifled industry, curbed innovation, and made it harder to raise capital and pay for troops. So what did Spain get wrong in its economic strategies in the seventeenth century, and then what did it get right in the eighteenth?

Spain's descent was many things, but a surprise it was not. Even contemporaries sounded the alarm. Cellorigo, for one, forecast Spain's fall. As a churchgoing man and a lawyer, he combined the urgency of a prophet with a keen grasp of power and profit. Cellorigo upbraided Spain's leaders for devising policies that seemed calculated to "turn these kingdoms into a republic of enchanted men, living outside the natural order."[72] In fact, one of the first uses of the word "decline" in Spain came from Cellorigo's pen when he warned that "our Spain ... is subject to the process of decline [*declinación*] to which all other republics are prone."[73]

The fall of Spain over the seventeenth century sprang from a tangle of causes: imperial overstretch and foreign wars, poor leadership, the rise of trade monopolies, excessive taxation, the collapse of shipping and industry, monetary inflation and bankruptcies, economic stagnation, and demographic decline. According to some estimates, the population of the Spanish region of Castile declined by 25 percent between 1600 and 1623. Residents fled the countryside and poured into towns.[74] Heavy tax burdens, abusive practices by wealthy landowners, and the sale of public offices for private gain accelerated the growing depopulation of rural areas.

A high incidence of plague, made worse in part by long drought, contributed to the mass exodus from the countryside. But history shows that bad luck often stems from bad policy. Malnutrition, agricultural decline, and the forced expulsion of some three hundred thousand Moriscos in the early seventeenth century stripped the Crown of Aragon of skilled workers, devastated agriculture, and sped the loss of revenue. The historian Pierre Vilar considers the drivers behind the decision to expel the Moriscos: "[The Moriscos] were a residue of the conquered Moors, converted by force but not assimilated. ... About 1600, after so many revolts, repressions, expulsions and mass displacements, the danger of a general uprising was probably only a myth. But suspicion towards the crypto-Christian, 'bad blood,' the spy, the marauder, the business man who laid his hand on too many ducats, turned the Morisco into an all-too-obvious scapegoat in a moment of crisis."[75]

The collapse of Spain's industry, farming productivity, and regional trade made the impact of demographic decline even harder to manage. Drought and wars in Catalonia and Portugal decimated livestock. Sheep ranchers in Castile suffered losses. Population decline in the region also took a toll on industry. The English, Dutch, and French were surging ahead, stiffening competition. Wool from Ireland and silk from Piedmont replaced Spanish wool and silk by midcentury. Efforts to adapt to these new conditions ran afoul of the Crown's belief that merely increasing the money supply would fuel needed growth. In reality, loose monetary policy and the influx of precious metals abetted inflation and triggered the crisis of 1680, when "the economy of Castile foundered completely."[76]

Unremitting warfare compounded Spain's difficulties. For much of the sixteenth and seventeenth centuries, Spain was embroiled in conflicts with an assortment of enemies, from the Dutch, English, and French in the Eighty Years' War (1568–1648) and the Thirty Years' War (1618–1648), to the Catalonians, Neapolitans, and Portuguese in the 1640s, to the Portuguese again in the 1660s, to the War of Devolution against Louis XIV of France in 1667–68. The costs of fielding large infantry forces and warships to compete with the British and Dutch exhausted Spain's resources. Troubling signs were evident as early as 1557, when the monarchy declared bankruptcy. As Kennedy notes, "[Spain] simply had too much to do, too many enemies to fight, too many fronts to defend. The stalwartness of the Spanish troops in battle could not compensate for the fact that these forces had to be dispersed, in homeland garrison, in North Africa, in Sicily and Italy, and in the New World, as well as in the Netherlands."[77] Because Spain was pinned down on so many fronts it was not able to stagger conflicts, retrench, or benefit from periods of relative calm.

Spanish political dysfunction and domestic fragmentation weakened the fiscal capacity of the state. Castilian taxpayers bore the brunt of financing Spain's numerous wars. This mismatch between defense commitments and available resources undermined the productive capacity of the state: "Unable to raise revenues by the most efficacious means, [Spain] resorted to a variety of expedients, easy in the short term but disastrous for the long-term good of the country."[78] These expedients included excessive taxes on the least well-off and the sale of government assets and privileges to the highest bidder. The Spanish leaned on deficit financing without limits, which created imbalances that Spain's rulers struggled to rectify.

The foundations of Spain's power weakened further over the course of the seventeenth century, largely because of disagreements over whether to embrace or limit free trade, the rise in contraband trade, excessive taxes, and burdensome customs arrangements. Trade monopolies in Seville and Cádiz distorted the economy, as did the neglect of Spain's merchant fleet. The powerful guilds bear much of the blame. Most of these elites governed trade and determined privileges across vast swathes of the Spanish economy, from cobblers and masons to shoemakers, pastry cooks, locksmiths, harness makers, and wool weavers. The declining share of foreign trade and the pressure on labor turned the guilds into equally powerful interest groups in favor of the status quo. Since the status quo meant stagnation and the Crown depended on elites to meet growing revenue needs, the guilds served as a bulwark and a brake on the Spanish economy in the latter part of the century.

Spain's leaders failed to boost national productivity by reforming the tax code, curtailing the influence of the guilds, and controlling royal spending. The economy stalled. Investors poured money into unproductive areas like personal loans (*census*) and government bonds (*juros*) as opposed to agriculture or industry. As the scholar J. H. Elliot observes, "The nature of the economic system was such that one became a student or a monk, a beggar or a bureaucrat. There was nothing else to be."[79] The Roman Catholic Church and the bureaucracy grew, while trade and industry shrank. The *arbitristas* proposed myriad solutions to Spain's economic crisis. But government policy was trapped in short-term thinking. It possessed, in Elliot's words, "neither the courage nor the will to look its problems squarely in the face," and it rested on a "social system and a psychological attitude which themselves blocked the way to radical reform."[80]

One historian called this privileged attitude "the hidalgo mentality," after the Spanish word for minor nobility. Attaining the status of the *hidalguía* became an obsession for the plebeian class. Rank became the measure of all things, while the value of work declined. The fate of the hidalgo inspires both comedy and tragedy. It is comic because the line separating the hidalgo from the commoner grew ever thinner. If the hidalgo aspired to nobility, freedom, and pride of place as a soldier of the kingdom, reality paled in comparison. It is tragic because the hidalgo held little power, courted financial ruin by putting honor above earnings, and fared poorly as soldiers in the age of professional armies. The hidalgo neither fought nor enjoyed exemption from taxation. Not least, the disdain of the hidalgo for the enterprising merchant and productive ordinary Spaniards deprived the Crown of a deep well of human capital. Thus absolute decline combined with relative decline to put Spain on a path of financial ruin and economic stagnation.

The story does not end there. As recent work has shown, Spain was not an absolutist state but a fiscal-military state that became "less monolithic and hidebound throughout the eighteenth century" and drew on "different growth factors to those that had been present during the sixteenth and seventeenth centuries."[81] Spain's fiscal challenges were both the source of its undoing in the seventeenth century and, learning from its errors, the wellspring of financial innovations in the eighteenth century. After the War of the Spanish Succession, Bourbon monarchs implemented fiscal and financial policies that allowed for more efficient debt servicing and the exploitation of resources from the New World. There were limits to the success of these practices: provincial tax farms proved stubborn to reform, and the regime lacked capacity to deal with the increased revenue and spending.[82] But the Spanish Crown managed to construct a fiscal-military state that remained competitive with its European counterparts and that underscored the importance of aligning sound institutions with the political will to reform. As the historian Rafael Torres Sánchez concludes, "There was nothing new in these reforms, only the will to enforce."[83]

Lessons for Statecraft

What can be gained from the study of how Spain's leaders managed the trade-offs between butter and guns? Can we derive lessons from Arati's leadership in an age of rapid technological advances?

First, avoid the trap of short-term gains and play the long game well. Too often leaders base their judgments on short-term political calculations instead of longer-term strategic consequences. The fashionable attractions of nobility in seventeenth-century Spain reveal the dangers of short-term thinking. Similarly, the practice in America today of accumulating unproductive debt widens inequality, tempts inflation, raises interest rates, and fuels deficits.

Failure to put America's programs for social well-being on a sound fiscal trajectory represents the expediency of politics in the extreme. The same could be said of the tendency among leaders in America to value military might over diplomatic acumen. It's easier to increase budgets for the military to fight future wars than to justify more dollars for diplomats and development professionals whose success depends on counterfactuals: the wars that didn't break out, the arms races that never occurred, and the terrorist attacks from distant sanctuaries that were averted.

The historians Richard Neustadt and Ernest May defined the practice of "thinking in time" for a generation of policy makers. In their study of the Cuban Missile Crisis they noted that President John F. Kennedy and his executive committee "saw the issues before them as part of a time sequence beginning long before the onset of crisis and continuing into an increasingly indistinct future."[84] The time horizons of leaders represent one of the intangibles of a nation's power. How far out does a leader cast his or her gaze? Do they consider the long-term implications of their policies? I asked Arati about what she looked for in new hires. "When I hired great program managers," she explains, "the first thing I looked for was expertise in a technical area; the second thing was the ability to navigate from atoms and bites to the systems context, to how a new capability could change the world. That requires seeing the temporal dimension of what you're working on."

It helps to think of time horizons as the lens through which policy makers assess relative threats and make decisions about how to allocate resources. This lens can be concave or convex depending on the willingness of a leader to trade present costs for future gains and play the long game. Political leaders who value long-term strategic thinking use history to imagine new possibilities. In the 1870s and 1880s the German statesman Otto von Bismarck was a master of wielding time for geostrategic advantage. He deflected attention from Germany's growing strength by convincing the great powers of Europe that Berlin was the pivot around which crises should be managed and contained.[85] In 1969, when conflict broke out between the Soviet Union and China over the Ussuri River boundary, President Richard Nixon and Secretary of State Henry Kissinger perceived the clash not as a routine spat between rivals but as "the culmination of a long-building rupture between the world's two largest communist nations."[86] By thinking in time, Nixon and Kissinger pulled China out of the Soviet orbit and deftly arrested a period of US decline relative to the Soviet Union.

Thinking in time is just as relevant in US decision making on domestic policy. When President George H. W. Bush agreed to raise taxes as part of a deal to avert a fiscal crisis in 1990, he reversed a campaign pledge. Playing the long game may have cost President Bush his reelection, but it served the greater good of the country and put America on a sustainable economic path. Unfortunately, many of today's leaders govern by immediate crises, not by long-term compromise. Farsighted agreements across the aisle seem almost as rare as they are politically treacherous to legislators who cling to the short term. In 2011 America faced another fiscal crisis of its own making. Instead of striking a bargain for the good of the country, congressional leaders courted a government shutdown, took the country to the brink of default, and agreed to a self-destructive process called sequestration, which took a hasty, short-sighted, one-year slash to the US budget rather than a deliberate calculation of where America's power and purpose should reach. Likewise, the unfunded tax cuts of 2017 exploded America's debt at a time of economic growth and recovery. Tax cuts produced short-term benefits for the wealthy, but at what cost for the financial health of the United States? The budgetary brinksmanship in late 2018 and early 2019 followed a distressingly similar pattern. Thinking in time can point the way to wisdom, but it doesn't guarantee it.

Second, craft the long-term strategy before the shock of decline. When Niccolò Machiavelli wrote his famous handbook for princes, he derived his principles of statecraft from a study of political orders at moments of maximum danger. Civil conflict and coups were his laboratory. To be successful, Machiavelli counseled princes, turn moments of peril into opportunity and imitate what he called the great "armed prophets," such as Moses, Theseus, and Romulus.[87] Leaders of great powers in decline should be wary of this advice. In

earlier eras the United States required an external shock to rouse it
from its strategic slumber. Examples include the Japanese attack on
Pearl Harbor of December 7, 1941, and US intervention into
World War II; the Korean War and the formulation in 1950 of National Security Council Memorandum 68; the Soviet Union's invasion of Afghanistan in 1979 triggering President Ronald Reagan's
decision to roll back Soviet power; and the terrorist attacks of 9/11
prompting an overhaul of US homeland security.[88] America requires an equivalent dose of strategic vision today, but, as Arati and
her team demonstrated when they developed the Safe Genes program, the spark for that vision must come from leaders who see the
future and prepare accordingly.

An important aspect of thinking long term is that the United
States is not organized effectively to deal with the realities of a
post-dominant world. As Casimir Yost of Georgetown University
argues in a report for Georgetown's Institute for the Study of Diplomacy, "The US Government has lost the capacity for sustained,
government-wide strategic assessment and anticipation."[89] This diminished capacity stems in part from the fact that the US economy
and governing institutions continue to reflect the imperatives and
assumptions of the Cold War. America's toolkit for macroeconomic
policy was developed to take pent-up demand for housing, civilian
goods, and reconstruction needs abroad and convert it into political and military advantage in the struggle with the Soviet Union.[90]

Today, the challenge isn't how to profit from excess demand
but how to revive flagging demand in an era of growing indebtedness, stagnant growth, limited monetary tools, and polarized politics. This task requires an understanding of fundamental dynamics
while anticipating new challenges. As in the Cold War, the United
States must design an enterprising strategy that attends to the connections between economic policy and foreign policy.[91] But those
basic connections need to be adapted and applied to a new suite of
challenges, including today's environmental crisis, rising nationalism, transnational networks of organized crime and corruption,
and the need to manage the impact on resources, ecosystems, and
supply chains of a swelling global middle class.[92] Strategic foresight
is critical, but even more important is the political will to act on
that foresight when the moment demands it.

Anticipating long-term requirements and summoning the investments and shared purpose to guide a nation through periods of relative decline require changes in culture and psychology as much as in politics and economics. All we have to do is consider the example of Spain in the seventeenth century. The Spanish hidalgo nurtured a culture that put nobility ahead of the necessity of statecraft. The path to fiscal and financial innovation in the eighteenth century ran through a series of defeats on the battlefield and poor economic decisions that consumed Spanish finances and undermined its long-term competitiveness. This example tells us that the United States should not wait for the next financial crisis to craft and implement a realistic, long-term strategy to arrest its descent. Great powers in decline can turn around from a modest setback or collapse with a bang. If a declining power waits for a bang before making important decisions, it's far too late.

Third, robust diplomacy backed by resources is the sharpest and most cost-effective tool in a declining power's arsenal. Striking the right balance between diplomatic acumen and military muscle is challenging in the best of times. It is infinitely harder in the worst of times, when conflict looms, political orders erode, and hostile powers seek vulnerabilities to exploit. Turbulence abroad makes it more difficult to manage the trade-offs at home. When leaders of a great power confront a threatening international landscape, as the case of Spain demonstrates, they are more likely to spend imprudent sums on the military and accumulate greater debt. Steady investments in cost-effective diplomatic initiatives worldwide can reduce foreign turmoil and free up resources for investment at home that strengthens a declining nation's power base instead of depleting it.

Diplomacy offers more bang for the buck in another way: it enables leaders of a declining power to wield influence against rivals in lieu of the use of military force. Part of the challenge in a world of shifting power and rising challengers is that rivals can erode a declining power's position incrementally through technological advances, economic competition, and other nonmilitary means.[93] Exhibit A is Russia's disinformation campaigns against democratic elections in the United States and Europe, or China's efforts to control global telecommunications infrastructure and mobile Internet standards.[94] US threats of a conventional military response in such cases would lack credibility and invite international backlash.

Instead, a realistic, long-term strategy would organize the machinery of the US government to compete effectively. Russian meddling and Chinese grand strategy pay little mind to US organizational charts or budgetary accounts that create artificial lines between diplomacy, international development, institution building, and defense. Strengthening the tools of diplomacy and development gives the declining nation a powerful arsenal with which to fend off attempts by rivals that test its commitments, weaken its alliances, and undercut its position in areas of vital interest. Paraphrasing the Chinese strategist Sun Tzu, the journalist David Ignatius counsels the United States to "win wars without fighting them."[95] This wise advice cannot be implemented under proposals to slash America's diplomatic corps by 30 percent.[96]

What's required is a more comprehensive and holistic vision for the national security budget. For the US military, a new approach will mean trimming bureaucracies and force structures unsuited to the current geopolitical competition with China and Russia and reducing investments in legacy platforms and military systems.[97] Savings from these investments should support improved readiness and modernized capabilities necessary for managing the long-term geopolitical competition, including long-range air power, advanced munitions, nonpermissive intelligence, surveillance, and reconnaissance assets, unmanned undersea vehicles, and robust human–machine teaming methods. By paring back investments in legacy systems and high-maintenance military platforms that bloat its defense budgets, the United States can free up resources to invest more in needed capabilities for diplomacy and development, including climate mitigation and adaptation, contesting the information space globally, supporting civil society, and promoting good governance and institutional reform in fragile states.

Masterful diplomacy can spell the difference between controlled risk taking and bluster that leads to war. A great power needs to assert the rules of the road for international cooperation and mutual benefit. During the Cold War, especially after the Cuban Missile Crisis and, later, in the Middle East, the United States and the Soviet Union maintained diplomatic relations and were able to reach informal understandings to dampen the threat of direct armed conflict between them. These skillful diplomatic initiatives put boundaries on US–Soviet conduct and helped to ensure that Cold War rivalry didn't escalate to nuclear war. Diplomacy is a tough tradecraft successfully accomplished by capable, seasoned professionals. In a world where the only certainty is change, we need more diplomacy, not less.

Finally, put the drivers of US productivity first: R&D, science and technology, education, and infrastructure. The real elixir of growth is productivity, or the ability to generate rising output from labor. One of the seminal facts about America today is that it suffers from a productivity problem: average annual growth in productivity declined from 2.1 percent over the 1987–2004 period to 1.2 percent over the 2004–14 period.[98] Declining productivity growth can prove fatal to great powers. If a nation loses the ability to innovate, it grows lethargic and consumes its seed corn for the future. Declining great powers are not fated to collapse. But prolonged slumps in productivity growth make that outcome more likely.[99]

The case of Imperial Spain suggests that institutional reform and enlightened leadership are essential to nurturing productivity. Guild control, demographic decline, foreign misadventures, and unproductive investments in *census* and *juros* held back the reforms necessary to spur growth in Spain in the seventeenth century. Innovations in the construction of a fiscal-military state sparked a revival of sorts in the eighteenth century.

America need not imitate the successes and failures of past cases. But it should learn from them. To jump-start the engines of productivity, the US government—in the spirit of the American engineer Vannevar Bush's 1945 report to President Franklin Roosevelt titled "Science—The Endless Frontier"—should launch a commission to study and propose new ways to organize and structure the US science and technology innovation ecosystem.[100] This pivotal reorganization should include a multiyear initiative to promote basic research among all potential contributors, from the federal level through such institutions as DARPA, the National Science Foundation, and the Department of Energy; to universities that rely on federal and private funding to conduct research in new areas of science that cut across traditional disciplinary boundaries;

to the private sector, foundations, and state and local governments, which are pioneering new ways to imagine America's science and technology ecosystem.[101]

Arati's and her team's success in driving the next generation of advances in bio- and nanotechnology, genetically based therapies, artificial intelligence, and other basic research is proof that huge gains in productivity are possible when government, universities, and the private sector work together. Nurturing a research ecosystem that supports this collaboration starts by adapting the role of government for the world we live in today. As Arati puts it, "Most research investors in government agencies have over-constrained their work in trying to avoid merely doing more of what the markets do anyway. As a result, I'd argue that federal agencies have contributed to too big a gap between the public role and where private capital can move forward."[102]

In the end, productivity is about people. One obvious step the United States could take to invest in people is to fix its broken immigration system. Demographic challenges coupled with exclusionary practices quickened the pace of decline in Spain. America need not follow this historical pattern. While it's true that the United States enjoys a more hopeful demographic profile than most developed countries, it must also contend with declining birthrates, rural depopulation, and an aging population.[103] The economist Ruchir Sharma notes that average annual growth in the labor force in America declined from 1.7 percent in the period 1960–2005 to 0.5 percent in the period of 2006–16.[104] Compounding these negative trends are declining rates of US life expectancy, lower employment rates for working-age American men, and lagging public health and educational attainment. The United States has long enjoyed a superior human capital base. As Nicholas Eberstadt observes, America also benefits from the fact that it accounts for nearly half of net immigration to the developed world over the past seventy years.[105]

The United States has the right, as does any nation, to set the terms for new arrivals. Border security and social cohesion are not incompatible with humane policies for asylum seekers or longtime residents. Still, we would do well to remember the benefits of America's identity as a nation of immigrants and the power that accrues to the country that welcomes newcomers instead of stig-matizing them. Immigrants are twice as likely to form a start-up as the native-born, less likely to commit a crime, and more confident in securing the American Dream.[106] In fact, immigrants or their children have founded nearly half of the high-tech firms in the Fortune 500.[107] That should matter at a time when competition be-tween democratic and authoritarian powers is on the rise. Ulti-mately, this competition is being waged over the fate of free and open societies. The stakes are too high to sacrifice America's natu-ral innovation advantages on the altar of short-term political gain.

The Next Choice

The strengths of the United States in this competition begin with its people, but they don't end there. It is commonplace to hear that international politics is a contact sport. In the absence of global government to enforce contracts, guarantee rights, adjudicate dis-putes, levy taxes, or serve as a lender of last resort, states are left to fend for themselves in a Hobbesian world that is equal parts nasty, brutish, and short. Yet this picture is incomplete. It's just as accu-rate to say that international politics is a team sport. The country that can rally more partners to its side has a crucial edge. One of the ironies of America's situation today is not that it lacks partners or allies but that some people see its vast network of alliances and partnerships as a burden to be sloughed off. Leaders face a choice: Should a great power in decline jettison allies and go its own way, unconstrained and unbridled? Or should it cement relationships with allies, find new partners, and make credible commitments to amplify national power and rally others to its cause? As the smoke hung over the ashen remains of the World Trade Center on Sep-tember 11, one US diplomat resolved to find the answers to those questions.

CHAPTER FOUR

Allies or Autonomy?

W HEN NICHOLAS BURNS, THE US ambassador to
NATO, called US National Security Advisor
Condoleezza Rice on the morning after 9/11, he
delivered a powerful expression of support from
America's European allies: "Condi, the NATO allies want to invoke
Article 5 [the mutual defense clause]. I need the president's permis-
sion." It was a call that Ambassador Burns was born to make.

Nick grew up in Boston. His was a life of barbeques and baseball,
hard work and family values. It was a typical upbringing in turbulent
times. When Nick turned seventeen in January 1973 the Vietnam
War was dominating the headlines. The Nixon administration announced that it had "reached agreement to end the war and bring
peace with honor in Vietnam and in Southeast Asia."[1] After nearly
two decades of grueling conflict and guerilla warfare, peace seemed
more elusive than ever. The horrors of the Vietnam War burrowed
deep in American life. "It came into my community, our church, and
to the family dinner table discussions," Nick told me. "It dominated
my high school years." That's when Nick resolved to pursue a career
in diplomacy. The old saying is that war represents a failure of diplomacy. The truth is more complicated. Nick reflects on the causes of
the Vietnam War still today: "The war had been a horrible mistake. I
knew that the United States had to do better as a global leader."

Nick was born to greatest-generation parents, who came of age during the Great Depression and World War II. "There are times when you have to fight—World War II and the Korean War are the obvious examples," Nick says. "But there are also times when you need to think about other ways to achieve your goals—and that's diplomacy." Nick learned about American diplomacy and the history of America's relations with the rest of the world during college and graduate school. "I came to understand that the great power differential between the United States and the Soviet Union was that we led the NATO alliance, and they led a much weaker alliance," Nick tells me. "America's allies are partners in democracy. We share a belief in human freedom, individual liberty, and democratic values. That's a precious thing, and we need to safeguard it."

On 9/11, Nick would be called to do just that. After less than two weeks on the job as US ambassador to NATO, Nick got a note from his staff during a meeting with his fellow NATO ambassadors. The note informed him that an airplane had struck the World Trade Center. "I thought it was probably a terrible accident," Nick says. Shortly thereafter another plane hit the second tower. That's when Nick and his colleagues knew that the United States was under attack: "We tried reaching the State Department, the Pentagon, and the White House, but all three buildings were evacuated in the hours after the attack." The Canadian ambassador to NATO, David Wright, called him and asked whether he'd thought about invoking Article 5, which states that an attack against one NATO member is an attack against all.

As a student of history and a participant in some of the high-stakes events that brought about the collapse of the Soviet Union, Nick knew the significance of the commitment in NATO's founding treaty. Despite the mutual balance of terror that gripped the world during the Cold War, the NATO allies hadn't once invoked Article 5. He appreciated the bitter irony. "There was always a presumption in NATO," Nick explains, "that if Article 5 were invoked, it would be for the Americans to come across the Atlantic for a third time to protect the Europeans." Instead, the Europeans rose up to defend the Americans. Within a few hours of the attacks Nick had spoken to every NATO ambassador. "To a person," Nick tells me, "they were resolute. They understood the severity of this attack and what it meant. We had to respond, and there was no hesitation." Early the next morning Nick called Rice to ask for President George W. Bush's permission to invoke Article 5. Her response summed up the pride and sense of purpose that Americans took from Europe's show of support. She answered simply, "It's good to have friends in the world."

When NATO's principal decision-making body convened late on September 11, its secretary general, Lord Robertson, asked Nick to brief the group. The permanent representatives of nineteen countries gathered at a moment of tribulation and tragedy. No one knew how many people had been killed or injured. "This could turn out to be one of the bloodiest days in American history since the Battle of Antietam," Nick said to his colleagues, in reference to the deadliest one-day battle of the American Civil War. NATO is a body that runs on consensus. When the time for decision came, the allies demonstrated courage and tenacity in the face of terror. "When Americans woke up on the morning of September 12," Nick affirms, "what they heard was that our allies were there with us."

A few days later Nick and his wife visited the town of Louvain in Flanders. The residents of Louvain were no strangers to tragedy. As Barbara Tuchman writes in *The Guns of August*, the city suffered grievously at the hands of the Germans during World War I. As the Rotterdam *Courant* reported, "The fact of destruction remains . . . so terrible that the whole world must have received the news with horror."[2] The Germans burned the library of the University of Louvain and its rare collections, an act of wanton destruction that befell the library again in World War II.

As Nick and his wife approached the ornate town hall at the center of the city, a long line of people gathered outside. Curious about the growing crowd, Nick inched closer. "That's when we realized," he recalls, "they were waiting in line to sign a condolence book for the American people. Hundreds of Belgians lined up to sign the book and lay flowers, as did citizens from every NATO country at diplomatic missions throughout Europe and Canada. This outpouring of emotion—that's what an alliance means."

In the months and years that followed, NATO allies joined the United States in its campaign in Afghanistan and paid a heavy price for their solidarity. NATO nations and partner countries have suffered more than a thousand combat deaths over eighteen years of war, and the fight continues. In his fourth inaugural address in 1945 President Roosevelt reflected on America's purpose in a new world order. He recalled the words of the essayist Ralph Waldo Emerson: "The only way to have a friend is to be one."[3] In the aftermath of 9/11 the United States counted many friends. Can its allies say the same about America today?

Even as NATO reinvents itself in a new age its purpose is once again subject to debate. Is it obsolete or the anchor of a fragile peace? A sucker's bet or a winning hand? A relic of the Cold War or a rampart in today's wars? A protection racket that drains America's coffers or a community of values that shares the burden?[4] Which is it? The answer depends on one's definition of alliances: what they're good for, why they form, what forms they take, and what dilemmas they solve. For a declining power these questions aren't hypothetical.

The Greek historian Thucydides famously observed, "The growth of the power of Athens, and the alarm which this inspired in Sparta, made war inevitable."[5] The trigger for that war turned on Athens's choice to form a defensive alliance with the island of Corcyra, which brought the Athenians into conflict with the Corinthians, who in turn brought in the Spartans. Human folly, cultural arrogance, spirals of insecurity, and unforeseen circumstances all played a role in sparking the nearly three-decade-long Peloponnesian War.[6] The choice to form alliances or maintain autonomy remained a paramount concern of the Athenians and the Spartans. In the timeless words of Thucydides, "The strong do what they can and the weak suffer what they must."[7]

Strategic Choice: Allies or Autonomy?

The tension between courting allies and asserting autonomy goes to the heart of the choices that declining powers face and that America faces today. Should the United States pursue its interests by going it alone, exerting regional might through spheres of influence, and using a heavy hand to advance political and security interests over compliant neighbors? Or should America defend its interests and project its influence through alliances, security guarantees, multilateral cooperation, and forward deployments of troops and equipment?

Autonomy is in vogue today. During his campaign and upon assuming office President Trump advocated going it alone and took a purely transactional approach to US alliances. The clearest evidence of this was his "cost plus 50" proposal, which would charge US allies for 100 percent of the costs of hosting US troops and a 50 percent premium on top of that. As one analyst notes, "In the most benign scenario, 'cost plus 50' would double Japan and South Korea's payments for US forces and quadruple the contribution from Germany."[8] This proposal damaged the credibility of US alliances and reflected the misguided belief that security commitments are a losing bet for America.

As for spheres of influence, consider the strategies of Russia in Eastern Europe and the Caucasus, China in the South China Sea, and Iran in the Levant and Persian Gulf. These powers seek to impose their will on smaller neighbors and deny the United States access to vital waterways, trade routes, energy resources, and global partners. Evidence of a more heavy-handed approach was Russia's invasion of eastern Ukraine and its annexation of Crimea in 2014. By keeping the conflict at a low boil Russia seeks to undermine Ukraine's government, delay and disrupt reforms, influence its political development, and prevent it from integrating with NATO and the EU. Some experts point to the growing political, military, and economic ties between Russia and China as proof of an emerging alliance between these two authoritarian powers.[9] Russia and China make common cause in pushing back against elements of the liberal international order. Yet both countries jealously guard their sovereignty, pursue at times divergent interests in Central Asia and the Far East, and show little appetite for a mutual defense pact obligating them to come to the aid of the other in the event of war. It would be more accurate to say that Russia and China operate as autonomous powers, establishing spheres of influence over lesser powers and using their strengthening partnership to assert their interests against the United States.

Unilateral action and the pursuit of spheres of influence are not the only ways to structure a major power's relations with other countries. Following World War II the United States promoted collective action through multilateral institutions and general rules of conduct. Multilateral institutions enhance the prospects for cooperation and make shared gains possible by creating a framework within which states can collaborate over time, monitor each other's behavior, reward compliance, and punish cheating.[10] Institutions mitigate the challenges of uncertainty in international politics and encourage leaders to see beyond immediate short-term interests to the prospect of long-term, mutually advantageous gains. This logic underpinned the creation of such international organizations as the United Nations, the World Trade Organization, the Organization of American States, and the Organization for Security and Cooperation in Europe.

Why Alliances Form

Alliances offer great powers a complementary path to security. At their core, alliances involve a commitment by one state to come to the aid of another when security is threatened. That aid can take different forms, from political consultations, diplomatic support, and economic assistance to the provision of weapons, basing arrangements, overflight rights, and a shared commitment to fight on behalf of the endangered ally. By aggregating diplomatic pressure with military capabilities members of the alliance bolster deterrence against threats and strengthen their hand in warfighting should conflict break out. An alliance can bring together strong states of commensurate capabilities or less capable states with unique contributions. It can form in response to specific threats or function as a general deterrent against unforeseen threats on the horizon. It can prove expedient by joining members with common interests, such as the alliance between the United States, Britain, and the Soviet Union in World War II; or it can prove exceptional by joining members with common values, such as the persistence of NATO in the post–Cold War period.[11] Alliances are distinct from strategic alignments and cooperative defense partnerships, both in how they form and the lasting purposes they serve.[12] America maintains mutual defense treaties with its allies in the core, such as its NATO allies, Japan, and South Korea. It maintains strategic and defense partnerships with countries in the near-core and periphery, such as India, Indonesia, Mongolia, and Afghanistan. Coalitions of the willing differ from formal alliances, though they may include treaty allies. Nations come together in a coalition to serve a specific need until their aims are accomplished without a longer-term commitment.

Why do alliances form, and what keeps them together? Alliances serve three goals in a competitive environment. First, alliances help states to aggregate capabilities against a threat and signal collective resolve to adversaries.[13] If a core component of power is the ability of institutions to transform resources into political influence, then alliances function as the lubricant for these gears of mobilization. For example, Britain's insular status gave it a certain margin of error. But when threats gathered on the horizon its leaders formed alliances to marshal resources and protect vital interests far from its homeland. Britain joined with France and the Ottoman Empire against Russia during the Crimean War of 1853–56. And it formed an alliance with Japan in 1902 to secure its interests in China and the Pacific. By combining strengths Britain increased its clout and confronted dangers in several parts of its empire.

Second, great powers rely on alliances to create stability in critical regions. Since World War II the United States has stationed troops in Europe and promoted the vision of a region "whole, free and at peace" not as a gift for the Europeans but as an expression of America's enlightened self-interest in aiding peaceful liberal democracies to thrive and prosper against old threats and new dangers.[14] The world wars of the early and mid-twentieth century and the violent collapse of Yugoslavia in the 1990s serve as powerful reminders of the fragility of peace and the need for constant vigilance. The flames of political disorder in Europe rarely extinguish themselves, and America has played the role of firefighter of last resort. By contrast, as Nick's diplomacy on 9/11 reminds us, a stable Europe offers the United States ready democratic partners to confront security threats to America. It is far wiser to buy insurance and pay modest costs up front than to forfeit the protections an alliance affords and pay untold sums later.

Finally, alliances operate as instruments of restraint and reassurance. It is well known that NATO played a crucial role in defending Western Europe against the Soviet Union and in deterring the threat of a land invasion across the Fulda Gap during the Cold War. Less well known is that NATO helped to assuage the fears and insecurities of its members toward one another. NATO's first secretary general, Lord Ismay, famously quipped that the alliance formed "to keep the Soviet Union out, the Americans in and the Germans down." After the Korean War, NATO improved its organizational capacity to keep the Soviets out. The alliance played the equally important role of guarding against the possibility of German revanchism and providing a security blanket for Europeans to move toward political and economic integration. This function persists today and reassures members who fear the consequences of getting dragged into conflicts in Central and Eastern Europe or coping with German power unbound.[15]

The Legacy of Autonomy

For more than a century and a half leading up to World War II, America's approach toward alliances could be summed up in a few words: stay out of our yard, and we'll stay out of yours. Indeed, skepticism of foreign entanglements is hardwired into the American psyche. George Washington warned the young Republic "to steer clear of permanent alliance with any portion of the foreign world."[16] Alexander Hamilton and Thomas Jefferson sparred over whether Britain or France posed a more immediate threat, with Jefferson espousing, "Peace, commerce, and honest friendship with all nations—entangling alliances with none."[17] John Quincy Adams counseled against going abroad "in search of monsters" and advocated instead a focus on nation building at home and neutrality in the great-power tussle between France and Britain. As the historian Charles Edel notes, Adams believed that "America's influence was best preserved by promoting its institutions at home and abstaining from direct interference in other nations' revolutions."[18] With few exceptions, the United States steered clear of alliances for much of its early history.[19]

The horrors of World War II transformed America's calculus and compelled its leaders to embrace a global role. Twice in the first half of the twentieth century European nations had descended into mutual bloodletting on a catastrophic scale; twice, America had intervened to save democracy and stem the tide of aggression. This tragic pattern called for a new bargain: the United States would augment its power through the establishment of multilateral rules and institutions, while granting opportunities for allies to influence its security policy; in return, allies would agree to support American leadership with access to bases, resources, and manpower while refraining from behavior that could jeopardize peace and prosperity in regions of vital interest to the United States.[20] In short, America would trade some autonomy for greater security, influence, and political legitimacy.

Today, this bargain is at risk of unraveling, for reasons old and new. The old reasons have to do with the blessings of America's geographic position, the advantages of technological superiority, and the illusions of a world that is moving toward routine, state-to-state cooperation.[21] After all, why make commitments to allies when America has oceans to the east and west and friends to the north and south, not to mention sufficient weaponry to deter enemy advances and project power into distant corners of the globe. Along with geography and technology, the temptation to pull up America's drawbridge is rooted in the presumption that spheres of influence are stable and that US involvement is unnecessary to maintain the balance of power in strategic regions of the world.[22] This view promises the best of both worlds: withdrawing from the burdens of leadership while pocketing the gains of cooperation. US engagement in the world need not entail a military first foreign policy. But to concede spheres of influence would only whet the appetite of aggressors and inject instability into regions where America can least afford it.[23] There is a difference between setting broad rules of the road and promoting crisis management, on the one hand, and ceding rival spheres of influence on the other. The former promotes stability, the latter jeopardizes it. That is why an enduring principle of US grand strategy in Eurasia and the Asia-Pacific since World War II has been to prevent the emergence of a hostile power that could lay claim to the vast resources of these regions, close off valuable markets to US firms, and threaten America.[24]

The postwar bargain is also at risk for new, surprising reasons. President Trump came into office with a penchant for autonomy.

The historian Robert Kagan aptly sums up this worldview: "It is unencumbered by historical memory. It recognizes no moral, political or strategic commitments. It feels free to pursue objectives without regard to the effect on allies or, for that matter, the world. It has no sense of responsibility to anything beyond itself."[25] Those who favor autonomy over alliances view security commitments in zero-sum terms: my loss is someone else's gain, and their loss is my gain. During his second year in office President Trump privately threatened to reverse decades of US policy and withdraw the United States from NATO, prompting the House of Representatives to pass a resolution in an effort to block the move.[26]

Beyond NATO, the United States has long maintained a posture of forward deployment of US troops and security guarantees for its allies in Asia, including Japan, South Korea, Australia, the Philippines, and Thailand. President Trump dismissed the value of these treaty commitments. His trade war with China unsettled America's allies and raised questions about US leadership in the region.[27] His disregard for Japan's concerns over North Korea and China increased tensions in Northeast Asia.[28] His decision to suspend military exercises with South Korea and his push for annual renegotiations of cost-sharing agreements for US troops on the Korean peninsula rankled this vital ally of the United States.[29] The former director of national intelligence Dan Coats observed the fallout in his statement on the Worldwide Threat Assessment for 2019: "Some US allies and partners are seeking greater independence from Washington in response to their perceptions of changing US policies on security and trade and are becoming more open to new bilateral and multilateral partnerships."[30]

The consequences of these policies are unmistakable, but there are deeper causes of America's drift toward autonomy. After two wars in Iraq and Afghanistan, the Great Recession, and bitter debates over burden sharing in NATO, some Americans question the benefits of a policy of forward engagement in Europe and Asia. Geopolitical chess moves matter little to those who live paycheck to paycheck. Why spend money on defending Prague when leaders could spend that money on roads, bridges, and schools in Peoria? Americans are right to expect allies to share more of the burden, but the question remains: Why pursue foreign entanglements in the first place?

Why Alliances Matter for America's Security

Alliances afford the United States crucial assets with which to manage the relative decline in its power and influence. If a declining great power anticipates the need to fight a war or win the peace, it helps to be able to count on allies that bring military manpower and specialized resources to the table.[31] The contributions of allies proved advantageous in both the first and second Persian Gulf Wars and in the coalition President Obama assembled to counter ISIS. If a great power needs to mobilize on short order, formal alliance structures give legitimacy to the operation. America's extensive network of bases and logistics chains also facilitate the deployment of forces and defray the costs of forward operations.[32] Allies that train, plan, and conduct exercises together with the United States are more effective than those who operate for the first time in a crisis. When a tsunami struck the coast of Indonesia in 2004 and created a massive humanitarian crisis in the Indian Ocean region, the Indonesian people benefited from the relief efforts of America and its allies Japan and Australia. Close cooperation among these countries was possible because they maintained interoperable forces and doctrine and conducted combined training and exercises annually in the region.[33]

Another advantage is that allies represent greater clout. Adversaries are more likely to think twice before attacking when they confront a military alliance of credible combat capability and unified resolve.[34] It's no coincidence that Russia invaded Georgia in 2008 and Ukraine in 2014 but refrained from doing so in the Baltic States or Poland, which are firmly anchored in NATO. US commitments and forward deployments enable allies to limit provocative deployments or large military buildups that would otherwise risk causing spirals of insecurity with neighbors. Security guarantees are just as useful for managing the risks of nuclear proliferation among allies as they are among adversaries. The United States made clever use of its alliances with Germany, South Korea, and Taiwan to prevent them from going nuclear and sparking arms races in Europe and Asia.[35] Even more, alliances are a ready-made framework for projecting US influence and promoting cooperation in key regions.[36] During the Cold War the United States used its alliance with West Germany to extract concessions during a balance of payments crisis. In the post–Cold War period both South Korea and Japan pursued trade agreements with the United States in part to bolster security cooperation.[37]

America's security guarantees also reduce the incentives and capability of allies to contest or balance US power in the future.[38] Far from bilking US taxpayers, America's alliances offer the best bargain on the dollar. The scholar Ashley Tellis observes that alliances free up resources and attention for the United States to focus on specific tasks, while allies protect the common interest.[39] In any alliance the benefits are not simply material. The United States also gains a more intangible benefit: legitimacy. It's good when a hegemon can rely on its friends, and a declining hegemon needs as many friends as it can find. This is especially true for a declining democratic great power whose identity is rooted in representative government and the rule of law. When the United States acts contrary to its stated values or spurns consultations with allies, it risks tarnishing its image and eroding its capacity for leadership.[40] When the United States undertakes action in concert with allies, it is more likely to garner public support and international approbation. This advantage defined, in Nick's phrase, America's "power differential" with the Soviet Union. Today, America's power differential with its nearest competitors is only magnified by shared values among its allies and friends.

Alliance Dilemmas

Alliances are vital to US security interests, and they require regular tending and prudent management. The political scientist Glenn Snyder highlights the importance of commitment and dependence in the context of a two-sided alliance dilemma: weak allies fear abandonment, and strong allies fear entrapment.[41] I expand this model to include emboldenment and abasement and develop the strategies that states use to navigate these dynamics.

It helps to think of this challenge as a quadrilemma that turns on the degree of dependence and commitment between allies. In situations of high dependence and strong commitment, the incentives to balance against threats is high, and the stronger ally fears entrapment.

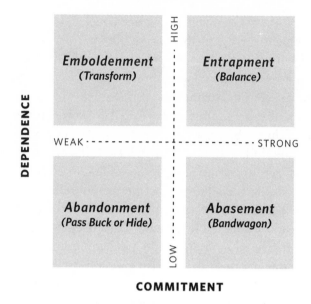

Figure 4.1. Alliance dilemma and coping strategies.

In situations of low dependence and weak commitment between allies, the incentives to hide or pass the buck are high, and the weaker ally fears abandonment. In situations of high dependence and weak commitment, the incentives to transform the system are high, and the stronger ally is inclined toward emboldenment. And in situations of low dependence and strong commitment, the incentives to jump on the threatening power's bandwagon are high, and the weaker ally is inclined toward abasement.

Fears of entrapment and abandonment constitute the familiar alliance dilemma.[42] Suppose Greece were to blunder into a war with Northern Macedonia. Should the United States allow itself to be entrapped by Greece's actions? Recent work on entrapment has shown that strong allies, such as the United States, perceive this risk and tailor their alliance agreements accordingly, making use of loopholes and cross-cutting commitments with various allies and partners.[43] While stronger allies may prove skilled at using these tactics to avoid getting dragged into costly wars, the risks of entrapment remain. As the political scientists David Edelstein and Joshua Shifrinson observe, stronger and weaker allies may agree that conflict is necessary, but a weaker ally can still entrap the stronger ally to fight sooner, aim higher, and spend faster than it would prefer.[44]

Fears of abandonment interact with fears of entrapment. Suppose Italy were to consider using force against Libya to stop the flow of migrants. Italy might fear that America would abandon it if the operation were to fail. As the going gets tough, so weaker allies worry, the tough get out. This fear was a major concern, not a minor irritant, of allied disputes within NATO during the Cold War. In the 1950s leaders in West Germany, France, and Italy feared that the United States would withdraw troops from Europe—and for good reason. Leaked documents from the Department of Defense in 1956 show that President Eisenhower came into office determined to retrench from Europe. He urged the State Department to "put the facts of life before the Europeans concerning reduction of our forces" and complained bitterly that the Europeans were "making a sucker out of Uncle Sam."[45] Chancellor Konrad Adenauer of Germany fretted behind closed doors that "NATO is finished."[46] Similarly, fears of abandonment permeated allied quarrels during President Kennedy's administration, when the United States explored ways to stabilize US–Soviet competition by recognizing Soviet ties in Eastern Europe and restraining the Federal Republic of Germany from developing nuclear weapons.[47] Disputes over nuclear sharing also roiled US–British relations, most notably during the so-called Skybolt Crisis, when the Kennedy administration announced plans to cancel the delivery of air-launched ballistic missiles that the United States had pledged to Britain in return for access to a submarine base in Scotland.[48]

Fears of abandonment are back with a vengeance today. During the Cold War allies bickered over whether the United States would sacrifice Boston for Bonn. The importance of Western unity in the Cold War meant that US pledges were credible enough to maintain a delicate balance on the Continent. Today, America's allies question whether it would trade Richmond for Riga. It's a legitimate concern. The United States and its NATO allies are no match for conventional Russian power in the Baltics.[49] While the US fears entrapment by Russian threats in Latvia, Latvia fears abandonment by NATO if tested by Russia. Given the asymmetry of interests between Russia and the United States in Eastern Europe, it strains credibility to think that the United States would escalate to nuclear conflict with Russia in defense of the Baltic States. The stakes are lower for the United States in the Baltics, and the hurdles to effective deterrence are much higher.[50] Add to this President Trump's equivocations on upholding America's commitment under Article 5 to defend NATO allies, and it is understandable why America's Eastern European allies fear abandonment in the extreme.[51]

Declining credibility and eroding trust among allies raise the incentives for emboldenment and abasement. The mood in some circles in Washington at present seems to be that allies are at best a nuisance and at worst a hindrance to the effective application of American power. In truth, a declining America needs allies more than ever. This combination of hubris and dependence can lead the stronger ally to entertain delusions of breaking with key allies and transforming the international system. America's invasion of Iraq in 2003 is a case in point. The UN Security Council would not authorize US military action as it had done in 1990, and NATO could not reach consensus beyond defending Turkey's borders against a potential Iraqi attack. When the temptations of regime change run up against unwarranted ambition in the periphery or counterbalancing coalitions in the core, hubris can turn to humility with whiplash speed. Weaker allies face the opposite dilemma. When allies are not dependent on each other, and when the weaker ally is more committed to the alliance, the incentive is for the weaker side to abase itself before the source of danger. Deprived of support from its stronger ally and lacking the wherewithal to defend its interests alone, the clearest path to security for the weaker side is to latch on to the aggressor. The hope for the weaker ally is that it will share in the spoils or divert the hostile power's designs on it.

The effects of this quadrilemma are frequently unpredictable, but farsighted leadership in nurturing alliance cohesion can help a declining great power manage the risks. One major risk is that the alliance dilemma overlaps with the security dilemma and creates spirals of instability.[52] Defensive moves by one power can appear to be threatening offensive moves by another. It all depends on which end of the gun sights a leader looks through. In the case of entrapment, fears and insecurity lead allies to mobilize their capabilities against the adversary. Rigid alliance agreements can trigger war between powers that seek nothing more than security. The Peloponnesian War of 431 to 404 BC, the War of the Spanish Succession of 1701–14, the Seven Years' War of 1756–63, the Sino–Indian War of 1962, and the Indian–Pakistani Wars of 1965 and 1971 are historical examples.[53]

In the case of abandonment, fears and insecurity can lead allies to pass the buck or hide. Shirking responsibility leads to conciliatory policies toward the adversary, increasing the danger by tempting aggression. British and French policies during the interwar years most closely resemble this conflict spiral.[54]

In the case of emboldenment, fears and insecurity splinter the alliance, with the stronger ally seeking to transform whole regions, such as the Middle East, in its image. The stronger ally will fulminate against the weaker one, diminishing the strength of the alliance and indirectly abetting the adversary.

Finally, in the case of abasement, fears and insecurity lead allies to embrace the stronger power, fueling aggression. In response to France's growing power in late 1793, Spain leaned toward France, and Prussia left the First Coalition and hid from danger.[55]

America's strategic choice between allies and autonomy depends on the mix of threats, opportunities, resources, and risks. Few declining powers managed these choices more skillfully than Austria's Habsburg Empire. Alliances strengthened its position at the heart of Europe, enhancing its ability to navigate centuries of warfare and the intrigues of enemies near and far.

Habsburg Austria and the Conquest of Time

In the search for historical cases of deft alliance management, the Habsburg Empire seems an unlikely fit. In addition to the bewildering array of names, personalities, and places, the monarchy was more byzantine than the Byzantine Empire. Institutionally complex and riven by ethnic and confessional divides, the Habsburg Empire occupied a precarious spot at the heart of Europe, kept alive more by marriage and its geographically central position than by cunning diplomacy and strategy. In the words of one historian,

"The Habsburg Monarchy offers no classical cases to the investi-
gator of world history. . . . [T]he historian . . . is unable to discover,
however well-intentioned he may be, anything that was pioneering
in Austrian history. All that happened in the Monarchy was nothing but a belated, second hand, and often distorted variant of Western European developments."[56] The empire's contemporaries were
no less scathing in their assessments. Napoleon is alleged to have
said that the monarchy was "nothing but an old maidservant," a
view many Prussian and, later, German officers shared.[57]

What this view misses—and even distorts—is that the
Habsburg Empire was anything but a faint replica of Western developments. Its distinctive approach to grand strategy merits con-
sideration today. As the historian Charles Ingrao notes, "It is only by
understanding the Monarchy's inherent individuality that we can
comprehend how it successfully dealt with problems that were present from the very beginning of its history and how it not only survived, but steadily grew in size and strength."[58] Surrounded by
enemies and plagued by internal divisions and unsound finances, the
Habsburg Monarchy managed to survive a succession of existential
wars on all fronts and endure for more than five centuries. Neither
the ambitions of Louis XIV and Napoleon nor the military genius
of Frederick the Great could defeat this unwieldy power. The
Habsburg Monarchy faced threats on all fronts and lacked the
means to deal with them simultaneously. The nightmare deepens
when one reflects on the fact that the empire was encircled and
lacked offensive military capabilities. Inclement weather, rugged
terrain, and vast distances meant that the monarchy faced porten-
tous challenges in projecting power, extending its writ, and collecting the revenues necessary to build up its state apparatus for
great-power competition.[59] The Danube River system alleviated the
strain of distance, as it was a conduit for trade and a bulwark against
conquest by neighbors. The Alps formed a security barrier around
the Danube heartland, but mountain ranges and river systems could
not obviate the monarchy's need for a successful strategy. How did
the empire survive the intensity of European great-power politics
with such meager resources and exposed frontiers?

In his study of the grand strategy of the Habsburg Empire, the
historian Wess Mitchell offers a clue. The Habsburg Monarchy

faced the classic tension between ends and means, between too many commitments and too few resources. Hence the need for a grand strategy that reconciled limited resources and military capabilities with potentially unlimited enemies and constraints. To succeed at this complex task, Habsburg Austria evolved a defensive security system that manipulated time to its advantage. Since the Habsburg Monarchy could not beat back all its enemies at once, it learned to stagger conflicts, limit their duration, and shape the environment diplomatically in ways that would allow it to confront adversaries at times and in places of its choosing. To achieve this feat Austria made use of fortifications and mountainous frontiers, mobile armies, natural advantages, and sometimes unnatural allies.[60]

Most interesting, in selecting allies Austria proved wilier than the stereotypes of its bungling diplomacy would suggest. It arrayed British and Dutch power against France, wielded the sizeable land power of the French against the offensive capability of Prussia, and courted Russia to safeguard its eastern frontier. Instead of extending the writ of empire over smaller, vassal entities, Austria cultivated buffer states to slow the advances of its enemies, buy time for mobilization, and prevent conflicts over borders with larger powers. Through sophisticated mapmaking, material planning, and conceptual innovations that rivaled Europe's most creative strategists, the Habsburg Monarchy preserved its influence and survived the onslaught of successive wars.[61]

Over the course of the eighteenth and nineteenth centuries, the monarchy's defensive security system faced trials by fire in existential battles with Frederick the Great's Prussia and, later, Napoleon's France. Prussia posed the gravest security threat to the Habsburg Empire for much of the eighteenth century. In addition to his military acumen, Frederick the Great was revisionist, predatory, and intent on subduing the monarchy. When conflict erupted over the succession to the Habsburg Monarchy in 1740, Empress Maria Theresa of Austria put all her wiles and willpower to use by forming alliances to defend the monarchy's strategic position. She courted Britain, Holland, and Russia and cultivated ties with status-quo powers that feared the advances of Prussia on their doorsteps. Hannover, Saxony, and Piedmont were brought into the Austrian circle through persistent diplomacy. Maria Theresa

learned the hard way that Austria needed time to mobilize its resources, buffer states to cushion the blow of attacks and keep the
fighting on foreign soil, and allies to add to the monarchy's resources. She turned time from a vulnerability into an advantage by
engaging with potential rivals before they turned against her,
defanging Prussia by seeking an interim truce, and focusing her
attention on defending Upper Austria from attack by France and
Bavaria. By the end of the War of the Austrian Succession (1740–
48), Maria Theresa had recovered Bohemia and Moravia, repelled
the Bavarians and the French, and turned the tables on Elector
Charles Albert of Bavaria by getting her husband elected as Holy
Roman Emperor.[62]

While these campaigns proved costly, Maria Theresa and her
foreign minister, Wenzel Anton von Kaunitz, emerged stronger for
it. Displaying the adept hand for which he became known, Kaunitz
spearheaded a diplomatic turning of the tables by allying Austria
with its nemesis France and securing a Russian commitment "'to
make war against the King of Prussia' in order to reconquer Silesia
and Glatz and place him in a position whereby he could no longer
disturb the peace."[63] Together with Saxony and Bavaria, the
Habsburg Monarchy took the fight to its enemy. This radial strategy of alliance management afforded Habsburg Austria the time
and space to bring the Reich states to heel, build up the army, and
mobilize its resources for the coming battles with Prussia.[64] The
Habsburg army faced setbacks in battle, but it staved off defeat.
Fighting raged from 1756 to 1763, by which point the sides had
settled into a stalemate. For a time it appeared that Austria might
best its Prussian rivals with the help of its Russian ally. After the
death of Empress Elizabeth of Russia, however, Austria's ally
abruptly pulled back from its alliance.[65] The monarchy failed to recover Silesia and struggled to align defensive means with offensive
goals. Nonetheless, Habsburg Austria improved its position. It secured Saxony as a buffer state, reaffirmed its critical role as a key-
stone in the European balance, and blunted Frederick's revisionist
designs on the monarchy.

The Habsburg Empire showed equal foresight and cunning in
fending off Ottoman threats along its southeastern frontier. For
much of the eighteenth century Austria's strategic approach to the

Ottoman Empire centered on frontier defenses and buffer states, while applying military tactics such as economy of force. Frederick posed the immediate threat from the north and west, so Habsburg diplomacy focused on defusing and blocking threats to its south. This strategy concentrated Habsburg forces in the most threatening areas, denying victory to Frederick's numerically superior forces.

Toward the end of the eighteenth century a new threat emerged from the east: an expansionary Russia. The Habsburg Monarchy wanted to keep the Ottoman Empire weak but stable enough to fend off Russian armies. The threat of Russian expansion was twofold. First, it would jeopardize the independence of the buffer states critical to Austria's security and bring Russia perilously close to its borders. Second, Russia's support was critical to achieving a concentration of force against the Prussian menace. As Mitchell astutely notes, the two goals were in tension: by blunting Russia's advances in the southeast, Austria endangered its alliance with Russia in the north and west; by solidifying its alliance with Russia, it risked losing the buffer states that formed the core of its defensive security system.

Once again Habsburg skillful diplomacy and alliance management opened a way out of this dilemma. The Habsburg Monarchy employed an alliance of restraint with Russia, signing the Austro–Russian Treaty of 1781. By forming a defensive alliance with Russia, Austria achieved several goals at once.[66] It secured a Russian commitment to fend off attacks from the Ottomans. It gained insight into Russian maneuvers, which restrained Russia's most aggressive tendencies against Turkey, thereby preserving a weak but stable buffer in Turkey and along the western approaches to the Danube.

Perhaps most important, Austria's defensive alliance with Russia forestalled the emergence of a strong Russo–Prussian axis that would spell doom for the Habsburg Monarchy. Foreign Minister Kaunitz grasped the necessity of allies to Austria's successful grand strategy. In his memoirs he wrote, "Every system of alliance, and also ours with Russia, is made advisable, useful and necessary based on two major considerations—one being the real benefits, which can be extracted from its existence, and the other being the drawbacks . . . if the alliance did not exist. . . . If the real [benefit] that we derive from [the alliance with Russia] seems accidental, then the real harm that would arise from the alliance not existing is inevitable, imminent, and highly worrying."[67]

Lessons for Statecraft

Austria's alliance strategies in the eighteenth century were not predicated on ideological commonality in the way they are for America's allies in the twenty-first century. Still, Kaunitz's insight encourages us to ask some hard questions. Even with its favorable geography, how would America fare today without allies by its side? Are treaty-based alliances a blessing or a burden? How can allies strengthen America's hand in the multifaceted competition of the future? Would the United States be better off sacrificing alliances for autonomy and pressing its advantage unilaterally from America's shores? What lessons can we learn from Habsburg Austria's strategies for managing geopolitical rivals and from Nick Burns's diplomatic engagement following the terrorist attacks of 9/11?

First, allies are net assets, not liabilities. When leaders tally up resources and commitments on the national balance sheet, they are tempted to place the costs of an alliance entirely on the commitment side of the ledger. Complaints about the costs of burden sharing never include the exorbitant costs that would be incurred if the alliance did not exist.[68] It is true that forward deployments of brigade combat teams, fuel for fighter jets, and funding for joint facilities and exercises add to the costs of a great power's defense. But these expenditures also confer vital benefits to America. Strong allied performance requires investments in time and resources, but anchoring American power around alliances magnifies US influence and extends its reach.

Discarding America's network of alliances to pursue autonomy is a fool's errand in today's world. Taking a transactional, zero-sum approach to alliances neglects a key strategic advantage for the United States in the competition with Russia and China: its vast network of allies and strategic partnerships. Alliances in early modern Europe often involved large, lump-sum payments for the supply and receipt of troops. America's alliances today represent an evolution from this imperfect system. The more the United States berates its allies and raises doubts about its commitments to them, the greater the damage to America's reputation for being reliable and resolved and the harder it will be to attract allies against unknown future threats from abroad.[69] A zero-sum, financial approach is a self-inflicted wound. Relative to earlier periods when security threats were primarily regional, Washington today needs to rely far more on allies and partners to deal with the threats of a globalized world. NATO allies have fought side by side with the United States in Afghanistan, promoted stability in Kosovo and the Mediterranean, supported the global coalition to defeat the terrorist group ISIS, and continued to play a vital role in deterring Russian aggression in Europe.

Habsburg Austria, perennially strapped for cash, was surrounded by multiple enemies on multiple fronts for much of its existence. If any great power had reason to free itself of undue commitments, it was the Habsburgs. And yet the monarchy skillfully relied on alliances to defend its frontiers, restrain potential enemies, bolster its capabilities, and concentrate force against near enemies while holding far ones at bay.

Today, there are few global challenges America can solve by going it alone. Alliances are ready-made coalitions for action on everything from countering cyber threats, to removing terrorist sanctuaries abroad, to containing the proliferation of weapons of mass destruction, to patrolling vital international waterways, to standing firm against aggression.[70] In a post-dominant world of shifting power and rising challengers the question isn't which individual country is stronger but which team is stronger, smarter, faster, broader, and deeper. America's allies and partners give it a bench that is broader and deeper than that of any rising power. During a period of relative decline the United States jettisons allies at its peril. As Condoleezza Rice told Nick on 9/11, friends make all the difference in the world because they are assets, not liabilities.

Second, alliances need to adapt to changing threats on the horizon. Compared with the early nineties, at present the combined military and economic clout of America's allies is on a downward trajectory. Long gone are the days when America's core treaty allies in

Europe and the Asia-Pacific could wield more than two-thirds of global economic power and spend more than two-thirds of global defense outlays. In fact, the share of global income held by authoritarian powers is set to outstrip the share held by liberal democracies.[71] The challenge grows when one considers the need for US allies and partners to adapt to the rapid modernization of Russian and Chinese militaries.

Much of the domestic political debate in the United States turns on whether America's NATO allies spend the minimum 2 percent of GDP on defense. Yet this debate is too simplistic. Disputes over burden sharing will persist, but it's important to remember that modest levels of European defense spending are baked into the DNA of NATO: precisely because of Europe's bloody history, US policy and troop deployments are designed to reduce the incentives for European states to build large militaries, amass offensive weaponry, and precipitate spirals of insecurity that can lead to a wider war.

While 2 percent serves as a reasonable financial target for burden sharing and holding allies to account, it can overlook the substantial contributions of allies in areas like foreign aid, peacekeeping, cyber security, counterterrorism, and sanctions enforcement that also strengthen the security of the US homeland.[72] Thus the United States must develop a more constructive approach to managing the imperative of burden sharing. Anthony Cordesman, a defense expert, notes that the target of spending 2 percent of GDP on defense is "actively counterproductive" for a reason. This target focuses attention on the wrong goals, prompts needless divisions within the alliance, defines priorities in the absence of a net assessment of the military balance, and distracts from the real need to improve force planning and the efficiency of resource allocations.[73] Allied investments and capabilities should be measured against their contributions to allied security and the threats Americans face today as well as those emerging over the horizon. Instead of berating a particular ally for not meeting its 2 percent target, the United States should focus on whether that ally is developing complementary capabilities and pursuing cost-effective strategies against America's likely strategic competitors, including future unconventional threats. More appropriate criteria would include measures for "alliance-wide" investments in modernization, force strength, and readiness needs.[74]

Reimagining roles and burdens requires the United States to assess more broadly the contribution of its allies. Habsburg Austria conceived of its alliance choices in the broader context of political geography, financial constraints, complementary capabilities, and temporal and spatial limitations. It reimagined its power by seeking allies that could ease financial burdens, such as Britain and Holland, or provide land power to supplement Austrian capabilities against Prussia, such as the large armies of Russia. The Habsburg Monarchy leaned on allies to help manage the duration and sequencing of conflicts and bought time to mobilize and reposition its military capabilities for war.

In reimagining NATO's benefits, America faces three challenges. First, while President Trump's policies have weakened America's alliances, much of the scar tissue in transatlantic relations had accumulated before he took office. America's unwise intervention in Iraq in 2003 and its uneven prosecution of the war in Afghanistan are never far from the minds of Europeans. America's swift response to Russian aggression in Ukraine alleviated some of the damage, but the tumultuous aftermath of NATO's intervention in Libya in 2011 and the absence of a coherent policy on Syria deepened rifts in US–European relations. Tomorrow's alliances will not look like those of 2001. Nick Burns powerfully reminds us of the resolve that America's allies showed on 9/11. The United States needs to bring that same resolve to adapting its alliances for a new era of rising powers, aggressive challengers, transnational threats, newly emerging dangers such as cyber, and existential risks, including climate change and nuclear proliferation.

The second challenge is to strengthen America's capacity for anticipating events, collecting strategic intelligence, and translating that intelligence into political decisions and actions.[75] Anticipating and assessing trends in the balance of power is not simply a nicety of great-power politics. It is crucial for managing alliance security dilemmas. Entrapment, abandonment, emboldenment, and abasement are more likely when great powers misread the trend lines and act without regard to underlying power dynamics.

The third challenge is to reimagine US and allied capabilities as an integrated whole, with an appropriate division of roles and responsibilities. The United States possesses unmatched advantages in air- and sealift, strategic and tactical communications, cyber security, assets for intelligence, surveillance and reconnaissance, and long-range strike capabilities. Its allies enjoy comparative advantages in local knowledge, local presence, and local ground troops that can alleviate the burdens of deterring and defending against adversaries in key theaters.[76] America should maintain its security guarantees and alliance commitments but reallocate burdens for deterrence and rely on smarter, more efficient coalitions for deploying its forces in trouble spots.[77] This shift would require greater coordination and investment to ensure that the capabilities and command and control systems of the United States and its allies remain interoperable as technologies advance. It would also entail some restructuring of the US force posture in theaters outside of Europe and the Asia-Pacific. US military capabilities and finances are not unlimited, and America needs to balance myriad national security priorities. It cannot wish away the trade-offs or tough policy choices. If the National Defense Strategy calls for strategic competition with China and Russia, other priorities need to give way to more sustainable strategies.[78] By thinking and planning holistically, America can invest in those military capabilities that promote collective defense, rebalance its national security toolkit to focus on preventing conflicts instead of fighting them, and benefit from the capabilities of allies, even as their combined share of global income declines in relative terms.

Third, alliance cohesion relies on domestic politics. The former Speaker of the House of Representatives Tip O'Neill had a phrase to characterize the power of the grassroots: "All politics is local." When it comes to great-power politics, all alliances are local, too. For evidence, look no further than Austria's struggles to manage its diverse coalition in the face of Frederick the Great's onslaughts from 1756 to 1763. Charles de Gaulle's decision to withdraw from NATO's integrated military command in 1967, the Philippines' demand that the United States exit the base at Subic Bay in 1992, and Japanese resistance to the US base in Okinawa are modern analogues of the same principle: no alliance can endure without a domestic base of support.

The good news is that polls show a reservoir of American support for internationalism. Majorities back NATO and the need to send in US troops should an ally come under attack.[79] But as President Trump's tweets have taken root, allied countries increasingly view American support for its alliances as conditional. Since 2017 fewer Americans think that compromising with allies is a good thing, and many believe that allies should take up more of the burden of providing for their defense and meeting common challenges.[80] According to a survey of 2018 midterm voters by the Pew Research Center, "a 38-percentage-point gap separates partisans on whether the US should take into account the interests of allies—one of the largest partisan gaps measured in the past 15 years."[81]

America should not risk its security by questioning its alliance commitments or allowing them to become the plaything of domestic partisan politics. A clear task of US policy makers is to talk about the benefits of alliances in enhancing the security and prosperity of ordinary Americans, and that conversation should occur not just on election day but on every day and among constituencies around the country. Leadership, institutions, and resolve are crucial variables in the strength of a great power. If leaders fail to build domestic political support for the alliances that enable America to defend its homeland from far away, project power, and preserve the peace, public resolve will weaken, and it will become harder to adapt in an era of declining US power.

Finally, keep friends close and democratic allies even closer. Austria expended considerable resources keeping its coalition against Prussia together, in part because its allies lacked common norms and political cultures. By contrast, shared democratic norms played an important role in assuring the peaceful transition of power between the United States and Britain in the nineteenth century. Scholars have long debated whether democracies are more likely than autocratic regimes to "flock together," and whether democracies are more effective warfighters than their authoritarian counterparts.[82]

These debates aside, the renewed threats democracies face from authoritarian powers call for democratic allies to stick together. The threat is global, so America needs to think and act globally. That means creating new linkages and cooperative arrangements that bind democratic allies in the Western Hemisphere, Europe, and the Asia-Pacific.[83] It means investing resources in creating a common intelligence picture and threat assessment among democratic allies who rely on the United States for their defense. And it means putting allies that backslide on democratic norms and institutions on notice, suspending aid to those that perpetually flout these norms and, in the extreme, dissolving alliances with countries that embrace outright authoritarianism.[84] To paraphrase Benjamin Franklin, democracies need to hang together; otherwise, they will hang separately.

The Next Choice

When power shifts and rivals gain momentum, the temptation runs high to deal with future threats by ordering preventive military attacks. Frazzled allies and fears of entrapment and abandonment compound the challenge. History is replete with cases of declining powers going to war with assertive challengers on the assumption that it is better to act now rather than later, when the rival will have grown stronger and will eventually press its advantage. What are the risks of launching a preventive war? Do the costs of preventive military attacks outweigh the benefits?

When North Korea threatened in 1993 to withdraw from the Nuclear Non-Proliferation Treaty (NPT), a decades-old international treaty intended to prevent the spread of nuclear weapons and further the goal of nuclear disarmament, the US diplomat Robert Gallucci engaged in high-stakes negotiations to ward off a future nuclear threat. Preventive air strikes against nuclear facilities at Yongbyon were on the table. Tensions ran high. The risk that the North Korea situation could go critical was very real. In the middle of it all was Bob Gallucci, charged with navigating the treacherous shoals of shifting regional power dynamics, rogue states, and the specter of nuclear war.

CHAPTER FIVE

Persuasion or Coercion?

O N THE EVE OF President Bill Clinton's inauguration in
1993 Bob Gallucci was out of a job. Or so he thought.
As assistant secretary of state for political military affairs in the outgoing George H. W. Bush administration, Bob knew the rules. During the administrations of Presidents
Jimmy Carter and Ronald Reagan, he had faced the Republican
chopping block. Now, he presumed, the Democrats were going to
show him the door. As a Clinton transition team official unceremo-
niously put it, he needed to clear out in short order.

Following the election of a new president, it's standard fare for
old political appointees to make room for a fresh crop of hungry
newcomers who want to leave their mark on government. Still, after
nearly two decades of public service in both Democratic and Republican administrations, Bob wasn't ready to say goodbye. He called
President Clinton's incoming national security advisor, Tony Lake,
and made his case. "I could be the first guy to be fired by Republicans
and Democrats!" Bob pleaded to Tony. As luck would have it, Tony
offered Bob a job at the White House. Bob took no small pleasure in
letting the Clinton transition official know of his recent promotion.
"So I guess we'll be working together," he quipped.

As it turned out, the new leadership at the State Department
kept Bob right where he was as assistant secretary of state, but with

a twist. His new portfolio included the North Korean nuclear file. By his own admission Bob was no North Korean hand. "I took a trip to Seoul once," he tells me, "but I didn't have any specialized knowledge." Expert or not, Bob had to learn the ropes—and fast. In the spring of 1993 North Korea announced it was pulling out of the NPT. The consequences were deadly serious. This treaty serves as the cornerstone of a global regime to control the world's most heinous weapons. When a rogue state lets the world know that it's intent on getting out from under those commitments, it sets off alarm bells, literally.

Bob assumed that the noted China hand Winston Lord would take the lead on the negotiations. Lord was the éminence grise of US Asia policy. A skillful practitioner in the mold of the legendary diplomats George Kennan and Charles Bohlen, Lord had served as director of policy planning and US ambassador to China. He knew the region cold and all its key players well. He was, in Bob's phrase, "Kissinger's Kissinger."

Senior Clinton officials worried, however, that Winston Lord was far too prominent. He would give too much diplomatic recognition to the North Koreans, who were dispatching a vice foreign minister to the talks in New York. The United States needed someone who wouldn't raise the meeting's profile too high. "Let's send them Bob," Gallucci recounts to me with a smile. "He's not known to the people on the block where he lives. He has no foreign languages and no real Asia experience. He'll be perfect." That's Bob's modest way of saying that the US government needed an expert in nuclear weapons policy. And Bob knew nuclear weapons, from the nuts and bolts of reactors to the intricate physics of chain reactions.

From the start Bob faced two big challenges. The first was the substantive challenge of understanding the North Korean nuclear weapons program: what they were trying to accomplish, what they were willing to give up, and what they wanted in return. Bob jokingly called this his "how-do-I-get-out-of-here-alive" challenge. The second challenge was the bureaucratic politics of the US government. "There were game qualities to this," Bob observes, referring to how complex interactions between players can yield surprising outcomes. Bob wrote his dissertation on the bureaucratic politics of US policy in Vietnam. Different countries, different challenges, but the knowledge he gained from the Vietnam case traveled surprisingly well to this assignment: "These challenges were on my mind from the beginning, but never left my mind. I faced the real-world challenge of North Korean substance and the unreal work of navigating the US policy process."

In the run-up to the first talks in New York between the US and North Korean delegations that spring, Bob got a lot of advice. "The hardliners came in and gave me books to read about how evil the North Koreans were," he recalls. "They'd say, 'You're going to negotiate with these commie bastards? Good luck!'" Suffice it to say, Bob faced more than a little skepticism in his quest to get anything useful out of talks with the North Koreans. To complicate matters, his marching orders kept growing longer and more uncompromising.

"We don't want them to separate any more plutonium from their spent nuclear fuel, so make sure they don't do that," Bob was told.

"We want them back in the NPT," Bob was instructed. "And make sure to get the inspections regime back up and running."

Bob struggled to understand how he was supposed to achieve all of these tough outcomes. In other words, the US approach was all take and no give. Bob pushed and prodded, asking, "By what mechanism does this magic of diplomacy succeed?" The answer he got was less than satisfactory. The bureaucracy coughed up a few vagaries of diplomatic parlance. He was instructed to tell the North Koreans that they could "become part of the Asian economic miracle." He could also offer the North Koreans the option of inspecting US bases in South Korea to ensure that the United States had no nuclear weapons stationed there. Bob's first thought was, How do the South Koreans feel about that? The answer? He would cross that bridge when he got to it.

Bob had only a thin briefing book and few carrots to dangle, so the talks got off to an inauspicious start. When Bob sat down with the North Korean negotiating team in New York in June the first thing he noticed was their ill-fitting suits, each with a lapel pin of the North Korean leader, Kim Il Sung, proudly displayed. "It made me think of the Mickey Mouse Club," Bob says. "There were a lot of circumstances that struck me as bizarre and bizarrely funny." The lead North Korean negotiator was known for his love of *Gone with the Wind*. Every now and then he would break out the line, "Dogs bark, but the caravan rolls on," which prompted more than a few curious stares among the US delegation. When the two sides exchanged gifts, as is customary in diplomatic talks, Bob gave his North Korean counterpart a leather-bound copy of *Gone with the Wind*. In return, Bob was given a wooden box with the best Ginseng tea in the world, or so the North Korean team claimed. He promptly handed the box over to the CIA.

During the talks in New York Bob followed his marching orders. He impressed on the North Koreans the need to return to compliance with its safeguard obligations under the NPT, cease the production of plutonium, and allow the International Atomic Energy Agency (IAEA) inspectors back in. The North Koreans wanted security guarantees along with improved relations with the United States. "Every time we tried to get agreement on a draft text," Bob tells me, "someone in Washington would scream 'concession!' We had a hard-right flank to worry about through the negotiations."

In a revealing moment during the talks a delegation member came over to Bob and showed him some draft language. Bob rejected it. "I can't say that," he exclaimed. "It sounds like we just made a treaty of peace with the North." His colleague reminded him that the language came from the UN Charter. Bob decided to see what Washington would think of it. He cabled over the text, and, sure enough, Washington cabled back that it was a nonstarter. When he reminded Washington that the language came straight out of the UN Charter, Bob got approval to try it out on the North Koreans. Sure enough, the North agreed, and both sides would continue talks in Geneva. In the meantime the North committed to suspend its intended withdrawal from the NPT and put the issue of IAEA safeguard obligations on the table. The first round of talks wrapped up, and the negotiations continued in Geneva.

"There's a view," Bob tells me in his office at Georgetown University, where he serves as distinguished professor of the practice of diplomacy in its School of Foreign Service, "that we weaken our security position by giving up anything—that it's naïve to negotiate over anything when all the North Koreans understand is force and power, and that the way to deal with them is to contain, isolate, and apply pressure until they crumble. That's how we won the Cold War, and that's how we deal with North Korea." That view may be right, Bob concedes. But he wanted to put the North Koreans to the test. "I felt conservative about expressions of confidence in what the North was thinking," he stresses. "I didn't know anyone who could speak with confidence about North Korean grand strategy: Is the myth of Korean unification under the North's rule truly operative—or is it just a national myth? Do they see nuclear weapons in offensive or defensive terms? Our confidence wasn't clear. My belief was that if we removed their security concerns, perhaps they would relax their grip and make concessions in areas of importance to the United States."

In the spring of 1994 the negotiations reached a critical moment. Many felt that dialogue had failed to achieve its purpose. Washington's patience was running out, and talk of confrontation came to the Senate floor. "We were days or perhaps even hours from the launch of a strike on North Korean nuclear facilities," Bob remembers. "There was detailed planning done for strikes at Yongbyon and the necessary ancillary strikes in order to destroy their plutonium separation capability." Officials in Washington knew that the North had taken fuel rods out of their nuclear reactors and put them in a pond to cool off. Once the North moved the rods from the storage pond to the reprocessing plant and separated the plutonium, the opportunity for a US strike would have passed. On May 18 Secretary of Defense William Perry and Joint Chiefs of Staff Chairman General John Shalikashvili convened the top brass in Washington. As one United States Navy captain who helped organize the meeting put it, "[This was] a real meeting of real war fighters to decide how they were going to fight a war."[1] No one knows whether President Clinton would have ordered military strikes against North Korea, but Bob felt the pressure and knew that time for his negotiations was running out.

The real process of preventing the North Koreans from going critical was hard enough. But the unreal process of navigating the bureaucracy also kept Bob up at night, with each of the major players focused on a different piece of the North Korean puzzle. At one White House meeting Bob confronted an array of objectives for the talks. Arms control officials wanted to make sure the North returned to the NPT and allowed for special inspections of nuclear waste sites at Yongbyon. The State Department wanted to make sure the South Koreans were onboard. The Joint Chiefs of Staff urged that any deal include the removal of artillery along the demilitarized zone that separated North and South Korea. "That's when Perry turned to me and said, 'Bob, with respect to my colleagues, you've got only one objective: stop plutonium separation. We've lived with the North's artillery for a long time. Your job is to stop the nuclear weapons program.' " Bob knew that pressure to launch US military strikes was growing. He needed someone to narrow the objectives. And that's exactly what Secretary Perry did. "We needed to zero in on the priorities," Bob says. "I knew that a deal would not be successful unless it could be defended as in the national security interest of the United States. Anyone can make a deal—the question is not any deal, but the right deal."

Amid these discussions former president Jimmy Carter made a surprise appearance. At the request of President Clinton, Bob and his colleagues kept Carter briefed on the situation. Bob traveled down to Plains, Georgia, to discuss the issue in person with the thirty-ninth US president. Carter obligingly sent Bob back to Washington with two huge bags of peanuts—and a message. Bob relayed to Deputy National Security Advisor Sandy Berger that Carter wanted to go to North Korea to see if he could resolve the crisis. Shortly thereafter Carter called Vice President Al Gore and informed him that the North Koreans had invited Carter to visit Pyongyang.

Events came to a head in early June 1994. The North Koreans had blocked the IAEA inspectors from doing their job. In response, the Clinton administration threatened sanctions. The North responded defiantly that sanctions would be a violation of the 1953 armistice that brought to a halt the fighting during the Korean War. And President Carter's visit created its own dynamic. "So I wasn't in control of the universe," Bob wryly notes.

By mid-June that universe started contracting. The Defense Department prepared to increase dramatically the American military presence on the Korean peninsula. At a White House meeting in the Cabinet Room to discuss the latest on sanctions, diplomacy at the UN Security Council, and plans for the military buildup, Secretary Perry raised the possibility that the deployments could resemble what Barbara Tuchman describes in *The Guns of August*, with rapid military buildups precipitating a slide to war.[2] Perry argued that the United States needed to recognize the risks in adopting a more aggressive course of action and take steps to mitigate them, even while knowing that a more assertive course might prove necessary.

At this point in the policy discussion the door to the room flew open and a White House aide informed the attendees that Jimmy Carter was on the line from Pyongyang: "President Carter wants to speak to you ... Mr. Gallucci." Without missing a beat, President Clinton turned to Bob and said, "Well, you better get it." Carter relayed to Bob that he had gotten the North Koreans to freeze the nuclear program and allow the IAEA inspectors to remain in the country. "What do you think?" Carter asked. "It doesn't matter what I think, Mr. President," said Bob. "President Clinton is in the next room—that's what matters." Before they hung up Carter mentioned that he had brought CNN with him and that he would be going on air after their discussion.

Bob walked back into the meeting room and explained that Carter's visit had yielded little in the way of a substantive breakthrough, but the former president would be going on CNN in a moment. Tony Lake leaned forward and gave Bob a quizzical look: "You told him not to go on CNN, didn't you?" he asked.

"No, I didn't," said Bob. "Why would he listen to me?"

"But you tried?" Tony asked.

President Clinton piled on, saying "You *did* try to tell him not to do this, didn't you?"

Then Secretary of State Warren Christopher asked, "You didn't try *at all*?"

Bob left that meeting with visions of his public hanging the next morning—but not before watching Carter being interviewed on CNN. In a photo of President Clinton and his national security team in that moment Bob is the man sitting with his legs crossed on the floor looking dispiritedly into the distance.

Shortly after Carter's surprising announcement of the North's offer to freeze, Bob was shoved in front of the White House press corps to give an update on the talks. "They looked like hungry lions," Bob recalls. For a moment a war between the United States and North Korea receded into the background as the press zeroed in on the potential war between Carter and Clinton.

The time to strike a reliable deal with the North was slipping away. Bob came under enormous pressure from the left and the right, from members of Congress and the press, and from various players across the US government. The road ahead was littered with minefields of plutonium. Bob needed to get the North to agree to shut down its reprocessing facility, close down its nuclear reactors, and accept South Korean reactors as a substitute. One request proved especially challenging: the United States wanted to include in the deal's language a line about the need for North and South Korea to resume direct, face-to-face talks. The North Korean team adamantly refused. Bob held firm: "I can't do a deal that fractures the alliance. This is a must-have." An interview by the South Korean president Kim Young Sam with the *New York Times* in mid-October underscored the high stakes as well as the complexities of getting to yes. President Kim opposed the agreement taking shape in Geneva, claiming, "North Korea faces the danger of imminent political and economic collapse . . . [and] any compromise with North Korea [at this point] will only help prolong its survival."[3]

Marathon talks between the US diplomat Tom Hubbard and his North Korean counterpart ironed out many of the wrinkles in the draft text. But the issue of North–South talks remained as thorny as ever. At a meeting in Geneva on October 15 Bob met with his counterpart, Kang Sok Ju. Kang refused to accept North–South dialogue. Conveying his refusal with admirable verve, the interpreter for Kang slammed his hand on the table and repeated, "I never want to hear the words North–South dialogue again!" Bob suppressed a smirk at the interpreter's fulminations, who was nothing if not committed to his boss's message. After a tense staredown and several slammed briefing books later, tempers cooled, but tensions remained high.

The negotiators had one more day to reach agreement. On the morning of October 16 the North Koreans agreed to a final session to iron out remaining differences. The diplomats Danny

Russel and Gary Samore bargained hard over the details of inter-Korean dialogue, including the issue of its timing and whether the provision of the South Korean reactors required dialogue first. Hubbard continued talks the following day. By October 17 the negotiators had reached a delicate compromise: "The DPRK [Democratic People's Republic of North Korea] will engage in North–South dialogue, as this Agreed Framework will help create an atmosphere that promotes such dialogue." As Gallucci and his colleagues reflected in their account of the negotiations, "Whether 'as' meant 'at the same time' or 'because' was unclear. But the words seemed to commit the North to talk to the South in the same timeframe as the construction of the new reactors."[4] With that, the negotiators shook hands on a deal to keep the North Korean nuclear freeze from becoming a nuclear winter.

Recalling the experience, Bob puts it this way: "I learned to be sensitive to what other people care most about. We always started with the challenge of North Korea's nukes—the real substance—but the different players in Washington had their own priorities and perspectives. You need to care about those, too—not as a gift, but as a way of bringing everyone onboard with the process."

Strategic Choice: Persuasion or Coercion?

As the 1994 crisis with North Korea reveals, skillful diplomacy is neither simple nor easy. The marathon negotiation sessions, bitter infighting, and uncertain outcomes reflect the turbulent world that diplomats must navigate in order to advance American interests and values. No agreement is perfect, and seasoned diplomats accept the principle of not letting the perfect be the enemy of the good. Too often, however, the bar for what counts as successful diplomacy is raised higher than the bar for successful military action.[5] The risk is that political leaders may stack the deck in favor of military force even when serious negotiations can achieve a better outcome for the United States at a much lower cost. The hazards grow when leaders see windows of opportunity closing and fear that time is not on America's side.

In addition to wrestling with the choice that addresses US military intervention in a peripheral state (see chapter 2), America today faces a distinctive strategic choice that involves ambitious regional powers: Should it deal with aggressive challengers through diplomatic tradecraft, commercial engagement for profit and contacts, and multilateral institutions to ensure compliance with international agreements? Or should it seek to avoid trading with the enemy and weaken threatening challengers by pursuing a range of preventive military actions before it's too late? In other words, should a declining great power favor persuasion or coercion?

This special challenge demands the daily attention of the United States because its competitors have or seek to have nuclear weapons; they can endanger valuable international commerce; they can sponsor terrorism and other attacks on American interests; or they can seek to dominate US allies and friends in critical regions. The challenge for the United States comes in two forms. One is the hostile rogue state, such as North Korea, which uses its conventional and nuclear capabilities to threaten America's allies and partners. The other is an antagonistic regional competitor, such as Iran, which plays on the fringes of international law and accepted practice while asserting its influence through the selective, often covert use of force and other coercive means. In the examples of these two countries—North Korea, the hostile rogue state, and Iran, the ambitious regional power—each is supported by America's competitors, namely, China vis-à-vis North Korea and Russia vis-à-vis Iran. Consequently, the choice of persuasion or coercion usually brings in the interests of China, Russia, or both at once.

America's strategic approach can run the gamut from preventive engagement to preventive war. The scholar Paul Stares defines the concept of preventive engagement to include strategies that aim to reduce the risks of crises, prevent crises from spiraling into conflicts, and mitigate the risk of conflicts escalating to full-blown war.[6] This approach is relevant to great powers in decline. Preventive engagement encompasses a range of strategies that aim to dissuade a threatening rival from challenging the interests of the declining power. Leaders can accomplish this goal via diplomatic strategies that pursue interests through hard-nosed negotiations; commercial strategies that entangle the rival through trade and investment regimes; and legal strategies that seek to bind and restrain challengers through institutions. Declining powers can also combine economic sanctions with deterrent strategies to constrain antagonists through the manipulation of costs, benefits, and risks. While deterrence involves the threat or limited use of force, the goal is to dissuade rivals from aggressing in the first place.[7]

These strategies of persuasion and dissuasion are mutually reinforcing and require careful management, sound judgment, and experienced leadership. Commercial engagement, for example, can generate interest groups with a stake in peaceful relations, promote greater understanding of and visibility into the workings of foreign governments, and entangle rivals in mutually beneficial trade and investment relationships that create barriers against conflict. As scholars have shown, however, commercial engagement can also create mutual vulnerabilities and incentives for conflict when expectations about the future are misaligned and mismanaged.[8] US–China relations today prove the point. American policy makers made a bet that commercial engagement would open China's economy and foster greater political liberalization. While debate continues about the successes and failures of this approach, it is clear that China took advantage of commercial engagement to steal intellectual property, advance its technology transfer programs, and block Western companies from equal access to its market. There are advantages to maintaining economic interdependence with China, but the United States and its allies will also need to protect sensitive technologies and reevaluate past assumptions about the trajectory of China's development.

Strategies of persuasion and dissuasion are forms of preventive engagement because they employ measures short of war to achieve important objectives. Alternatively, instead of relying on preventive engagement, a declining great power can undertake preventive military actions to nip aggressive challengers in the bud. Weighing the costs and benefits of these two approaches requires distinguishing between preemptive and preventive uses of force. The preemptive use of force entails acting rapidly against an imminent threat; the preventive use of force requires acting against a threat that may be months, if not years, away from materializing. The logic and stakes are different.[9] The preventer says better now than later; the preemptor says it's now or never. The preventer looks to the future and seeks to curb the growth of its adversary's military and economic capabilities; the preemptor looks to the present and seeks to deal with its adversary's current military and economic capabilities. Whereas the preventer may wish to bait the aggressive challenger into lashing out first in the interest of attracting diplomatic or domestic political support, the preemptor will often be seized by strong incentives to strike first in hopes of avoiding a damaging blow.[10]

A Negotiator's Mind-set

In tracing debates around the decision of persuasion or coercion with a dangerous North Korea, one can imagine Bob asking three questions about the merits of preventive military actions that should guide leaders of a declining America today: What is a leader's motivation? What are the strategic alternatives? And from what position is the great power falling?

Each question corresponds to a different image of analysis that enables us to fully appreciate the complexities of this strategic choice.[11] In the first image we care about the motives of political leaders: their belief systems, their perceptions and biases, and their fears and expectations. In the second image we care about the costs, benefits, and risks of different alternatives; the influence of domestic political and social structures; and the role of bureaucratic politics. In the third image we care about the balance of power among nations: Who's growing stronger and who's threatening whom? By looking at these three images simultaneously, we arrive at a more complete picture of the logic of preventive military action and the risks of pursuing it by a great power in decline.

Consider the first image and the question of a political leader's motivation. The temptation to resort to military force is especially strong when a great power is in decline and its political leaders confront a threatening challenger. As the historian Paul Schroeder observes, "Preventive wars, even risky preventive wars, are not extreme anomalies in politics. ... They are normal, even common, tools of statecraft."[12] The dominant power may initiate military strikes to take out an adversary before it's too late. Fear is a powerful motivator, and fear of harmful consequences posed by a threatening rival can trigger dangerous spirals.

The debate over whether the dominant power is more inclined to launch a preventive strike against a potential aggressor is not just an academic point. It cuts to the heart of a leader's motivation to pursue preventive war. As the political scientist Jack Levy points out, "The key question is not whether a particular war is preventive; instead, it concerns the relative importance of the preventive motivation with respect to other variables in the process leading to war and the conditions affecting its intensity."[13] The motivation to launch military attacks stems from a leader's fear that national power is eroding relative to a dangerous challenger and that time is not on his side. In Bob's case, he negotiated with the clock ticking, skillfully navigating pressures from Congress and administration hardliners to take more aggressive measures. The motivation of prevention compels action: the sooner a political leader decides to strike, so the argument runs, the better.

The second image and the matter of alternative strategic approaches raise questions like these: Is America destined for preventive war? Will the rise of China compel America to take military action before it's too late? Will rogue states and aggressive challengers tempt America to reach for preventive military strikes as a tool of first resort? The political scientist Graham Allison studied the prospects for peaceful hegemonic transitions and found that rising and ruling powers came to blows in twelve of sixteen cases over the past five hundred years.[14] The scholar Kori Schake, however, sees only one case of peaceful hegemonic transition, the Anglo–American transition in the nineteenth century.[15]

When power shifts in favor of an assertive challenger, the risk is that a leader's field of vision narrows, and that leader discounts all options except for the use of force. Domestic politics add pressure and can distort how leaders value the range of available options. Bob's study of the Vietnam War made him acutely aware of the role of bureaucratic politics. Regime type further complicates these dynamics. The political scientist Randall Schweller asks the right question: "Why do some power shifts result in preventive war while others do not?" To find the answer, he surveyed the history of preventive wars and reached a surprising conclusion: liberal norms and electoral accountability, among other qualities associated with democracy, limit the strategic choices of declining democratic powers

to defensive alliances (if the challenger is autocratic) or accommodation (if the challenger is democratic). On the other hand,
Schweller says, declining autocratic powers will pursue preventive
war irrespective of the regime type of the challenging power.

If only autocracies are prone to launch preventive military action, perhaps the choice facing America as a declining power today
is no choice at all. Instead of favoring preventive war, US policy
makers may simply rely on the clout of alliances and pursue diplomacy with a threatening challenger. Even a cursory glance at the
historical record shows, however, that regime type is an imperfect
predictor of which countries are most likely to launch preventive
military strikes.[16] The rush to preventive war against Iraq in 2003
is instructive.

First, US political leaders failed to assess rigorously whether
Iraq actually held weapons of mass destruction. The threat of nuclear terrorism, while ominous, was not the only threat America
faced at the time, nor was it as pervasive as some suggested. If we
calculate the risk of nuclear terrorism by multiplying its probabil-
ity by the consequences, then US policy makers owe it to the
American people to thoroughly assess the likelihood that terrorists
will obtain and deploy nuclear weapons.[17] It may be that the risks
are high enough to justify armed attacks, but political leaders
should be mindful of the costs of this judgment.

Second, the preventive use of force may not be the most effective or prudent strategy to employ against the threat of rogue state
proliferation. Again, the benefits of preventive war must be weighed
against costly armed misadventures, often caused by poor intelligence assessments following regime change, military blunders, the
unintended and uncontrollable consequences of war, the difficulties
of regime change, and the impact such an action will have on mod-
erate, pro-American movements within the target country.[18]

Third, America claimed the right to wage preventive war at
times and places of its choosing. While national security imperatives weigh on the minds of all political leaders, this approach of-
fended the strategic and moral sensibilities of US allies. The
erosion of allied support has serious consequences for the efficacy
and durability of US power. In addition to the political, financial,
military, and intelligence support allies provide, the United States

depends on their moral approbation. Robert Kagan is correct to point out that America's democratic system tethers it powerfully to the opinions of liberal democratic societies.[19] If the United States becomes a pariah in the eyes of democracies in the West and elsewhere, it is unlikely to sustain its power and position in the world.

This discussion leads to the third image: From what position is the great power falling? One could argue that a dominant power has more at stake and therefore greater incentives to use force to preserve its position. Much depends on the magnitude and rate of the power shift and at what stage the dominant power starts to decline.[20] The risks of pursuing preventive war vary depending on whether a great power is rising, growing but at a decelerating rate, peaking, descending, or entering a phase of "acute relative decline."[21] A precarious situation emerges when a dominant power's role and expectations in the international system no longer reflect the underlying balance of power in key regions. This condition is most likely to appear when a great power is rising at a slowing rate, peaking, or falling into acute relative decline. The incentives to strike first can be just as powerful for declining challengers that fear the consequences of inaction as for a dominant power that fears the consequences of slipping to second place.

In summary, why is it so important that leaders ask these three broad questions and pursue objective, rigorous assessments? Shifts in the distribution of power and assertive regional challengers tempt political leaders of a dominant power to rush headlong into conflict. While it is easy to plan for the best-case scenario without appropriate skepticism, preventive military attacks often lead to worse outcomes. History shows that Britain's leaders wisely understood this lesson. Britain's cooperative approach toward an assertive America in the nineteenth century demonstrates the potential of balanced strategies short of military force to improve a declining power's security relative to a rising rival.

Britain and the Wisdom of Preventive Engagement

By the middle of the nineteenth century the British Empire was at the zenith of its power. It held at least 15 percent of world GDP. It served as the global financial center and dominated the terms of international trade. As the world's foremost naval power, Britain enjoyed mastery of the high seas. This position gave it a marked geostrategic advantage in interstate disputes and a prominent role in the scramble for colonies from Africa to Asia.

Decades later Britain's fortunes had slipped. Its share of global commerce dropped from 23.2 percent in 1880 to 14.1 percent over 1911 to 1913. Its share of manufacturing output declined from 22.9 percent in 1880 to 13.6 percent by 1913.[22] Not all indicators pointed in a negative direction, but the overall trends were clear: Britain was falling behind as rising competitors jockeyed for position. Two countries in particular surged ahead in relative terms: the United States and Germany. The United States increased its share of world manufacturing output from 14.7 percent in 1880 to 32 percent in 1913; Germany also registered notable growth in manufacturing output, rising from an 8.5 percent share of world manufacturing output in 1880 to a 14.8 percent share in 1913.[23] Britain's average annual growth in output did increase by 2.4 percent over the 1860 to 1880 period, but that of the United States grew by an average of 5 percent.[24] The United States and Germany excelled in other areas as well. America's steel output soared from 9.3 million tons to 26.5 million between 1890 and 1910; Germany's steel production also rose, from 4.1 million tons in 1890 to 13.6 million by 1910. By contrast, Britain's production levels declined from 8 million tons in 1890 to 6.5 million by 1910.[25]

Britain's relative economic decline was accompanied by fiscal decline. As Prime Minister Arthur Balfour put it in a secret memorandum in 1904, "We cannot say that the country could pay so much for its army: that another 100,000 pounds would mean either a violent anti-military reaction or financial ruin. ... There is a point at which the reduction of troops would leave the Empire defenseless. There is a point at which expenditure would become unbearable."[26]

Compounding this sense of fiscal crisis, Britain's navy was stretched thin. It commanded the high seas through its so-called two-power standard, meaning that the Royal Navy should have "a battlefield strength equal to that of any two potential foes," most likely France and its ally Russia.[27] During the later years of the nineteenth century the United States and Germany moved ahead.

Russia, France, and Japan were next in line, forcing Britain to limit its expansive reach to only its surrounding waters.

Even in the late nineteenth century British leaders viewed America as an ambitious challenger to their interests. How did they manage this competition during a period of relative decline? Following the American Revolution the power transition between the United States and Britain proceeded gradually. Differences over trading rights with Napoleonic France, among other points of tension, spilled over into the War of 1812, which threatened to upend an already adversarial relationship. During the American Civil War Britain recognized the belligerent status of the Confederacy and strained relations further by allowing the ironclad warship *Alabama* to be constructed and enter into service on the side of the Confederacy.

Starting in the early 1870s, however, US–British relations underwent a remarkable transformation from mutual antagonism to mutual restraint and cooperative engagement. Both sides left the Canadian border undefended, accepting vulnerabilities and demonstrating a newfound level of trust. In 1895 Britain and the United States resolved the Venezuelan boundary dispute. This crisis involved a border disagreement between British Guiana and Venezuela, which solicited help from the United States. After protracted negotiations the British cabinet voted in favor of arbitration to resolve the dispute, conceding to the means of resolution proposed by the United States: the agreement placed the decision in the hands of the US Commission on the Venezuelan–British Guiana border. Like other aspects of the Anglo–American rapprochement, this outcome reflected a series of decisions and reciprocal negotiations, not one-sided appeasement. Negotiation involves compromise; appeasement involves asymmetric and sustained concessions to satisfy grievances or, in some cases, to buy time in a strategic context of multiple rivals.[28] As the historian Bradford Perkins writes of the outcome of the Venezuelan border dispute, "The tangled negotiations ... saw compromise on both sides. ... Salisbury's government had retreated from its insistence that a dispute with Venezuela was no concern of the United States ... [but] Olney offered a compromise by which areas settled for more than fifty years would be excluded from arbitration."[29]

The transformation continued through the Spanish–American War of 1898. American involvement reflected what Schake calls its "revolutionary creed," which equated the right to rule with the consent of the governed.[30] Britain's support for the United States in this conflict was not without risks. Indeed, as Schake notes, Britain's decision "risked war with both Spain and Germany, cementing its isolation from Europe."[31] While British leaders expected the United States to temper its ideological commitments in foreign policy with the passage of time, the foundation for the Anglo–American rapprochement rested on practical realities: agreements on territorial disputes and a new hierarchy of relations that allowed the United States to exert supremacy in the Western Hemisphere and Britain to retain authority in the Mediterranean.[32]

The modus vivendi on the Alaskan boundary dispute with Canada is another case of increased cooperation. Previous agreements had forced Great Britain and the United States into a crisis with respect to contested boundaries. In the spring of 1899 a comprehensive settlement of the remaining issues eluded them. US Secretary of State John Hay and Sir Julian Pauncefote, the British ambassador to the United States, and, later, Hay and the British chargé d'affaires in Washington Reginald Tower, worked constructively to hammer out the details of an agreement that would, as one historian notes, "reserve their countries' full rights as to the boundary's final course, [while providing] sufficient stability to tide things over in the disputed areas for the time being."[33] To be sure, Britain was less than satisfied with the Canadian boundary arrangement and would soon press for arbitration. But the benefits of negotiation outweighed the costs: the new diplomatic understanding reduced tensions along the border and mitigated the risk that misperceptions and miscalculations would lead to conflict.[34]

In short, over the decades leading up to World War I a declining Britain pursued cooperative engagement with a rising, ambitious United States. Instead of embroiling itself in costly military adventures London sought to negotiate on the principles of order through a strategy of mutual restraint and reciprocity. As one historian of the period observes, "Lasting improvement in relations could ... come only from settling specific disputes through hard, persistent negotiations."[35] The United States and Britain reached agreement that rested on four pillars of order: a new hierarchy of power, reciprocity in trade, spheres of influence, and management of territorial disputes.[36] Traditionally, Britain relied on the United States for raw materials and basic foodstuffs, whereas the United States imported British manufactured goods. Before long, the United States gained a comparative advantage in manufactured goods, and a yawning trade imbalance opened up between the two countries. The British tolerated this imbalance, in part, because the United States demonstrated reciprocity in advocating for British commercial interests toward China, specifically by limiting imports of foreign machinery from Britain.

To be sure, the two sides disagreed over the merits of free trade and protectionism. But they agreed on rules of the road that would govern the international monetary system, with the United States moving toward the British "gold standard." Agreement on spheres of influence followed, with the British respecting the Monroe Doctrine's application in the Western Hemisphere and the Americans deferring to British influence in European affairs. As Prime Minster Balfour put it in a speech in Liverpool, "The Monroe doctrine has no enemies in this country. . . . We welcome any increase of the great influence of the United States of America upon the great Western Hemisphere."[37]

Pathways to Peaceful Transition

The common cultural heritage between the United States and Britain facilitated a peaceful transition in power. As Schake and Charles Kupchan both observe, however, cultural commonality is not a guarantee of peace.[38] Perceptions and misperceptions among decision makers in the United States and Britain all too often complicated relations, despite the overlap in cultural perspectives.[39] Peaceful transitions are more likely when leaders of the declining power show a willingness to adapt, balance resources and commitments, sacrifice short-term costs for long-term gains, instantiate shared values, and practice restraint. Britain's strategy of preventive engagement toward an assertive America incorporated elements of all five policy approaches.

First, Britain adapted to the limitations of its declining power. British leaders perceived the relative threat of a rising Germany and Russia to be greater than the threat posed by the United States. To be sure, Britain did not thrill to the idea of ceding its place in the Western Hemisphere. The United States presented a long-term threat to British naval superiority in the Atlantic, as did a rising Japan in the Pacific.[40] But Germany's naval buildup posed a greater short-term, immediate danger to British interests. Yuen Foong Khong of Oxford University observes that, although the United States was perceived as a great power at the end of the American Civil War in 1865, it "only really 'arrived' after the Spanish–American War in 1898."[41] Particularly before 1890 the United States was something of an anomaly: "The country's central decision-makers noticed and considered clear opportunities to expand American influence abroad and rejected them."[42]

Second, Britain's leaders made the hard choices of balancing commitments with available resources. Germany's rapid growth after Bismarck's involuntary resignation shaped Britain's assessment of its international position. The British secretary of state for the colonies Joseph Chamberlain drives this point home in a March 1898 letter: "We have in hand difficulties of the most serious character with France, Russia and Germany. We are engaged in an important expedition in the Soudan; and it is uncertain as yet whether the war on the North-west frontier of India has been finally concluded. We may emerge from all these troubles without a war, but I cannot conceal from myself that the prospect is more gloomy than it has ever been in my recollection."[43] Britain's revision of the naval two-power standard to focus on superiority closer to home reflected its perceptions of relative decline.[44] By the turn of the century, as Perkins notes, London simply did not have the resources to sustain a "battlefield strength equal to that of any two potential foes."[45]

Third, British leaders sacrificed short-term costs for long-term gains and considered the future implications of their policies. Put another way, British leaders from William Gladstone to Benjamin Disraeli held longer time horizons for assessing the costs of confronting an assertive America. This strategic approach enabled them to test the proposition that the United States could be integrated without jeopardizing mutual strategic interests.

Fourth, shared political and cultural values fortified the Anglo–American rapprochement.[46] During this period Princeton and Yale assumed a Gothic cast, mirroring the British universities of Oxford and Cambridge. The upper classes of the two societies adopted similar cultural practices, and rates of intermarriage began to rise. That both countries were part of the English-speaking world eased the passing of the torch between a declining Britain and a rising America.

Regime type matters, and concordant changes in regime type matter even more.[47] Because democracies trust and respect one another and because they are governed by institutions that restrain power and clarify intentions, Britain could direct its energies against an autocratic Germany as opposed to a more distant, democratic power across the Atlantic. As Schake observes, the United States and Britain grew to resemble each other during the nineteenth century in that the United States become more internationally engaged after the closing of the western frontier, and Britain became more democratic as a result of the Great Reform Act of 1832 and the advance of industrialization. Both countries focused more on their combined power than on the relative power differences between them.[48]

This "sense of sameness," in Schake's description, counsels caution about the prospects for future peaceful transitions of power, particularly in the case of two powers with as vastly different conceptions of domestic political arrangements as the United States and China.[49] While Beijing will likely seek to impose its own conception of international order, the US–China relationship is not fixed in enmity, and war is not inevitable. The choices both sides make in the coming years will determine whether the two countries learn the lessons from history or repeat them to their great mutual detriment.

Finally, British leaders were vigilant, adapted their strategic approach, and employed skillful statecraft. In reaction to its horrendous experience in the War of 1812, where disagreements over trading rights led to the gravest crisis in US–British relations since the War of Independence, British elites, businesses, and interest groups ultimately accepted the merits of a restrained approach to an assertive United States.[50] This course reaped the benefits of an emerging new cooperative relationship that would shore up Britain's power compared with that of Germany, Russia, and France.

Lessons for Statecraft

What lessons lie in the strategic decisions of Britain and in Bob Gallucci's approach toward negotiations with North Korea? Should a declining power pursue preventive engagement or preventive war? Should it militarily thwart an aggressive challenger before it becomes an existential threat? Or should it seek to persuade the challenger that its interests are better served through cooperative arrangements?

First, the best way out of the lure of preventive war is through constructive dialogue. In dealing with the North Korea nuclear crisis, Bob confronted a ticking clock and dwindling options. Instead of embracing military strikes, however, he tested the intentions of North Korea through hard-nosed diplomacy and constructive dialogue. Secretary Perry and Gallucci recognized that diplomacy goes hand in hand with the credible threat of force, but they also perceived the risks of self-reinforcing spirals of hostility.

The Clinton-era negotiations averted a costly war, but years later North Korea ultimately failed to abide by the terms of that deal. Successive diplomatic talks under multiple US administrations of both parties have failed to achieve the ultimate goal of a denuclearized Korean peninsula. This outcome need not imply that preventive military actions are the sole remaining solution, but this case highlights the potential uncertainties of preventive engagement when tensions are high and leverage is low.

In 2017 the United States and North Korea ratcheted up the rhetoric and brought the Korean peninsula dangerously close to nuclear war. The Trump administration's pivot from maximum pressure to maximum engagement the following year was executed poorly and haphazardly. Instead of building leverage by coordinating with allies, the administration failed to consult the South Koreans on its decision to suspend military exercises with them. Instead of working with China to maintain pressure on the North Koreans until they took concrete, verifiable steps toward denuclearization, the administration waged a trade war on China without rallying allies to its side and allowed serious gaps to emerge in the sanctions regime against Pyongyang. Preventive engagement requires more than the pomp and circumstance of presidential summitry. It requires distinct goals, a clear engagement strategy, and an unambiguous diplomatic path forward for generating and applying the leverage necessary to achieve one's goals.

Fortunately, there are instructive historical examples. British leaders saw the risks of negotiating with an aggressive America; after all, the two sides had fought a series of costly wars from the end of the eighteenth century through the early nineteenth century. This history of mutual antagonism was never far from the minds of Britain's leaders. To their credit British politicians in the late 1800s grasped the wisdom of preventive engagement and relied on diplomacy to secure their interests without going to war.

Political leaders who judge mistakenly that cooperation with a rising power is impossible may make preventive war inevitable. This path leads to what might be called Bismarck's dilemma, named after the German chancellor who allegedly said, "Preventive war is like committing suicide for fear of death." Misperceptions of the sources and inevitability of decline can produce high-risk, aggressive strategies that hasten the very outcome great powers seek to avoid.[51]

When political leaders of a declining power fear the worst, they adopt policies based on hostile images of the adversary.[52] Nationalist tempers flare, bureaucracies prepare for war, and offensive military plans encourage the illusion of an easy victory. Just as the automaticity of military timetables pushed European great powers toward war in 1914, rigid strategic cultures pressure declining great powers toward military options that, after deliberation, they would otherwise have set aside.[53] To escape Bismarck's dilemma is to recognize the dangers of self-fulfilling prophecies and worst-case thinking and to substitute in their place long-term, flexible, and comprehensive strategies for dealing with threatening rivals.

Second, rigorous policy analysis protects against false, silver-bullet certainty. There are no silver bullets in today's world. The eminent historian of the Cold War John Lewis Gaddis noted in 1992 that "surprise is still very much with us."[54] His insight bears repeating.

Few experts predicted the timing, nature, causes, or asymmetrical outcome of the Cold War's endgame.[55] Indeed, Soviet retrenchment from Eastern Europe was not a foregone conclusion in the late 1980s. Moscow could have attempted to muddle through or even lash out. Similarly, few predicted the terrorist attacks of 9/11 or the Arab revolutions that convulsed the Middle East in 2011, whose aftershocks are still being felt.

The decision to launch preventive war rests on an assumption of near certainty in a messy world of unpredictability and surprise. All policy recommendations involve predictions about the future; some are realistic, while others are fantasy. The difference between preventive engagement and preventive war is that aggression forecloses options while persuasion creates time and space to test intentions and reveal hidden assumptions. Bob recognized this fact when he questioned US officials who were overly confident in their assertions about North Korea's nuclear capability, grand strategy, and ultimate aims.

The scholar and former naval officer Scott Silverstone asks, "Can leaders see the future clearly enough to justify launching such wars with true confidence that the risks are essential for long-term self-defense? Are they actually preventing future aggression and more costly armed conflict by ordering military attacks against rivals that appear to be rising in power? Or are they simply bringing on the costs of war unnecessarily?"[56] Opting for preventive war means embarking on an extreme course of action over which leaders in the declining power have little control. There is no telling how assertive challengers will react to military attacks, and there's no predicting how simple miscalculations will combine to frustrate even the most basic objectives.

The security dilemma in international politics is rooted in the idea that states seeking nothing more than security can wind up fighting each other because of misperceptions about intentions. Actually, the challenge runs deeper. Great powers can come to blows even if they enjoy access to the same information.[57] Uncertainty about the meaning of security and the military capabilities needed to guarantee it can spell war between states who harbor only defensive intentions.[58] The odds of war climb higher when leaders of a declining power are more risk tolerant or hungry for status than leaders of the threatening challenger. The solution to the challenge of uncertainty is not to avoid it but to embrace it, understand its sources, and manage it skillfully. In the case of the United States, this route would require treating power shifts and the prospects of war less as a science and more as an art, applying methods of rigorous analysis along with a cautious disposition that reflects history's ironies, paradoxes, and tragic consequences.[59]

Third, erect guardrails against dangerous, short-sighted policies for preventive war. There's an old saying in politics known as Miles's Law: "Where you stand depends on where you sit."[60] Named for the former official Rugus E. Miles, who served in the US government in the 1950s and 1960s, his assertion is that perspective matters. When policy makers face a crisis or engage in a high-stakes negotiation, their view of the situation reflects the office they hold, the experiences they've had, the information they see, and the bureaucratic interests they represent. For a great power in decline, there is an analogous maxim: where and when a great power strikes depends on where it sits in the international hierarchy and how it sees its decline.

The odds of a military attack increase when fears grow as a nation's power descends at an accelerating rate or when an aggressive challenger approaches parity and begins to overtake it.[61] The risks also vary depending on who rules the regional and global roosts. The most dangerous situation is when global and regional hierarchies are misaligned. We've learned from history that the bloodiest wars occurred precisely when power was in transition globally but concentrated locally under the leadership of a dominant regional power.[62] Sun Tzu's advice is on the mark: "If you know the enemy and know yourself, you need not fear the result of a hundred battles."[63]

In a post-dominant world, policy makers in the United States will need to keep an objective mind about aggressive challengers and be realistic about the declining West. They will need to reassess America's position continually not only at the international level but also in key regions of interest. And they will need to recognize that the temptation to launch preventive war is not a constant but instead ebbs and flows at different stages of the life cycle of great powers. By acknowledging the danger zones, great powers in decline can erect guardrails against short-sighted policies.

Finally, preventive engagement is not surrender; it is a valuable policy alternative. Time and again Bob confronted the challenge of a US approach to negotiation that was all take and no give. If advocates of preventive war downplay the costs and risks of military action, they also exaggerate the losses and fears of alternative strategies for dealing with an aggressive challenger. Preventive engagement can be time-consuming and less satisfying to great powers that seek decisive outcomes, but these strategies are critical for adapting to relative decline. The use of force is only one arrow in a great power's quiver. Declining powers err not when they contemplate military action but when they reach for the military arrow first.

There are times when it may prove necessary to use force. But the tragic history of declining powers and preventive war should warn America's leaders about the perils of unintended consequences. What's more, there are good reasons for exercising patience during power transitions. Aggressive challengers may threaten a declining power or they may stumble along the way. Economic growth is hard to sustain, and aggressive policies can provoke counterbalancing coalitions or domestic backlash.[64]

To advocate restraint during power transitions is not to counsel passivity or surrender. The choice for great powers in decline is not simply to go to war now or face eventual subjugation. In fact, there are many strategies available to declining powers as they manage geopolitical competition. Diplomatic engagement can buy time for a faltering power to mobilize its resources and link arms with allies, strengthening its ability to deter the rising challenger short of war. Declining great powers can also manipulate the time horizons and threat perceptions of leaders of an assertive challenger, inclining them toward cooperation and away from confrontation.[65] In the nineteenth century, for example, Prussia forestalled opposition to its ascent by showing restraint, appealing to common values, and shaping the environment within which its rise took place.[66] Likewise, the United States should explore ways to shape the regional context of China's rise through coordination with allies, economic statecraft, and skillful diplomacy.[67]

Following the Second World War, America established a set of multilateral institutions to encourage cooperation, safeguard democracy, extend free trade, and promote shared prosperity. This model points to another form of preventive engagement. The United States wisely chose to disperse and restrain power in cooperative international and regional institutions, giving allies a voice in US decision making and gaining their broad support for an American-led global order.[68] Many of America's most salient diplomatic successes, such as the NPT and the peaceful transition of Eastern Europe after the end of the Cold War, were achieved through persistent diplomatic cooperation in multilateral fora.

Multilateral institutions and balance of power dynamics are not mutually exclusive. Indeed, US institution building during the Cold War coincided with assertive balancing against the Soviet Union. America also proved adept at wielding these institutions to its geopolitical advantage.[69] Multilateral institutions do not resolve all tensions among allies or temper the impulse toward hard bargaining. But they allow these frictions to play out in the context of densely woven interactions and tight linkages that make cooperation easier to achieve.

The Next Choice

Preventive engagement rests on the idea that focused, early, and cooperative action is critical in addressing threats before they become crises. This pathway is just as relevant for domestic challenges as for international challenges. The scholar and activist Sarah Chayes learned this lesson the hard way. After bearing witness to the effects of corruption and bad governance abroad, she is sounding the alarm over the rot in American democracy at home.

CHAPTER SIX

People Power or Pinstripe Rule?

"**I**F AN OFFICIAL ASSESSES a farmer more than is due to the authorities, the sum he unjustly raised should be demanded of him and returned to the farmer, and if the official has any property, it should be confiscated as an example to other agents, so they refrain from tyrannical acts." When Sarah Chayes read these words in her workshop in Kandahar, Afghanistan, a light went on in her head. "Now *there* was an anticorruption measure that would make an impact," she thought.[1] The admonition came from Nizam al-Mulk's *A Treatise on Government*. Sarah came upon this ancient text in a Parisian bookstore and took it with her to Afghanistan. Nizam al-Mulk served as chief minister to two sultans of the Ghaznavid Empire in the eleventh century. His manual forms part of a literary genre called mirror for princes, of which Machiavelli's *The Prince* is perhaps the most well-known installment.

Sarah couldn't help but notice the raw contemporary application of this Persian administrator's wise counsel. Nizam al-Mulk warned against forcible seizure of property: "It is reported that [the powerful eighth-century governor of Basra] Umara b. Hamza attended Caliph Wasiq's audience on the day the caliph was meting out justice for those complaining of arbitrary conduct. A man . . . rose and accused Umara in these terms: 'Umara b. Hamza forcibly commandeered a property that belongs to me.' " In addition, Nizam al-Mulk advised the sultans to protect the independence of judges, and for judges to rule with impartiality: "The salaries and emoluments accorded to judges assure their independence and keep them from unfairness. This point is extremely important and extremely sensitive, for judges ... dispose of the lives and fortunes of Muslims." Equally striking, Nizam al-Mulk emphasized the importance of accountability between the ruler and the ruled "because the good and the bad that they do reflects on the prince and his government."

As Sarah pored over the pages of this manual from the Islamic Middle Ages, she recognized a truth fully relevant to present times. Corruption is not just morally wrong, Sarah tells me. "Corruption brings about the ruin of a kingdom." Sarah made this discussion an anchor of her second book on the link between kleptocratic governance and global insecurity. Most would not expect to find a work on contemporary international corruption that weaves in passages of unheard-of medieval authors. But that's the kind of unusual connecting of dots across genres and epochs that is typical of Sarah's thinking.

I asked Sarah what might bring about the ruin of the American kingdom today. "What ails us," she told me, "goes beyond specific policy lapses and remedies. What ails us is deeply cultural, and that's why I've found myself resonating with some ancient tales." When we sat down to talk, Sarah was in the throes of writing. She told me she had found herself using what she calls "sacred stories" in her current book about corruption in the United States, much as she drew on the mirrors for princes in her earlier volume.

Sarah's path to becoming an interpreter of ancient myths for application to present times is long and winding. She cut her teeth as a journalist for National Public Radio. Sarah didn't shrink from the dangers of reporting on the front lines; in fact, she relished them. She covered the civil war in Algeria in the late 1990s and in Kosovo in 1999. Not three years later, in December 2001, she made her way to Kandahar to cover the US intervention in Afghanistan. She entered Afghanistan to report on the war, but she stayed to help Afghans win the peace. She learned Pashto and set up a cooperative to make and sell soap. She learned about

Afghanistan and its people. Above all, she listened to their complaints. She heard stories of shakedowns and bribery, of power grabs and theft. She could see and feel the anger boiling among ordinary Afghans. "It's not just that many were denied redress," Sarah tells me. "There's no such thing as redress. The courts and the police were in on the system." Her friend Nurallah told her a story of how the police shook down his brother at a checkpoint and smacked him when he refused to pay a bribe. "You call that law?" Nurallah fumed to Sarah. "They're the police! They should be showing people what the law is; they should be enforcing the law. And they're the ones breaking it."[2]

That's when it all clicked for Sarah. Corruption wasn't a *result* of the insurgency; it was the major driver—and not just in Afghanistan. Sarah knew that the shakedowns and petty bribes added up to something more than the daily violence and depredations to which Afghans had grown accustomed. Corruption robs people of the future and offends one's most basic sense of human dignity. When political leaders use their public office for private gain, it alienates people from one another and from their government. In Afghanistan that sense of alienation and indignation was driving Sarah's neighbors into the arms of the Taliban.

After seeing the debilitating effects of corruption in Afghanistan firsthand, Sarah returned to the United States with an urgent message for the world, appropriately summed up in the title of her book, *Thieves of State: Why Corruption Threatens Global Security*, published in 2015. Even then, Sarah tells me, she knew that her message applied as well to the United States. "I just thought there would be more time before the American version of other countries' extreme reactions to systemic corruption hit," Sarah admits. "This isn't just Afghanistan, and it isn't just the United States. It's a global zeitgeist."

In 2017 Sarah decided to pivot and apply her international experience to examining what seems to be rotten in the state of American democracy. "Look at how our culture is set up," Sarah explains. "The leaders of our political economy are engaged in a race counted in dollars, where your social standing is measured by the size of your wallet. That means they need to convert everything to cash, and what can't be converted to cash gets bulldozed out of the way or destroyed. Mining companies call mountaintops 'overburden.' People in this race will bulldoze a mountain or raze a forest to get at the coal or gas beneath it. They convert everything of irreplaceable value into zeroes in a bank account."

Sarah offers a compelling take on the US Constitution as "an anti-corruption device." America's founders were fixated on the dangers of corruption and its potential stranglehold on their young republic. When John Adams remarked that in France "there is everything here too which can seduce, betray, deceive, corrupt, and debauch," he meant it as both an observation and a warning.[3] Corruption in France was farce; corruption in Britain was tragedy. The French openly traded riches for rule; the British claimed ideals their leaders quietly ignored.

Sarah shares a warning of her own. She points to the Gilded Age of the late nineteenth century as a period when systemic corruption reigned in America but was fiercely challenged by some of its most badly hurt victims: "How incredibly vibrant and multidimensional and creative the protests were against Gilded Age practices. Look at the labor movement of the late nineteenth and early twentieth centuries and how persistently they worked to bind themselves across the divides of identity, ethnicity, and religion that were every bit as virulent as ours are now. I don't sense that same spirit today. We are fractured, and therefore at a real disadvantage in our effort to challenge the power of money to rig our system and undermine our democracy."

The platforms of American movements such as the Knights of Labor and the Populist Party inspired much of the legislation ascribed to the Progressive Era on everything from working conditions to antitrust laws. But what's enforced in law actually matters. As Sarah points out, "When you drill down on how the legislation of the Progressive Era was applied, it's a different story. The Sherman Antitrust Act, for example, was applied more often against unions than against the big monopolies."

For Sarah, the roots of America's current obsession with money stretch back to the 1980s. "The 1980s is the rebirth of the money obsession; and it starts morphing into kleptocracy in the 1990s," Sarah continued. "Once infinite wealth is the objective, the only way to secure it is to rig the system." Sarah sees the history of corruption as a series of ebbs and flows. "Violence is present in every society, always," Sarah tells me. "So is corruption. But organized, intense, widespread, socially sanctioned violence is war, and that only happens periodically. Similarly with systemic corruption. The last time we had this kind of kleptocracy on a global scale was the Gilded Age." Sarah hypothesizes that what it took to get us out then was a series of calamities: two world wars, two genocides, and mass starvation in Europe. "What is the scale of the disaster it will take this time?" Sarah asks.

The tragedy of American democracy today is that money has become the measure of all things. This false promise has entwined itself so completely in political and economic life now that few recognize it as a myth. "What corrupt networks do," Sarah explains, "is grasp certain institutions and agencies and elements of state function, and then weaponize them. The way I've boiled it down—in emblematic language—is . . . the power of the scales (justice), the power of the pen (lawmaking), the mace (force), and the purse (control over the budget or public resources, such as land). The kleptocratic network weaponizes these four powers, but they sabotage those powers aimed at protecting ordinary people."

In short, public goods become endowments for modern-day robber barons in pinstripe suits. The institutions of the state don't serve ordinary people but work for the privileged few. This pattern is much bigger than any one individual or bad apple. As Sarah shows in her research, the institutions of kleptocracies are more than fronts for illicit activities; they are the means by which corrupt networks channel loot to the winners—their members—and shake down the losers. What makes this plunder all the more difficult to expose and prevent is that the hidden gains from corruption are concentrated whereas the benefits of collective action in the name of the general public are diffuse.[4]

Strategic Choice: People Power or Pinstripe Rule?

The story of political corruption is common to great powers in decline. Power is about more than the possession of resources; it is also about the ability of states to use those resources to achieve important ends. When privileged elites, corporations, and special interests determine who governs, they undermine the public's trust, corrode the institutions of government, and weaken the ability of states to convert wealth into national power. In relative terms China and Russia are materially more corrupt than the United States, but in absolute terms corruption in America poses an acute threat to its long-term power.[5] Corruption narrows the tax base, decreases state revenues, and creates entrenched interest groups that limit the investments necessary to sustain a productive economy and advanced military capabilities over the long term. Little wonder that the scholars Daron Acemoğlu and James Robinson point to extractive political and economic institutions as a primary cause of why nations fail.[6] Systems based on plunder may work well for privileged elites; indeed, they operate efficiently and exclusively for that purpose. Corruption is not mere opportunism; it is, in Sarah's phrase, "the deliberate operating system of sophisticated networks bent on self-enrichment."[7] Corrupt networks are widespread, systematic, and resilient. They are also deeply corrosive of power. Self-enrichment is not a recipe for national advancement.

In practice, leaders of declining powers face a choice between people power and pinstripe rule. Do political leaders govern in the interests of the people as a whole and distribute the resources of the state based on merit and the rule of law? Or do political leaders govern in the interest of self-enrichment, self-preservation, and self-interest by targeting resources to specific groups and wealthy elites based on insider privileges? In his 1982 book *The Rise and Decline of Nations* the economist Mancur Olson warned of the dangers to democracy of pure rent-seeking behavior by privileged elites. When the rot sets in, it's hard to treat short of invasive procedures. Olson concluded that war and revolution are common, if catastrophic, remedies.

Corruption in a democracy takes many forms. One widely used definition is "the abuse of public office for private gain."[8] The anticorruption watchdog Transparency International distinguishes between three types of corruption: petty, political, and grand corruption. Petty corruption involves the abuse of public office by lower-level officials who prey on citizens seeking access to the benefits and services of the state. Grand corruption occurs when high-level government officials wield the instruments of state in the interests of self-enrichment or to advance the interests of a privileged few. In many countries, petty and grand corruption are tightly linked. As Sarah points out, "These structures are almost always vertically integrated, meaning some proportion of the street-level shakedowns that plague the people is funneled up to those at the top."[9] Another type of abuse of power for private gain is political corruption, which involves the "manipulation of policies, institutions, and rules of procedure in the allocation of resources and financing by political decision makers, who abuse their position to sustain their power, status and wealth."[10]

The charge of corruption is appropriate when an individual or group vested with public authority seeks to use an office to benefit themselves or their client group and wealthy benefactors and then conceals this act from the general public.[11] Not all theft is properly termed an act of corruption, but in a general sense every act of corruption is a form of theft. It robs average citizens of the opportunity to shape their future, sell their wares, and sustain their lives by means of hard work and fair play. Corrupted democracy is no democracy at all.

In America today political corruption threatens the integrity of democracy. Individuals and groups paying cash and other rewards manipulate policies, laws, and rules of procedure with near impunity. Privileged elites, corporations, and special interests dominate the selection of who governs in the United States—at the federal, state, and local levels.[12] Many of their shady activities have legal cover given by weak laws and constrained enforcement.

The historian Edward Watts draws a disturbing parallel between the United States today and the decline of the Roman Republic: "The erosion of norms really start[ed] when Roman politicians convince[d] themselves that their personal ambitions and the good of the republic [were] one and the same. In other words, they started acting in their own self-interest but deluded themselves into thinking that it was really for the betterment of Rome."[13] Watts's message is that the decline of American democracy today is inseparable from the decline of the behavioral norms and institutions that put a check on greed and open a window into unsavory dealings.

How far America sinks will depend on the willingness of political leaders and citizens to unmask the myth of money and embrace a movement against political corruption. To extend Sarah's metaphor, this movement would harness her four powers to work differently: it would wield a wiser pen; tip the scales in favor of justice; use the mace primarily to curb the abuse of power by those who wield it rather than to keep the powerless submissive; and employ the purse for the public good.

A Wiser Pen

The founding fathers were concerned about the threat of state capture by moneyed elites. State capture also lies at the heart of theories about when and under what conditions political institutions erode and decay. When institutions fail to adapt, it's generally because leaders are unable or unwilling to reform and because reforms pose a threat to the wealth of powerful elites.[14] Consider the amount of dark money sloshing around in American politics. In her investigation of dark money's nefarious reach, the journalist Jane Mayer paints a disturbing portrait of a democracy in thrall to big moneyed interests. At the center of the storm are the billionaires Charles and the late David Koch, the Koch brothers, owners of one of the largest private companies in the United States. As Mayer shows, the Koch brothers have used their fortune to influence the workings of government to suit their own agenda.

In her book *Democracy in Chains* the historian Nancy MacLean traces the ideology and tactics of the Koch brothers to the ideas of the political economist James McGill Buchanan and his fight to preserve the privileges of a wealthy elite. MacLean writes of one of the key decisions in the Koch brothers' evolution: "In his first big gift to Buchanan's program, Charles Koch signaled his desire for the work he funded to be conducted behind the backs of the majority. 'Since we are greatly outnumbered,' Koch conceded to the assembled team, the movement could not win simply by persuasion. Instead, the cause's insiders had to use their knowledge of 'the rules of the game'—that game being how modern democratic governance works—'to create winning strategies.' "[15]

The Koch brothers pursue their winning strategies through what one of their operatives called a "fully integrated network."[16] This network includes direct campaign contributions, a stable of think tanks and academic programs that churn out studies favorable to their cause, a multitude of corporate lobbyists and legal groups, and tax-exempt nonprofit organizations that do not have to disclose the sources of their funding. The reach of this tightly led network of influential actors is unequaled in the history of American politics. Mayer cites the work of the scholars Theda Skocpol and Alexander Hertel-Fernandez to reveal a startling statistic: "In 2016 the Kochs' private network of political groups had a bigger payroll than the Republican National Committee. The Koch network had 1,600 paid staffers in thirty-five states and boasted that its operation covered 80 percent of the population. ... In Texas alone, they supported candidates in seventy-four different races."[17]

Privileged elites, corporations, and special interests rely on lobbying government officials to advance their interests. As the political scientist Francis Fukuyama writes, "The explosion of interest groups and lobbying in Washington has been astonishing, with the number of firms with registered lobbyists rising from 175 in 1971 to roughly 2,500 a decade later, and then to 13,700 lobbyists spending about $3.5 billion by 2009."[18] Between 2007 and 2012, according to another estimate, lobbyists spent $5.8 billion on political influence campaigns, which resulted in roughly $4.4 trillion in federal largesse being returned to two hundred of the biggest corporations.[19] Is it any wonder that US public policies benefit the privileged few at the expense of the middle class and working poor?

To be sure, Americans have the right to petition their government. Lobbyists bring expertise to issues and represent major sectors of the American economy. And some registered lobby groups allow for a degree of transparency and oversight. Still, it's undeniable that billions of dollars from special interest groups and lobbyists adversely sway the legislative process against the interests of ordinary Americans. If US citizens want to know why the tax code is thousands of pages long or why it resembles a Swiss cheese of loopholes and carve-outs, look no further than the reach of the pharmaceutical lobby, the banking lobby, or the insurance lobby. The Affordable Care Act and the Dodd–Frank Wall Street Reform and Consumer Protection Act are needlessly complex for a reason. The Tax Cut and Jobs Act of 2017 is only a recent example of where people power is losing to pinstripe rule. The issue is not simply that lobby groups are proliferating. It is that the practice of democracy in America today favors those groups that are most organized, better funded, and more extreme in their positions than the majorities who support compromise positions, to say nothing of poorer and marginalized communities that lack a similar voice in the process.[20]

The power of the legislative pen is biased for another reason. For much of the post–Cold War period American officials preached the gospel of globalization. Free trade and open markets, they said, were the future and would bring peace and prosperity to more people in more countries than ever before. In retrospect, that view was not wrong but it was blind to the darker side of globalization. More and more the global playing field tilts in favor of oligarchs, kleptocrats, and moneyed interests. Many of these professional plunderers exploit the processes of globalization to their advantage through offshore bank accounts, shell corporations, and money laundering, and America's return to pinstripe rule gives them an open field. As the journalist Franklin Foer reports, while Congress tightened restrictions on the banking sector after 9/11 in response to concerns about terrorism and money laundering, lobbying and special interest group pressure managed to carve out an exception for the real estate sector. This loophole allowed oligarchs and kleptocrats overseas to set up anonymous shell companies in places like Delaware and Nevada to launder their ill-gotten gains in luxury real estate or US markets. "Those states, along with a few others, had turned the registration of shell companies into a hugely lucrative racket," observes Foer, "and it was stunningly simple to arrange such a Potemkin front on behalf of a dictator, a drug dealer, or an oligarch."[21]

America set out to transform the world in its image. Increasingly, however, the kleptocracies of the world have transformed America in theirs.[22] The decline in principles of behavior among the privileged classes abets this corruption. Foer refers to the decay in standards in the "white-shoe world" as a struggle for survival of the fittest, where the norms that keep human instincts in check are bent toward power and personal enrichment. Such depreciation is evident across a range of global service providers. Daniel Nexon gives a sense of how broad and deep the rot goes: "International service providers such as bankers, accountants, lawyers, wealth managers, second-citizenship providers and real estate brokers enable these transactions, creating an increasingly globalized system of corruption and concentration of wealth."[23] One of the consequences of permitting the growth of a pay-to-play system at home is that the world's oligarchs and kleptocrats are flush with cash and all too happy to play as well.

Tipping the Scales in Favor of Justice

The need to rebalance the scales in order to ensure justice, equality, and fair play is acute. The former Supreme Court justice Louis Brandeis wrote, "We must make our choice. We may have democracy, or we may have wealth concentrated in the hands of a few, but we can't have both."[24] In the 2010 *Citizens United v. Federal Elections Commission* decision the Supreme Court accelerated an alarming trend that allows wealth and power to concentrate in the hands of the few who have dominant impact on public policy. The court ruled five to four that political contributions are free speech, thereby allowing corporations to spend without limit on political campaigns. In delivering the majority opinion, Justice Anthony Kennedy wrote, "If the First Amendment has any force, it prohibits Congress from fining or jailing citizens, or associations of citizens, for simply engaging in political speech."[25] The phrase "associations of citizens" is ripe with ambiguity. Are corporations actually "associations of citizens"? If foreign nationals are prohibited from making political contributions in America's elections, what are the ramifications for corporations with wealthy foreign shareholders?[26] While there is precedent for the Supreme Court extending protections to corporations under the First Amendment, *Citizens United* deepens the rot of a system in which seemingly everything, even one's vote, is up for sale.

The *Citizens United* decision raises another question: If corporate spending is speech, under what conditions can it be limited? By precedent, the court has acknowledged a "compelling state interest" in preventing corruption. In *Citizens United*, however, the court narrowed the terms of corruption merely to bribery in the form of a quid pro quo.[27] Kennedy cited the Supreme Court's 1976 decision in

Buckley v. Valeo to support his argument: "The Buckley Court explained that the potential for quid pro quo corruption distinguished direct contributions to candidates from independent expenditures. The Court emphasized that 'the independent expenditure ceiling ... fails to serve any substantial governmental interest in stemming the reality or appearance of corruption in the electoral process ...' because '[t]he absence of prearrangement and coordination ... alleviates the danger that expenditures will be given as a quid pro quo for improper commitments from the candidate.' "[28] By limiting the definition of corruption to simple bribery, the court opened the door to more powerful venal influences that have corrupted the American political system. How far could this go?

The Supreme Court opened that door further in 2017 when it ruled to overturn the conviction of the former governor of Virginia Bob McDonnell on eleven counts of corruption, including fraud and extortion. In his majority opinion Chief Justice John Roberts expressed distaste for the facts of the case, which, as one journalist noted, included clear evidence that the governor and his wife had accepted "over $175,000 worth of loans and gifts, such as vacations, designer clothes and a Rolex watch, from a businessman seeking the state's help in promoting a tobacco-based dietary supplement."[29] Concerns about the facts of the case, however, did not prevent the court from narrowing the definition of bribery. Chief Justice Roberts put it this way: "There is no doubt that this case is distasteful; it may be worse than that. But our concern is not with tawdry tales of Ferraris, Rolexes, and ball gowns. It is instead with the broader legal implications of the Government's boundless interpretation of the federal bribery statute. A more limited interpretation of the term 'official act' leaves ample room for prosecuting corruption, while comporting with the text of the statute and the precedent of this Court."[30]

This ruling will make it more difficult for prosecutors to bring cases in the absence of an explicit quid pro quo. The problem is both a political and legal concern. It is a political concern because the ultimate responsibility for keeping vast sums of dark money out of US politics lies with the Congress; it is a legal problem in that the Supreme Court has narrowed the definition of corruption in a way that will make the task of rooting out deep-seated corruption all the more challenging. If the definition of corruption is the "abuse of public office for private gain," the court's decision in McDonnell v. the United States strikes a blow against one of democracy's essential guardrails. As the attorney and campaign finance reform expert Fred Wertheimer concludes, "The Court's decision opens the door to a corrupt 'pay to play' culture in government so long as the official receiving the benefits does not make an actual government decision or take an official government action in response to the benefits given. But short of an official action, the Court has said that it is perfectly legal for an officeholder to exchange access and various types of other actions in return for financial benefits going into the officeholder's pocket."[31] The impact? Today, political corruption has been made attractive to pinstripe power brokers, and, with the advice of an average lawyer, bribery is now legal. Where is Justice Louis Brandeis now?

Curbing the Mace

If corruption is about the abuse of power, curbing the mace is about putting restraints on the power of government officials in order to protect the interests of ordinary citizens. The question for America is this: Should wealth determine who is empowered to govern and how they govern? On issue after issue, from campaign finance and revolving doors to gerrymandering and voter suppression, the answer increasingly is yes.

Curbing the mace will require eliminating, reducing, or containing massive donations of dark money through political campaigns. These opaque donations enable powerful elites and corporations to select their candidates over the preferences of ordinary citizens. By one estimate more than 90 percent of the candidates who outspend their political opponents in campaigns for the US House of Representatives are successful.[32] Absent campaign finance controls, elections create unbridled opportunities for abuse.

As for revolving doors, it is imperative to maintain a clear distinction between the lobbying apparatus and those who write laws and regulations. This revolving door needs to be controlled, restricted, and transparent. Lobbyists and lawmakers who violate these rules and codes of conduct must be held accountable.

Gerrymandering is the quiet political agenda of those in office, used to manipulate the system and retain their hold on power. It distorts the ideal of one person, one vote. And it undermines public trust in government by eliminating effective competition between parties and empowering the more extreme ends of the political spectrum. The Supreme Court has yet to elaborate criteria for deciding when gerrymandering is permissible and when it crosses an impermissible line. Sooner than later, gerrymandering needs to be brought under control for a simple reason: it violates the fundamental principle that citizens are entitled to equal protection under the law.

Perhaps the most egregious use of the mace is voter suppression. Privileged elites, corporations, and special interests maintain their grip on power by disenfranchising voters from minority communities. In the 2018 midterm elections in the United States rampant voter suppression was on full display in Georgia, Florida, North Dakota, and many other states. Since 2010 twenty-five states in America have adopted measures that restrict the people's right to vote.[33] As in the case of gerrymandering, the task of combating voter suppression demands action from the federal government. All citizens must be able to conveniently register on time, vote when the polls open, have their ballots counted, and make their voices heard. The list of steps that need to be taken to secure American democracy is long and sometimes technical, but the principle is simple: one person, one vote. And every vote should count.

Using the Purse for Public Good

The final power needing reform is use of the purse for the public good. The purse refers to how officeholders oversee public assets, such as federal, state, and local budgets and the management of public land. In a functioning democracy leaders should pass budgets that support the interests of ordinary citizens on the economy and public health, among other issues. Such support includes the protection of public lands from environmental degradation, the prevention of lethal toxins and wastewater from being dumped in rivers, and regulations that bar logging companies from ravaging forested landscapes.[34]

In America today the public's purse belongs to the highest bidder. In a 2014 study the political scientists Martin Gilens and Benjamin Page reviewed 1,779 policy issues over two decades to see whether they tracked more closely with the interests of average citizens, mass interest groups, industry groups, or economic elites. Overwhelmingly, the evidence shows that business groups and economic elites fare best.[35] This finding reflects, in part, the pervasive influence of money in politics. It also explains why so many voters are driven to extremes: when the political system ignores the concerns of ordinary people over a generation, many Americans see little reason to work within a corrupt system or to support candidates who claim they respect its norms and procedures. This is not an argument for abandoning the US political system; it is an argument for enacting policies and laws that more closely reflect the preferences of ordinary Americans.

The pen, the scales, the mace, and the purse are all central aspects of dealing with corruption. In the end, however, national leaders must stand up against venality and institute good governance. In *How Democracies Die* Steven Levitsky and Daniel Ziblatt of Harvard University identify critical warning signs: Do leaders flout the constitutional order? Do they condone violence against minorities? Do they attack independent institutions, such as the media and judiciary, or threaten civil liberties? And do they dismiss their political opponents as enemies of the state instead of respecting them as legitimate participants in a democratic order?[36]

How does the presidency score? The degeneration of American democracy began long before President Trump assumed office, but his presidency has deepened the crisis in alarming ways. As the journalist and author David Frum warns of the Trump administration's ethical lapses, "If one gauge of authoritarianism is the merger of state power with familial economic interests, the needle is approaching the red zone."[37] The lights have been flashing red in any number of areas, most notably in the failure to separate private business interests from public duties, thereby creating a potential opening for foreign governments to purchase influence at the highest levels of the US government. Add to these myriad conflicts of interest the persistent erosion of norms intended to safeguard the presidency from being used as a bully pulpit to threaten companies, the media, individuals, and organizations, and there is a recipe for abuse of power in the extreme.[38]

We know what happens when political leaders succumb to the lure of dark money and use their position to advance the power and wealth of privileged elites above the well-being of ordinary citizens. We know because history offers us lessons and a way out of the danger zone. We have seen how Spanish political leaders allowed privileged interests in society to dominate the policies of government, a practice that contributed to its longer-term decline (see chapter 3).

Ottoman Decay, Experimentation, and Reform

To understand the dangers of corruption and how to arrest the slide into patronage and decay, the United States would do well to consider the case of the Ottoman Empire in the sixteenth and seventeenth centuries. The causes and character of Ottoman decline have been subject to considerable debate and reinterpretation among historians.[39] For centuries the Ottoman state and society were a textbook example of an empire that rose to great heights only to deteriorate and decay in the seventeenth century. Since the 1970s, however, historians have challenged this picture of a "diseased system" by examining the lives of ordinary people from a comparative perspective.[40] What emerges is a more subtle rendering of an empire that underwent profound changes in the seventeenth century, changes marked by decay, experimentation, and reform. Its example is worthy of study for a simple reason: like Spain, the Ottoman Empire sheds light on the causes and character of decline as well as on the means by which declining powers seek to adapt and renew the sources of their strength.

At its height in the early to mid-sixteenth century the Ottoman Empire stretched from Algeria and Egypt in the west to Hungary, Bulgaria, and Macedonia in the north to Syria, Lebanon, Jordan, and parts of Arabia in the east. How did a ragtag group of principalities in western Asia Minor reach such grand proportions and last so long? Equally perplexing, how and why did the Ottoman Empire unravel? Historians have long debated this story, and its contours reveal important lessons about the proper functioning of state institutions and the perils of political corruption.

The Ottomans were arguably one of Asia Minor's greatest innovators, at least initially. After the Seljuks suffered defeat at the hands of the Mongols in the thirteenth century, the Ottomans gathered strength on the outer edges of the Byzantine Empire. One of the leaders of the frontier tribes, Osman, won a crucial victory at Baphaeon in the early fourteenth century and staked his claim to rule over the other tribes. The Ottomans emerged as the dominant group among the Turco-Muslim principalities and carved out a strategic position from which to defend their gains and attack the increasingly overstretched Byzantine forces.

The Ottomans leveraged several advantages.[41] They were inconspicuous relative to other principalities, which gave them time to grow and conquer territory without provoking the ire of the Mongols. They were innovative, pioneering new forms of organization, forging alliances, and tolerating a degree of pluralism in their domains. And they were skillful centralizers and consolidators, co-opting social groups through bargaining. The Ottomans pursued a path to centralization different from that of western Europe. Whereas European states moved from feudalism and indirect control to what the sociologist Karen Barkey terms "contested centralization and bureaucratization," the Ottomans developed a more negotiated centralization process. As Barkey observes, "Even the bandits—who were seen as the major threat of the state—were used by the central authorities to consolidate their power."[42]

From early on the Ottomans took steps to prevent the emergence of a hereditary warrior class that would control land and pass it on to their family members. Under the practice of *devshirme* the Ottomans would take young boys from their families, convert them to Islam, train them in the metropole, and impress them into service as part of the Janissary corps. Cemal Kafadar of Harvard University notes that the Janissaries, the sultan's palace guard, "provided the central administration with an effective check on the power of the warrior aristocracies of Anatolia and the Balkans. . . . Thus the center prevented the parceling of sovereignty through the creation of a socially uprooted but loyal force—an artificial extension of the royal household that produced no lineage but ensured the continued rule of the dynasty."[43] The Ottomans achieved this centralized administration through a system of military enslavement and strict rules of social control, which separated the civil and military spheres and prohibited nepotism.[44]

The Ottomans organized cavalrymen, or *sipahi*, in ways that would guard against the tendency to favor one's own. Through rotation and other methods the ruling elite maintained centralized control and prevented "the solidification of claims on land, resources and positions within family lines."[45] In effect, the state granted a cavalryman a fief, or *timar*, for the duration of his service to the state. In contrast to the feudal system in Europe, as Fukuyama notes, "the Turkish appanages could not be turned into heritable property and given to the sipahis' descendants."[46]

Then there were the intangibles. The founding father of the Ottoman Empire, Osman I, was reputed to be a " 'self-made man' with no glorious lineage to automatically legitimate him and his descendants or to tie him to 'timeless' traditions."[47] Perhaps as a consequence, the early Ottomans displayed creativity and adapted institutions to suit their political and strategic needs. The central administration understood the power of legitimacy. The dynasty could endure disruptions, disorder, and even decapitation of a specific ruler and still retain its hold on the Ottoman state and its sprawling empire.

During the seventeenth century, however, internal and external pressures combined to weaken the Ottoman state from multiple directions. Inflation and financial crises, the unsustainability of the timar system, the spread of banditry, and natural disasters all played a part in eroding the empire's foundations.[48] Elements of the Ottoman state returned to earlier forms of patrimony, with government officials distributing rents and providing favors to friends, family, and insiders based on ties of personal loyalty.[49] Inflation exposed vulnerabilities in the timar system. Unable to sustain themselves, cavalrymen broke ranks and descended into banditry. Timars were sold to the highest bidder. Private individuals called tax farmers, who collected revenue on behalf of the state, became more prevalent and took advantage of the peasantry.[50] The rising costs of military modernization brought about changes in the Janissary corps. As the Ottoman scholar Norman Itzkowitz notes, "Revoked and abandoned *timars* fell into the hands of leading janissaries. . . . In the mid-seventeenth century several leading janissary officers ... somehow managed appointments as chief financial officer of the empire, under whose control were the bureaus that substantiated title to timars and issued the appropriate documents to timar-holders."[51] The Janissaries grew undisciplined, less effective in projecting force, more aligned with business and commercial interests, and increasingly willing to enroll their sons in military service.[52]

As certain institutions of the empire deteriorated, however, others adapted and strengthened. The decay of the Ottoman Empire in the seventeenth century coincided with notable experimentation and reform of fiscal policy and administration. Finance officials explored alternate sources of revenue. Elites demonstrated an ability to jettison the old, such as the land survey registers for agricultural revenue, and usher in the new, such as lifetime tax farms, "a device which recognized the positive involvement of non-government elites in collecting revenue, and which ultimately created new allies for the state among wealthy provincials from diverse backgrounds."[53] As the historian Linda Darling shows, the seventeenth century was a period of both continuity and change.[54] Traditional models were no longer operative, which explains in part the tendency toward decay and stagnation in certain corners of the empire. It also explains the willingness of officials to adopt new methods to meet growing demands on the state at the elite and local levels.

The Ottoman state was not a democracy as we know it, but the seventeenth century saw changes in the relationship between officials in Istanbul and local elites in the provinces. Central authority faced challenges as local officials pressed their advantage and employed bribery to secure coveted positions. Decentralization of authority, however, did not entail the destruction of state authority. The historian Dina Rizk Khoury notes that governance structures at the provincial level adapted by incorporating local elites into positions of leadership. The integration of local elites into provincial military and financial offices, as the historians Christine Woodward and Khoury observe, bolstered central–provincial relations and helped to " 'Ottomanise' [*sic*] local societies and to draw them closer to their imperial patron."[55]

The Ottoman Empire died a slow death. "If one could graph the relative position of the Ottoman state in the world in terms of delivery of forces and the ability to command obedience and awe," Kafadar argues, "internally as well as externally, the line would zig-zag but incline steadily downward after the turn of the seventeenth century."[56] The empire persisted for another three centuries, leaving behind a complex legacy of institutional decay and reform, power hoarding and power sharing, administrative inefficiency, and financial adaptation.

Lessons for Statecraft

What can we learn from the decay, experimentation, and reform of the Ottoman Empire and from Sarah Chayes's insights into the workings of corrupt networks? Are there lessons we can draw about the fate of great powers that allow wealthy, privileged elites, rather than ordinary citizens, to decide on who rules and how public policy is made?

We can distill warnings that are relevant to present times, from the spread of corruption to the weakening of Ottoman institutions. The erosion of the Ottoman state in the seventeenth century was the work of many hands: unscrupulous tax farmers, blundering caliphs, disgruntled cavalrymen, and greedy Janissaries. Later bursts of reform prolonged the Ottoman Empire, but these efforts were not enough to stave off the empire's eventual collapse. Corrupt networks rebound and regenerate. If the decay of institutions is the work of many hands, the fight to repair them requires just as many.

First, attack the hydra of American corruption on multiple fronts. Sarah emphasizes that one sole strategy against corruption is not enough. In her paper "Fighting the Hydra" she analyzes the recent worldwide protests against corruption. She quotes the anticorruption activist Cosmin Pojoranu, who remarks that corruption is "like a hydra. You cut off one head and another grows."[57] Hercules, a hero of Greek and Roman lore, defeated the hydra by enlisting the help of his nephew Iolaus. When Hercules cut off one of the heads, Iolaus cauterized the neck to prevent another head from growing in its place. In our discussion Sarah recommends a similar strategy for today's corrupt networks: "Too often the fight against kleptocratic networks focuses on individuals who hold key positions in that network. Almost every time, those networks bounce back—replacing the individuals or working around the holes. To deal with kleptocratic networks, systemic policy solutions are necessary to prevent a resurgence."

Successful anticorruption strategies deploy three tools: legislation, enforcement, and behavioral norms. Strict rules and accountability, anticorruption commissions, transparency measures, and regulations that close off lucrative sectors like real estate to money launderers are important first steps. Enforcement requires the full spectrum of capabilities, from criminal intelligence, policing, and prosecution to courts and prisons. Recent experience tells us that these instruments of enforcement need to be clean, honest, and responsive to the public. Just as vital is the creation of new standards of behavior for governing elites for which ordinary Americans can hold them accountable. The only way to fight corrupt networks sustainably is to create norms against the abuse of public office for personal enrichment.

When a great power declines and the gains from economic growth dissipate, as happened when a fiscal crisis devastated the Ottoman Empire in the late sixteenth century, the temptation for corrupt officials is to grab a share of the spoils, thereby compromising the integrity of public institutions. Behavioral norms guard against the tendency of officeholders to entrench themselves in power by rewriting the rules. In the United States today these norms would limit campaign contributions and the reach of special interest groups in the legislative and rulemaking processes. New behavioral norms would shine a bright light on the dark money that surges through US politics and impose tough ethical standards on those in positions of authority.[58] Having the right laws on the books, laws upheld by independent judges, lops off the head of the hydra; instituting the right behavioral norms prevents the hydra's head from growing back.

Second, name the crook to fight the crooked. To fight corruption, we need to understand it; to understand it, we need to name it accurately. "If we begin naming things for what they are instead of using polite terms," Sarah tells me, "we can make progress. I do think it's helpful to call a crime a crime—and to bring the weight of public opprobrium down on it and to empower the public to reject this type of practice—and to show them how they can do that."

The history of the Ottoman Empire shows how bad actors flourish and institutions decay when societies become inured to corruption. It also reveals the possibilities for adaptation when officials create inclusive governance structures, disperse power, and encourage financial and administrative reform at the local level.

As the scholar Rachel Kleinfeld observes in her study of the origins and "recivilizing" of violent societies, "Change begins when the middle class, the people with enough voice and power to change the system, mobilize. ... The middle class rouses only when its sense of invulnerability breaks."[59] Corrupt networks flourish not because of state weakness; states are weak precisely because powerful political elites manipulate them for private gain. Sarah puts it this way: "Corrupt acts often do not represent rational responses to a permissive environment ... rather, they are a professional requirement."[60] The police and judges are corrupt because politicians and kleptocrats want to escape accountability. Privileged elites and special interests accrue more power and privilege because political leaders benefit from their largesse, especially in the form of campaign contributions and other desirable incentives.

Third, reinforce norms of behavior for good governance. The deeper challenge is cultural. When great powers decline and degenerate into corrupt governance, that process shapes and reflects a particular culture around money and power. For the United States, this means that political leaders and social activists need to do more than constrain the *power* of money; they also need to change the *culture* of money.

Sarah agrees that everyone should have the right to a materially comfortable life. The philosophers Amartya Sen and Martha Nussbaum call this aspiration "the capabilities approach" to human development.[61] The capabilities approach asks us to shift our perspective: instead of focusing on what people have, we should focus on the conditions that empower them to live a life of human flourishing.

The call in the US Declaration of Independence for equality and human dignity is incompatible with the desire for infinite human wealth. "The pursuit of infinite wealth," Sarah argues, "should be contemptible instead of admirable—because it is impossible to achieve without rigging the system and because it is based on extractive processes. It is based on converting mountaintops into money—or, for those further down the ladder, on exchanging meaning for convenience." To change that narrative and to challenge the myth of money that lies at the heart of democracy there needs to be a transformation in what we value and in how we demand those values in our government leaders. In Sarah's words, we need to decide that "we want more meaning even if it comes at the expense of some convenience."

Finally, find the lever and move the world. US leadership is vital to a world in turmoil. The question is, Leadership to what end? If American leadership nurtures transparent and accountable governance and sparks a cultural reawakening that values ordinary citizens more than the few with privileged power, its purpose is beyond reproach and much needed. If America applies its power to bolster a failed status quo of transnational kleptocracy, or what Sarah refers to as "the global race for more zeroes in bank accounts," its purpose is suspect. Who can doubt that money and the quest for money are at the heart of America's identity; but so, too, is the quest for liberty, equality, and democratic accountability. The two are intertwined and twist around each other in what Sarah calls "the double helix in America's DNA."

The question is, Which part of America's identity will its citizens and leaders choose to augment and amplify in a time of decline? If we look to history, there are some intriguing paradoxes. For example, as Sarah notes, Athenian democracy appears after the introduction of money by the Lydians around 700 BC. And the explosion of paper money in America coincided with the launch of constitutional democracy in the United States. Sarah calls these "perplexing examples of the co-evolution of democracy and a newly monetized economy." I asked her about how democracies slide into kleptocracy. "When money starts becoming the end rather than the means," Sarah observes, "politics starts shifting from democracy toward kleptocracy. It recreates a new money-based aristocracy in place of the blood-based one it destroyed."

To reverse this slide and protect the integrity of democracy, leaders of great powers in decline would do well to consult another classic text. The Greek mathematician and scientist Archimedes said, "Give me a place to stand and with a lever I will move the whole world."[62] Today, money moves the world. America needs to use its leverage and take a stand to change the culture around money at home and in an ever more globalized economy. As Nexon argues, today's reformers could pull on any number of levers, including "ending the secrecy of all US-based LLCs, creating a national database of beneficial owners, and expanding the scope of the Treasury Department's Geographic Targeting Orders that mandate title insurance providers to identify the individuals who pay all-cash for luxury residential real estate purchases in major markets."[63]

For the United States, this agenda could also include working with allies to close the space in which kleptocrats operate, including through "the freezing of financial assets through 'unexplained wealth orders' of individuals who attempt to launder dirty money within Western financial systems."[64] Such measures are only a start, but they are a necessary start to combat corruption and restore integrity to the system of democratic self-government and international cooperation founded on multilateral institutions, the protection of rights, free trade, and the rule of law.

What does all of this mean for the average American? It means that if political corruption persists or worsens, Americans will lose the ability to hold their government to account. The words of the poet Langston Hughes capture this aspiration: "O, let America be America again—The land that never has been yet—And yet must be."[65] The promise of America is the slow, painstaking work of bending the arc of democracy toward inclusion, equality, and justice. No work is more important, and no time is more urgent than now.

The Next Choice

Is there any cause for optimism in this post-dominant world? How can leaders manage the new divides in Western politics between those who favor open economies and free societies and those who fear that rapid accelerations in global trade and technology have left them behind? For answers to these questions I turned to the former US secretary of state John Kerry, who has spent a lifetime in service to democratic ideals, from the Mekong Delta in Vietnam to the Maidan in Ukraine, and is a veteran of battles foreign and domestic.

CHAPTER SEVEN

Open or Closed?

I CAUGHT UP WITH John Kerry at a revealing moment, just as he was looking both forward and backward. The former secretary of state and United States senator was heading into a lunch with the students he mentors at Yale. Right after lunch he gave an interview for a documentary on Vietnam in 1969. One part of his mind looked forward to the next generation who could make things right. The other part looked backward to a generation mired in a war gone wrong. I wondered if I could get him to talk about America's challenges in the present.

"If you want to empower the forces of evil, do nothing," he told me, echoing the famous dictum of the statesman and philosopher Edmund Burke. I've collaborated with Secretary Kerry on literally hundreds of public addresses, but few statements more powerfully capture the animating philosophy of his life. Many people think of John Kerry as a politician. But I've always seen him as an activist in the best sense of the word. His warning to act in the face of adversity stood out for me not only for what it reveals about his life's purpose but also for what America needs at this moment of testing. It's more than the power of activism that defines Kerry's journey; it's the perspective he brings and the principles he puts into action. As leaders seek to repair cracks in the postwar liberal international order they will need all three qualities—power, perspective, and principle—now more than ever.

I learned about the power of the grassroots during my first prep session for a speech with then Senator Kerry in the fall of 2011. I was a newly minted speechwriter raised on generous helpings of *West Wing* idealism and Bobby Kennedy rhetoric. I was in a hurry to make a difference on the big issues, and now I had my chance. Kerry was scheduled to give remarks about combating poverty and the future of foreign aid at an event for the Millennium Campus Network, a nonprofit in Boston that trains students across the globe in the fight for social justice and sustainable development. I'd watched dozens of videos of Kerry speaking on the floor of the Senate and during his 2004 presidential campaign. I'd read nearly as many books about his life and politics. I could hear his deep, booming voice in my head. I was ready to craft a speech for the history books. The only thing to fear was the draft itself.

I sat down at my laptop and composed a lengthy address on the relevant legislation pending in Congress, the mechanics of foreign aid, and the need for bold leadership at the highest levels of government. Apart from the clichés, heavy jargon, and meandering structure, the speech was brilliant . . . or so I thought. The next day I watched Kerry as he read the draft. He got about three paragraphs in before putting it down on his desk and turning to me with a pained expression on his face. I made a quick calculation: either my draft was so good that it was about to bring tears of joy to the senator's face, or my draft was so bad that the senator was unable to hide his disappointment. I concluded that the latter was considerably, if not sadly, more likely.

To my surprise, Kerry didn't fire me that day or lean into me for my boilerplate prose. He simply told me a story. When he and his fellow vets came back from Vietnam and wanted to protest the war, some scorned their patriotism with the words "my country, right or wrong." Kerry the activist had a simple answer to that taunt: "Yes, my country right or wrong. When right, keep it right. When wrong, make it right."[1] It was Kerry's way of saying that real power comes from the grassroots, not from Congress or the cramped offices of the West Wing. He schooled me on his activism and that of millions of others across the country on Earth Day in 1970, when citizens protested the so-called Dirty Dozen members of Congress and demanded change on the environment. "You need to make it real. Connect with the energy and activism on college campuses," he said. As I got up to leave, feeling equal parts deflated and determined to get it right on the second draft, he added, "And try not to make me sound like a robot!"

I gave it another try, and with the help of a talented writer on Kerry's team we pulled together a new draft that reflected Kerry's voice and vision more closely. To my great delight we quoted Bobby Kennedy's remarks at the University of Cape Town in 1966. As the shadow of apartheid hung over South Africa, Kennedy traveled to Cape Town and challenged students with the indelible words, "Each time a man stands up for an ideal, or acts to improve the lot of others, he sends forth a tiny ripple of hope." Kerry could recite the passage from memory. I realized why he loved that speech. It wasn't just that he felt a personal connection to the Kennedy mystique. What resonated with Kerry was the message it sends about how every voice matters in creating the momentum for lasting change.

If America wants to update and modernize the liberal order, Kerry tells me from his office at Yale, "its leaders need to recognize that people are not going to fall on their swords for an idea, but over something they can see that makes their lives better." Just as important as Kerry's view of grassroots power is the perspective he brings to diplomacy. After surviving that first speech prep session I went on to draft many more remarks and eventually joined Secretary Kerry at the State Department as one of his speechwriters. We were in New York one afternoon for the preparation of his commencement speech at the UN International School, a high school that welcomes students from more than forty countries. I struggled to home in on a theme that would speak to the many different students from so many distinct countries and cultures. In our prep session before the speech Kerry reminded me of the lesson he learned from his father, Richard Kerry, who, like my father, served as an American diplomat: "My dad used to tell me that the art of diplomacy is seeing another country through its eyes." That morsel of wisdom helped me finish drafting the speech; but even more, it helped me to see a common thread in Kerry's life and learn another lesson.

In 1968, when he was serving in Vietnam as a young lieutenant in the United States Navy, Kerry wrote home to his parents about seeing a young Vietnamese boy on an operating table, struggling in the last moments of his life. Kerry gave him the name Nguyen in his letter because he felt compelled to find a piece of humanity amid the horrors of war. Kerry wondered what this boy thought of American soldiers in Vietnam and how the war looked from his perspective. He agonized over the boy dying completely alone, without anyone there to speak his language to comfort him. It was one of Kerry's earliest and most vivid memories of death. It was also an early sign that he took his father's advice to heart.

Many years later Kerry visited Gaza after its war with Israel in 2009. At one point he spotted a young girl playing in the rubble, and his mind jumped back to Vietnam and the young boy struggling for his life on the operating table. He wondered again what the conflict looked like from her perspective. He wanted to jump out of his armored vehicle and talk with her and show her that he cared. Kerry would have the same impulse in Afghanistan as chairman of the Foreign Relations Committee in 2009. As he writes in his memoir, "On my first trip to Afghanistan as chairman, I looked out the window of the armored Humvee as we drove through the dusty streets of Kabul. A little girl was playing with some toys on the side of the road. My mind immediately flashed back to Vietnam and the kids who often lined the canals or streets, staring at us with a 'what are you doing here?' look. Right away I thought, *What do we look like to that young girl?* I might as well be from another planet."[2]

For anyone to see a country through the eyes of its children reflects the best form of empathy, namely, empathy that inspires action. If power comes from the grassroots, the motivation to act in diplomacy comes from the perspective we take and the principles that guide us along the way.

By any standard the liberal international order seems abstract and distant to most people. But the principles it enshrines are every bit as real as a dying boy's desire to live, the food on one's table, and the chance to vote on election day. That's the final lesson Kerry taught me, and it intersects with my life in personal ways. My younger brother Chris has autism. More than a little I've struggled with how to be the best brother for him and how to see the world through his eyes. I remember growing up trying to stay silent for whole days at a time just to see what it was like to live my life without the ability to speak. It was agony, and Chris has to do that, and a lot more, every day. I'm in awe of his courage and willingness to forgive those who call him names or who stare at him and whisper things about him just because he's different. Many people refrain from speaking such obvious insults, preferring to keep their distance. Not so John Kerry. He met my brother in Brussels a few years ago, and the two hit it off immediately. I've rarely seen Chris take to someone with such immediacy and warmth. Kerry hugged him, spent time with him, and asked him about his studies and artwork, one of Chris's passions. There were no cameras and no reporters to tell the tale. It was just two people connecting on an emotional level.

I thought about that encounter during my final year in the Senate, when I worked with Senator Kerry and his team on the Convention on the Rights of Persons with Disabilities. If the liberal order is a cathedral, treaties and conventions are its foundation: they reflect shared understandings, define common obligations, and make cooperation among nations possible. Yet those shared understandings and common obligations are not automatic. Such beliefs develop slowly, often through painstaking diplomacy and negotiation.

The United States has long championed disability rights through its domestic legislation, particularly the Americans with Disabilities Act of 1991, or ADA. During the debates over whether the United States should ratify the convention, Senator Kerry referred to the ADA as the "gold standard" for disability rights. He spoke with conviction on the floor of the Senate, urging his colleagues to export that standard to the world. I knew from his interactions with Chris that those were more than just words. Kerry understood what disability rights meant for people like my brother and how America can lead the world to think and act differently. He also understood that an international standard that protects disability rights isn't just an abstraction. It means that Americans can work, study, and travel abroad without fear of discrimination. It means buildings having fire alarms with flashing lights so a parent's son or daughter who is hard of hearing knows there's an emergency. It means tactile steps at train stations and sidewalks with curb cuts for veterans like Dan Berschinski who've lost their legs. Even more, it means progress toward a world in which people are not defined by their disability but recognized everywhere for their common dignity. I asked Kerry about the future of the liberal international order and how to defend a grand design that feels so abstract to nearly everyone. "A lot of people take it for granted," he told me. "They've forgotten the number of Americans who died defeating tyranny in World War II or the horrors of the Holocaust. They've forgotten the killing fields in Cambodia, the bloody wars in the Balkans, or the Ukrainians who marched for their future in the Maidan. You have to defend rights; you can't just proclaim them. You have to engage as citizens and stand up and fight for an agenda. If you want to guarantee failure, sit on the sidelines." America cannot afford to take its future for granted or to sit on the sidelines and wait for others to fill the void. The stakes are too high and the risks too great.

Strategic Choice: Open or Closed?

The foundations of the liberal international order were weakening before President Trump took office in 2017. Some might respond with a shrug of the shoulders and a bemused, "So what?" After all, the United States has committed its share of blunders—through sins of commission, omission, or both. Why should it matter that America is a great power in decline? Should we really mourn the loss of a liberal order that was created in its image?

Declining powers must not only set the balance between the core or periphery, butter or guns, allies or autonomy, persuasion or coercion, and people power or pinstripe rule. A great power must also envision the form of world order it seeks to promote. This vision is all the more important when power among nations is in transition and new rivals challenge basic principles. The survival of the liberal order depends on the material capabilities of its leading supporter, the United States. That is why the renewal of liberal order is inseparable from the renewal of US power and hence from the issue of America's decline.

It is clear that the world order needs to remake itself. The question is, but how? For the United States today, this choice is about America's vision of international order. Should it modernize a liberal world order for the twenty-first century founded on the principles of democratic governance, multilateral collaboration through newly reformed and adapted institutions, greater popular support for free trade, and lawful regulation of financial markets in service of the international common good? Or should America disengage from today's liberal international order and allow it to be replaced with a loose global arrangement of competing spheres of control by regional hegemons, authoritarian governance, mercantilist trade practices, and state-controlled economic activity?

One reason to care about today's liberal order is what might appear in its wake. Scholars note the long peace that has prevailed since 1945. Debates rage over how to define the terms of that peace, its primary causes, whether it reflects a decline in the capability or willingness of states to aggress, and whether it is a blip between major wars that tend to appear every century or indicative of an enduring trend.[3] Was the timing of the long peace unrelated to its principal sponsor? As Robert Kagan observes, it coincides with the rise of the American world order that established norms and institutions to protect the rights of the individual against arbitrary governance and the machinations of self-aggrandizing leaders.[4] The United States created the liberal order after World War II and led it for over seventy years by extending its security umbrella to allies in Europe and Asia, promoting democratic principles, and fostering the growth of widespread peace and prosperity.

Despite its successes, this order contained vulnerabilities that undermined its promise for many. "Those who question the benefits of the liberal order have a completely legitimate complaint," Kerry asserted to me. "The fruits of labor haven't been shared fairly, and that's got a lot of people angry and rightly so. Government depends on credibility and the trust of the people who elected you. If you don't make the right choices, you break that trust. In America right now people feel disconnected from their government. It's an albatross that weighs them down when we need to be thinking about how to lift people up and make governance actually deliver for people. Go back to our founding documents. It's all there in the Federalist Papers."

America's Enduring Principles

I've come to appreciate over the years that Kerry has subtle ways of assigning homework. So I went back and read the Declaration of Independence. As the historian David Armitage shows, the Declaration is rich with meaning. It is a statement of principle, a declaration of rights, a summons to the American people to institute a new government based on their consent, and a plea to other nations to apply its revolutionary creed. Above all, it is a document with a national and global history.[5]

To understand why America's third president, Thomas Jefferson, called the Declaration "an instrument pregnant with . . . the fate of the world," one should understand its second sentence in full.[6] The sentence reads as follows: "We hold these truths to be self-evident, that all men are created equal, that they are endowed by their Creator with certain unalienable Rights, that among these are Life, Liberty and the pursuit of Happiness.—That to secure these rights, Governments are instituted among Men, deriving their just powers from the consent of the governed.—That whenever any Form of Government becomes destructive of these ends, it is the Right of the People to alter or to abolish it, and to institute new Government, laying its foundation on such principles and organizing its powers in such form, as to them shall seem most likely to effect their Safety and Happiness."[7]

The political philosopher Danielle Allen rightly calls this sentence the "most efficient account of the basic work of citizenship ever written."[8] The Declaration enshrined principles and powers for a new domestic order, but its message is fully relevant today as America confronts the need to modernize the current world order. Just as successive generations of Americans reaffirmed the principles of the Declaration while reforming the powers of government to reflect those principles in practice, so the United States today must reaffirm the principles of the liberal international order while modernizing its rules, powers, and structures to reflect the realities of the twenty-first century more precisely. By adapting the global rules of the road without discarding the basic principles, America can bolster its influence in a post-dominant world.

The principles of the Declaration are fundamental to the American experiment in self-government: people are endowed with inalienable rights, including life, liberty, and the pursuit of happiness; governments are formed to guarantee those rights; and power derives from the consent of the governed. If political leaders run roughshod over these principles, the Declaration enshrines the right of the people to alter or abolish it, thereby adapting the powers of government to reflect the principles of democratic self-government. Allen observes that the founders intended for the principles of the Declaration to apply to all people, even though the powers of government were held in the hands of a few.

If the principles of the Declaration endure, the powers of government have evolved. The American Civil War from 1861 to 1865 was nothing if not a refutation of blood-and-soil nationalism as the bedrock principle of the nation. As President Abraham Lincoln observed in his Gettysburg address, America's founders "brought forth on this continent a new nation, conceived in liberty and dedicated to the proposition that all men are created equal."[9] What defines America is not a common bloodline or religious creed. In Lincoln's telling, America is defined by its commitment to a core idea. It is dedicated *to the proposition* that a new nation could be founded on the principles of liberty and equality. The proof would come through the hard work of citizenship, the extension of rights, and the determination to proceed "with malice toward none, with charity for all . . . to bind up the nation's wounds . . . to do all which may achieve and cherish a just and lasting peace among ourselves and with all nations."[10] Lincoln counseled "firmness in the right," but also humility in the attempt to rebuild the nation after war and chart a course for the future. In the historian John Gaddis's phrase, he showed "the practicality, in politics, of a moral standard."[11]

The Rise of the Liberal International Order

In the twentieth century America took its principles of democratic self-government embodied in the Declaration and extended them, at first to countries along the Atlantic rim and key Pacific allies and then globally. World War I marked a turning point. In an address before Congress on January 8, 1918, President Woodrow Wilson articulated his Fourteen Points for a new order based not on the balance of power but on collective security. Each nation would act in the interest of all nations. The world must be made, in Wilson's phrase, "fit and safe to live in; and particularly that it be made safe for every peace-loving nation which, like our own, wishes to live its own life, determine its own institutions, be assured of justice and fair dealing by the other peoples of the world as against force and selfish aggression."[12]

The principles at the heart of Wilson's vision attracted broad international support, broader than perhaps he ever intended. In his global history of what he calls "the Wilsonian moment," Erez Manela shows just how powerful the vision of self-determining nation-states was for Egyptian, Indian, Chinese, and South Korean nationalists.[13] These anticolonial movements pressed their claims in Paris and appealed to Wilson's Fourteen Points in their political programs.

The Fourteen Points enshrined the principles of America's democratic creed, but the organization of powers in a League of Nations to safeguard these principles proved inadequate to the challenge. Wilson's League of Nations required the overwhelming majority of countries to renounce the use of force, eschew narrow interests, and trust other states to behave in good faith.[14] Since the international system lacked a sovereign entity with power to enforce legitimate decisions, sort out the aggressors from the victims, and promote cooperation over self-serving aggression, the post–World War I experiment in collective security foundered in its core pursuit. The seminal challenge was to construct a world order that reflected the common will of its members and "a guaranty of peace."[15]

During and after World War II, President Franklin Roosevelt assumed the mantle of creator of a new international system. In August 1941 FDR met with Prime Minister Winston Churchill aboard the *USS Augusta* in Newfoundland, Canada. The two leaders gathered at a perilous moment, shortly after Hitler launched his assault on the Soviet Union and prior to the US entry into the war. Even as the fighting inflamed the world, FDR and Churchill looked beyond war to the peace that would follow. FDR supported many of the principles contained in Wilson's Fourteen Points, but he recognized the shortcomings of the League of Nations and the critical need for a "wider and permanent system of general security."[16] FDR and Churchill released a joint declaration that outlined a postwar agenda for peace. Churchill cabled to London that President Roosevelt emphasized the "importance of the Joint Declaration, which he believes will affect the whole movement of United States opinion."[17] FDR captured the significance of what came to be called the Atlantic Charter at a news conference a few days after the signing of the joint declaration. He drew a parallel with Lincoln's struggles during the Civil War and argued that America "hadn't yet waked up to the fact that they had a war to win."[18] Returning to the present day, FDR made his point explicit: "I think there are a lot of people who haven't waked up to the . . . danger. A great many people."[19]

Armed with a statement of principles, FDR set about coordinating wartime strategy with America's allies and building a new architecture for international order. This order reflected three core principles: a network of alliances to guarantee security; an open, international economy to promote shared prosperity; and a set of interlocking political, economic, and social institutions to safeguard democracy.[20] John Ikenberry of Princeton University rightly argues that the postwar order was created not to escape great-power competition but to manage it more effectively.[21] US leaders acted in their enlightened self-interest by recognizing that America would prosper in a world of rule-based market democracies freely trading with one another. As the historian Warren Kimball observes, the British "well understood Roosevelt's desire to propagate Americanism, that version of liberalism set forth broadly in the Atlantic Charter."[22] The charter embraced the lessons of the 1930s: that isolated economic blocs and beggar-thy-neighbor policies undermine prosperity, that spheres of influence are rarely stable, and that unchecked aggression invites further armed hostilities. This new order may have taken shape in the postwar period, but its inspiration came from lessons learned the hard way following Wilson's failed experiment with the League of Nations.

The principles that inspired the US Declaration of Independence were now applied to rules-based international relations: America encoded its democratic values in global institutions to make the world truly "fit and safe to live in." Compared with the postwar settlements of 1648 at the end of the Thirty Years' War, of 1713 at the end of the War of the Spanish Succession, of 1815 at the end of the Napoleonic Wars, and that of 1919 at the end of the Great War, the unprecedented settlement following World War II reflected liberal principles.[23] America would restrain its power and give others a voice in decision making on international concerns. In return, the beneficiaries of this order would adhere to a common set of rules and support America in its stewardship of global order. The genius of this system was that it constrained American power at its height so that its influence might be preserved if it were to fall.

International Cooperation Meets Power Politics

America's lofty principles soon met harsh realities. This new world order emerged in parallel with the new confrontation in great-power politics. The bipolarity of the Cold War rested largely on the material resources and military capabilities of the United States and the Soviet Union. Because power was at the center of this order, America made compromises on principle that challenged its reputation for benevolent hegemony.[24] It backed Saudi Arabia and other autocracies in the Middle East to ensure the free flow of oil into Europe, facilitating its economic recovery from the war. The United States tolerated spheres of influence in Eastern Europe and frequently showed little regard for the United Nations or the sovereignty of minor powers, such as when it orchestrated a coup in Guatemala in 1954. At times, the United States and its liberal brethren stood tall for principle and assertively promoted democracy; at other times, democratic principle was sacrificed on the altar of national security.[25]

Following the demise of the Soviet Union in 1991 the United States embarked on an ambitious campaign to extend the postwar order to the rest of the world. It encountered favorable winds initially. Democratic capitalism had triumphed, and state-managed economies were consigned to the dustbin of history. Russia lay prostrate, and under President Boris Yeltsin grudgingly accepted NATO enlargement. Fearful of popular resentment after its brutal response to the protests at Tiananmen Square, China clamped down on incipient democratic movements, but it seemed to accept the economic principles of liberal order. As the international system entered its so-called unipolar moment, developing nations embraced the Washington Consensus and clamored for invitations to join this exclusive club. Economic interdependence appeared to stitch the world together in a seamless whole, with the information revolution turbocharging the trend lines in favor of liberal democracy, free markets, and multilateral governance.

The euphoria surrounding the post–Cold War unipolar moment gave rise to three assumptions, each of which has either failed to materialize or come under renewed scrutiny.[26] First, the United States believed that China, Russia, and other authoritarian powers would seek to integrate into the Western, rules-based international order. Policy makers hoped that by treating Beijing and Moscow as responsible stakeholders in this order, these powers would embrace liberal norms and play a constructive role.[27] Second, the United States believed that the liberal order could accommodate new actors, greater movement toward regional cooperation, and common aspirations for economic equality, political autonomy, and dignity in countries across Asia, Africa, and Latin America.[28] Third, the United States and its Western allies presumed there would be durable public support of the liberal international order. A new decade of great-power peace, sustained growth, and the third wave of democratic transitions convinced many Western leaders that popular backing for extending the liberal order would be forthcoming.[29]

Well before President Trump took office these assumptions were put to the test. China and Russia resisted integration into the liberal order and then diverged on separate paths. Instead of embracing liberal norms and multilateral institutions Moscow and Beijing hunkered down and pushed back on what they perceived to be malign Western influences. While Moscow pursued a vengeful agenda to tear down the liberal order, China pursued a revisionist agenda to redefine and remake the liberal order in its image. Both powers saw the liberal order as a threat to their regimes, and both acted to constrain American power and leadership.[30]

To the extent that authoritarian powers abided by the principles of liberal order, this strategy often reflected an opportunistic ploy to use the liberal norms of sovereignty and noninterference as a shield against international scrutiny of domestic abuses.[31] Chinese and Russian appeals to sovereignty in order to deflect criticism of human rights violations at the UN Security Council were a case in point.

At the same time, the United States took actions that exacerbated tensions with its Cold War foe. It sought to integrate Russia into an expanded G-8 and the Asia-Pacific Economic Cooperation forum, but it overpromised and underdelivered on aid to Moscow in the 1990s.[32] The US-led expansion of NATO helped to stabilize Central and Eastern Europe and responded to the demand of those countries for closer integration into Euro–Atlantic structures, but it also deepened Russia's perceptions of insecurity along its borders. The United States and its European partners intervened in the Balkans in the 1990s to halt the brutal violence following the breakup of Yugoslavia; to Russian sensibilities, NATO's military involvement in the Balkan conflicts showed a disregard for Russian interests with its longtime ally Serbia. It is unclear whether these strains could have been avoided given the long-standing differences in Russian and American political, economic, cultural, and security concerns. What is clear is that in pursuing its interests in the post–Cold War period while at the peak of its power, the United States took actions that complicated its future relations with Russia.

Regarding the second assumption, that of accommodating the wider world, the United States failed to integrate nonstate actors, such as international humanitarian NGOs, into the workings of the liberal order. It also missed an opportunity to empower regional organizations like the African Union and the Association of Southeast Asian Nations (ASEAN) in areas where America could afford to devolve responsibility for the management of this order.

As for the third assumption, that of domestic support, the United States and Western elites failed to appreciate the tensions between democracy and capitalism. Postwar economies were mixed economies. They combined private control of the means of production with democratic checks on capital and social safety nets for those who fell behind. This "embedded liberalism" paved the way for decades of growth, rising wages, and reduced inequality in the

Western world.[33] By the 1970s, however, democracies had become intertwined with global markets and lifted more controls on the movement of capital.[34] As the political economist Dani Rodrick notes, "The central lesson of the [Bretton Woods system, which created international monetary arrangements based on the convertibility of the US dollar into gold] was forgotten. Globalization became the end, national economies the means."[35] Starting in the 1980s the United States rolled back regulations, decimated unions, distorted the tax code, and gutted antitrust legislation designed to keep a lid on oligopolistic concentrations of wealth and power. The result was a popular domestic backlash against globalization at a time when economic sluggishness became the new normal.[36]

President Trump's vision of America First should not be dismissed as merely a tweet or campaign slogan. Many Americans agree with his views and support his rhetoric, which disparages today's liberal order as a treacherous scheme for other nations to prey on America's money and goodwill. The Trump administration has removed the United States from several multilateral agreements and disengaged America further from the rules-based system of international cooperation and commitments that have guided US leaders since 1945. Still, we should ask tough questions: What does America First mean in practice? If the United States adopts President Trump's vision of America First, would its allies, partners, and friends cooperate? Or join his cause? Or follow his lead? If so, for how long?

As we consider the stakes for America in the twenty-first century, we can gain valuable insights by looking to the early twentieth century. Rival visions of global order emerged during this period and intersected powerfully with domestic battles in the United States. Just as we need to understand the origins of the liberal international order, we need to appreciate the origins of America First and its warnings for today.

America First in the 1940s

Fearful of becoming involved in another bloody European war, the United States watched and waited as the great powers went down different paths leading to World War II. Should the United States be Fortress America? Or should it be an international force for the common good? Should America wall itself off from the world, declare its neutrality, and ward off foreign influences with immigration quotas and tariff barriers? Or should it embrace its role as a world power and become, in President Roosevelt's phrase, "the great arsenal of democracy?"[37]

For much of the 1930s the balance of domestic opinion tilted decidedly in favor of Fortress America. Congress passed restrictive immigration quotas in 1924. Six years later it raised tariffs on thousands of imported goods through the protectionist Smoot-Hawley Tariff, worsening the effects of the Great Depression and contributing to a plunge in the value of global trade. In April 1934 Congress passed the Johnson Act, which prevented foreign nations in arrears on debt payments from securing private loans.[38] Congress followed this measure with a suite of Neutrality Acts that limited America's involvement in another European war. FDR worked cleverly to support European powers that were resisting aggression, but American public opinion was deeply divided and the stakes were growing more dire by the day.

By the late 1930s one of the most contentious debates in American history unfolded. On one side were the Anglophile interventionists, who believed that Britain's fate was America's cause. They urged the United States to supply material aid to the British and to make preparations to enter the war on the side of the Allies. In an essay for the *Atlantic Monthly* the Yale history professor Arnold Whitridge chided American isolationists for refusing to see the dangers on the horizon. "Much as we hate war," Whitridge wrote, "we shall have to fight, and the sooner we get ready for it, the better."[39]

On the other side were the antiwar isolationists, who made it their mission to keep America out of World War II and limit aid to Britain to "cash and carry," under which London could purchase nonlethal supplies from Washington so long as it paid in cash and arranged the transport. These anti-interventionist currents swirled around the country and caught the attention of the young Kingman Brewster, a Yale graduate and future president of Yale University. Brewster applied his focus and energies to transforming this inchoate sentiment into a nationwide movement. In response to Whitridge,

Brewster and a student from Harvard took aim at the Yale professor
for what they called his casuistry and argued for taking a "stand on
this side of the Atlantic ... because at least it offers a chance for the
maintenance of all the things we care about in America."[40] Brewster
wielded a fiery pen and harbored big ambitions.

Together with another Yale student, Robert Douglas Stuart Jr.,
Brewster set about establishing the America First Committee to
counter what they viewed as the prowar, pro-British propaganda
issuing from the Committee to Defend America by Aiding the
Allies, an organization founded by the Republican journalist and
progressive leader William Allen White. Stuart and Brewster advocated isolationism up and down the East coast, circulating petitions
and recruiting volunteers for their movement. Yet the Yale students
faced an uphill battle. To become a national organization, they
needed name recognition, so they courted the most famous isolationist of them all: the famed aviator Charles Lindbergh. Stuart
and Brewster convinced Lindbergh to speak at Yale in the fall of
1940, but it wasn't until April 1941 that he joined the group as an
official member.[41]

At its height the America First Committee boasted of eight
hundred thousand members and more than four hundred local
chapters. Prominent supporters included Teddy Roosevelt's daughter Alice Roosevelt Longworth; a future American president, Ger-
ald Ford; a future Supreme Court justice, Potter Stewart; and the
chief executive of Sears Roebuck and former quartermaster general
of the US Army in World War I, Robert Wood. Just out of college
and not yet in the navy, the young John F. Kennedy wrote a one-
hundred-dollar check to the organization with the note, "What
you are all doing is vital."[42]

The showdown between the pro-British interventionists and
the isolationists of the America First Committee came over the
symbolically numbered H.R. 1776, a bill to "further promote the
defense of the United States." Known as the Lend-Lease Act,
the legislation was intended to provide military supplies to Britain
and "the government of any country whose defense the President
deems vital to the defense of the United States."[43] The isolationist
bloc in Congress knew that if passed, this bill would spell the end of
neutrality in the United States and put a stake through the heart of

the anti-interventionist cause. More than a few members of Congress opposed intervention. When FDR tried to get senators to amend the Neutrality Act in 1939, Senator William Borah locked eyes with the president and said bluntly, "There is not going to be any war in Europe this year. All this hysteria is manufactured and artificial."[44] The two most senior Republicans on the Senate Foreign Relations Committee were Senators Borah and Hiram Johnson. Both were leading isolationists.

FDR benefited from the fact that most Americans supported the Lend-Lease Act, but that didn't stop the America First Committee. Opposition to H.R. 1776 became a cause célèbre of America First volunteers and the galvanizing spark they needed to attract more members. As the historian Lynne Olson recounts in her narrative of America's domestic fight about entering World War II, "Within weeks, hundreds of new chapters sprang up, and tens of thousands of America First volunteers circulated anti-Lend-Lease petitions, put up posters, staged rallies, and showered Capitol Hill and the White House with letters and telegrams. In Washington, America First staff members became unofficial staffers for isolationist senators and congressmen, providing them with research and writing speeches opposing the legislation."[45]

Against this concerted pressure, Roosevelt implored White's committee and other interventionist groups to make the case to the country.[46] The debates were acrimonious to say the least. The journalist Nicholas Wapshott wrote that America was "as deeply divided over Lend-Lease as it had been over any issue since emancipation."[47] The *Chicago Tribune* called the Lend-Lease bill the "war dictatorship bill," and antiwar activists brandished signs that read Kill Bill 1776, Not Our Boys.[48] Lindbergh's testimony before the House Foreign Affairs Committee in support of the isolationist cause drew thunderous reactions.

But even Lindbergh's statement was not enough to prevent the bill from passing in March 1941. The staunch advocacy of FDR, White, and their allies in Congress tipped the balance of support in favor of the interventionists. America First lost this vote, but many of its leaders continued to pursue their isolationist campaign. Brewster glimpsed the future: "Whether we like it or not, America has decided what its ends are. . . . A national pressure group therefore is not aiming to determine policy, it is seeking to obstruct it. I cannot be a part of that effort."[49] Others were not so willing to silence their voices.

As momentum for the cause of America First waned, so did its reputation. The partisans of America First suffered from guilt by association: irrespective of the motives of its leaders and volunteers, and there were many, the cause of America First was also the cause of Hitler's Germany.[50] The director of America First's Washington, DC, branch summed up the challenge: "Because it was to Germany's advantage for the United States to stay out of war, it was inevitable that America First would be accused of pro-Nazism. . . . Likewise, it was inevitable that real pro-Nazis would attempt to get on the America First bandwagon."[51] The movement also suffered from a number of self-inflicted wounds and reprehensible decisions. As *The Atlantic* magazine notes in a retrospective on the group, the America First crowd initially welcomed "socialists, conservatives and some of the most prominent Americans from some of the most prominent families."[52] When the group moved its base of operations to Chicago under the leadership of Robert Wood, however, it took on a more conservative, isolationist cast.

As America First grew, it failed to weed out extremists of all kinds from its local chapters. Racists and pro-Nazi sympathizers, including Laura Ingalls, an aviator and America First volunteer who was a German agent, increasingly found a voice and a venue at America First events. Notorious anti-Semites from Father Charles Coughlin, a Catholic priest who was infamous for his fiery, anti-Semitic broadsides over the radio, and William Dudley Pelley, a fascist political leader and writer in America, to the president of the US Olympic Committee Avery Brundage and the auto executive Henry Ford were also drawn to the noninterventionist camp. Lindbergh sullied his reputation and that of America First even further by giving a speech in Des Moines, Iowa, on September 11, 1941, in which he said, "Tolerance is a virtue that depends upon peace and strength. History shows that it cannot survive war and devastations. A few far-sighted Jewish people realize this and stand opposed to intervention. But the majority still do not. Their greatest danger to this country lies in their large ownership and influence in our motion pictures, our press, our radio and our government."[53]

These dark currents of America First reflect an even darker history in American politics and society.[54] The phrase "America First" emerged in the context of trade disputes with the British in the nineteenth century. It entered the political lexicon when the Republican Party adopted it as a slogan in 1894. The future president and then Senate candidate Warren Harding employed the phrase as part of his campaign for Prosper America First. Woodrow Wilson picked up the slogan as a means of rallying public support for staying out of World War I. In the 1920s America First became intermingled with domestic nativist, anti-Semitic, and white supremacist movements, such as the advocates of 100 percent Americanism in the 1920s and as a rallying cry of the Ku Klux Klan.

The Legacy of America First

In its ugliest incarnations and in its opposition to interventionism abroad America First continues even to the present to stir controversy and shape the public debate. At the UN General Assembly in 2018 President Trump announced America's retreat from multilateralism: "We will never surrender America's sovereignty to an unelected, unaccountable, global bureaucracy. . . . We reject the ideology of globalism, and we embrace the doctrine of patriotism."[55] Never mind that patriotism is not a doctrine, and globalism is not an ideology, but a description of the world characterized by networks of interdependence.[56]

To defend sovereignty at all costs is to beg a more fundamental question: What purpose is American power meant to serve? Abraham Lincoln called on the nation to make real the promise of liberty and equality for all. FDR declared that America's purpose in the world is to create a new "moral order" based on the four freedoms: the freedoms of speech and worship and the freedoms from want and fear.[57] Ronald Reagan summoned the nation to defend freedom and opportunity, and Barack Obama challenged us all to form a more perfect union at home and a "just and lasting peace"

in the world. In whose name and to what end, in the Trump administration's conception, would America defend sovereignty and
disengage from international cooperation?

The United States is no stranger to hubris and hypocrisy, but
its animating purpose in the world is not to restrict liberty but to
spread it. Secretary Kerry underscores the stakes with a simple insight: "A government that fails to respect human rights, no matter
how lofty its pretentions, has very little to boast about, to teach,
and very little indeed in the way of reaching its full potential."[58]
The United States loses in the long run when it attempts to spread
its ideals through the barrel of a gun. It gains immeasurably when
it defines its enlightened self-interest as the pursuit of the national
and international common good. And yet the greatest threat to
American leadership today may be not self-righteousness and du-
plicity but the short-sighted hell of partisan infighting.

The burning question for the future of the liberal order is clear:
Should the United States and its allies seek to reaffirm, reform, or
reject it? A growing chorus of analysts favors rejection. Patrick Porter of the Cato Institute argues that the concept of liberal international order is so riddled with contradictions and hypocrisy that it
is time to cast it aside: "At times the liberal order was neither very
liberal nor very orderly. . . . Efforts to spread liberalism often contained the seeds of illiberalism. Multiple orders collided and met
the limits of their reach and power. Efforts to create a liberal order
ended up accommodating illiberalism."[59] Graham Allison of Harvard agrees. By his lights, the liberal international order is nothing
more than "conceptual Jell-O." It hides the fact that the balance of
power did most of the work in winning the Cold War and that
America engages in the world not "to advance liberalism abroad or
to build an international order but . . . to do what [is] necessary to
preserve liberal democracy at home."[60] The political scientist John
Mearsheimer takes aim at the guiding ideology of the liberal order,
which he calls "liberal hegemony." According to Mearsheimer, this
ideology reflects America's liberal traditions, but America was able
to extend these principles globally only because of its great power
after the end of World War II. He argues that liberal hegemony is
"at odds with nationalism and realism, which ultimately have far
more influence on international politics than liberalism does."[61]

Achievements of the Liberal Order

America's history of holding competing visions of world order reveals several key issues about the evolution, purpose, and overall appeal of the liberal international order. One of the most notable achievements of the liberal order is that its principles continue to inspire leaders and publics around the world. While the United States served as the order's principal architect, it is not its only advocate. The rules and norms of the liberal order we know today emerged from decades of persistent diplomatic engagement, institutional development, legal evolution, and cooperation from many states.[62] The scholars Mira Rapp-Hooper and Rebecca Friedman Lissner highlight this broad support: "When Canadian Prime Minister Justin Trudeau, German Chancellor Angela Merkel, Japanese Premier Shinzo Abe, and other US allies invoke the beleaguered liberal order today, it is because they want to preserve those achievements. Far from dismissing the order as a mere euphemism for US hegemony, they see their own national interests and values at stake in it. They also recognize that those interests and values cannot be protected without a powerful—and committed—United States."[63]

The concept of liberal order embraces various forms of democratic governance, and it is not reducible to any single method of organizing political and economic communities. Liberalism is a big tent that incorporates everything from the minimalist state advocated by the economist Milton Friedman to the embedded liberalism of the postwar economies in Europe and the United States, from the imperial order of the British Empire in the nineteenth century to the multilateral order of the post-1945, US-led international system.[64] The point is not that there are contradictions in the liberal tradition, but that there are "a lot of different ways to do liberalism, and different ways of being liberal."[65] This fact should open up the possibility of bringing the practices and powers of today's liberal order more into line with the principles of democratic self-government, representative democracy, individual liberty, and the rule of law.

The liberal order not only enjoys broader support and embraces a wider set of traditions than is commonly assumed but also benefits from a third advantage: sedimentary foundations. Just as the settled remains of minerals and organic particles accumulate on an ocean seabed, eventually forming sedimentary rocks, so the liberal order is the agglomeration of myriad principles that developed over the centuries: Westphalian precepts of sovereignty and domestic authority structures, norms of equality and freedom that took shape in the Age of Enlightenment, representative institutions that trace their roots to medieval political traditions, and the rise of twin liberal powers in Britain and America that asserted global leadership in peaceful succession.[66]

If the liberal order is composed of American power, democratic principles, and complementary political and economic institutions, the United States and its allies should pursue a common agenda: reaffirm its ideals, adapt its institutions to emerging challenges, and put both to work in advancing the liberal values on which the United States was founded.[67]

Lessons for Statecraft

Lord Ismay's rallying cry to the Western alliance of free nations during the Cold War was "keep the Soviet Union out, the Americans in and the Germans down." Today's rallying cry demands equal clarity and conviction: bolster democratic governance, bring in aspirants, keep the spoilers at bay, and create a compelling narrative that will mobilize popular support.

First, bolster the political will and collaboration of Western and non-Western democracies. The mark of a statesman is knowing when to advance consensus and when to consolidate one's gains. Western and non-Western democracies today need to protect their gains.[68] Power buttresses order, but the collective power that the United States and its allies can bring to bear in defense of Western and non-Western democracies is declining.

In a post-dominant world the United States and its allies will need to engage Russia, China, and other authoritarian powers from a position of strength. That strength will come from shoring up the foundations of liberal democracy. To get back on track, liberal democracies need to develop new compacts that provide tangible improvements to people everywhere—both domestically and internationally. On the home front there are a multitude of ideas circulating on how to widen access to health care and educational opportunities, increase labor force participation, reform immigration systems, and invest in the workforce of the future. What's needed is the political will of national leaders to put a modernization agenda on the table and restore faith in democracy as a system of government that can deliver for its citizens. As Secretary Kerry puts it, "Nostalgia won't defeat neo-populism; progress will."[69] Likewise, on the international front the United States needs to advance policies that contribute to a broad modernization agenda for the common good, including updated arrangements for security, for inclusive societies, for legitimate free markets and trade, for individual liberty and human rights, for healthy communities, and for environmental protection of a planet in crisis.

In a globalized world the domestic and international levels are powerfully linked. Progress on one front will reinforce progress on the other. To build support for free trade at home, the United States and its allies should not retreat from international leadership under the guise of America First. On the contrary, liberal democracies need to band together to write new rules for the digital era and enforce existing ones. Leaders should define national economic interests more broadly to include the perspectives of consumers and corporations, small businesses and Internet companies, rural workers and urban employees.[70] Free trade and globalization produce winners and losers, and the gains of the winners must fund more comprehensive and innovative programs to help those left behind to move up the socioeconomic ladder. The solutions need to go beyond worker retraining schemes and trade adjustment assistance to include apprenticeships and vocational training, regional infrastructure planning, and other measures to help workers and communities stay competitive.[71] In liberal democracies this modernization agenda should include putting in place sensible democratic checks on capital, from coordinating national policies on taxation of multinationals to devising new rules that limit the power of monopolies from stifling innovation, entrepreneurship, and growth.

Second, bring aspiring democratic states into the community. The United States and its European allies are not the only backers of the liberal order. Many non-Western powers support its norms and principles, even if they take exception to rules and procedures that benefit the old Western powers.[72] From international trade and finance to nuclear nonproliferation and climate adaptation and mitigation regimes, rising powers such as Brazil, India, South Africa, Argentina, and Indonesia all benefit from the liberal order.

The regional powers that make up the Global South are not passive recipients of these benefits. In fact, many of them took an active role in shaping the norms and rules of today's order, from human development to gender equality.[73] Perhaps that's why these countries are willing to defend America's principles even as the country retreats from promoting them. After the United States withdrew from negotiations on the Trans-Pacific Partnership, Japan took the lead in negotiating and concluding a pact for the deal that succeeded it. India is stepping into the vacuum left by the withdrawal of the United States from the Paris climate agreement. And many non-Western states, from South Africa and Indonesia to Japan and India, play a dynamic role in supporting democracy at both the regional and global levels.[74]

The counterpart to bolstering democratic governance is to bring in aspiring democracies. In a post-dominant world, rising powers will seek equal voice with and recognition from their peers. There's much agreement in principle between the West and the emerging economies of Asia, Latin America, and Africa. What's needed is a concerted effort to adapt the powers and procedures of the institutions of liberal order to accommodate new players.

The path toward inclusion of aspiring democracies is straightforward. Western powers need to bring in the rest in three ways: by expanding participation in existing institutions, for example, broadening the membership of the UN Security Council, and increasing the vote shares and quotas in the World Bank and the International Monetary Fund; enlisting the support of non-Western powers in defending and promoting democracy, with a focus on strengthening checks and balances and combating corruption; and evolving a more layered liberal international order that incorporates the private sector, civil society, and other nonstate actors that play an increasingly vital role in such areas as global health, conflict prevention and mitigation, good governance, infrastructure development, education, climate change, and clean energy.[75]

Third, manage spoilers and obstructionists skillfully. Spoilers come in various shapes and sizes, and they each require different modes of management. In examining the conditions that lead to successful peace processes, the scholar Stephen Stedman identifies spoilers according to their goals and level of commitment: limited, greedy, and total spoilers.[76] Each type poses a distinct challenge to those managing a peace process, and each type requires a particular strategy. For limited spoilers Stedman recommends the use of positive inducements. For greedy spoilers he advocates the use of carrots and sticks to socialize and persuade them to abide by democratic norms. And for total, all or nothing spoilers he counsels the application of deterrence and other coercive measures. Know your competitor, know your spoiler.

The United States and its allies and partners must be steadfast, vigilant, and nimble in dealing with a range of spoilers of the liberal international order, especially rival powers. China and Russia are, to use Stedman's typology, limited spoilers on some issues, for example, trade and investment. They act as more assertive, greedy spoilers in their search for raw materials and commodities in the Arctic and across the developing world. Most concerning, both China and Russia act as total spoilers in their efforts to undermine and destabilize vulnerable leaders and the institutions, rules, and practices of the world's democracies, including America's democracy.

The challenge for the United States and its allies is to simultaneously manage the competition in areas where China and Russia act as limited spoilers and push back forcefully in areas where they act as ambitiously greedy or total spoilers. In doing so, the United States should take care not to adopt policies that push China and Russia closer together. China relies on exports to the developed world to fuel its domestic economic growth. And for all the headlines about Russia turning east and reversing the Cold War Sino–Soviet split, Moscow depends on European markets and Western capital and technology. Globalization entangles autocracies as surely as it does democracies.

Notwithstanding these benefits, Russia and China appreciate the conundrum at the heart of the liberal order: Can illiberal states embrace the institutions and norms of the liberal order and retain their essential authoritarian characteristics?[77] Increasingly, Moscow and Beijing answer with a resounding no. They scan the horizon and see nefarious liberal influences everywhere, among them Google and other technology companies that carry subversive democratic ideas, civil society activists who defend human rights, and exposés in the *New York Times* and the Panama Papers that shine a bright light on corruption and kleptocratic networks.[78] These pressures and points of friction are not bugs in the global system but essential features of liberal order. China and Russia understand this dilemma, which is why they are pushing back with a vengeance.

If the tensions between democratic states and those led by autocrats are built into the system, friction will not abate. The question for the United States is how to manage those tensions without drifting into needless confrontation. Three principles should guide America's approach to managing spoilers of the international order.

The first principle is to engage in competition, not conflict. The United States and its allies need to recognize the limits of an approach that treats China and Russia as "responsible stakeholders."[79] Beijing and Moscow are bent on exploiting the liberal order in some areas, revising it in others, and replacing it whenever the opportunity arises. Where the interests of the United States and its allies align with those of China and Russia, the two sides should exploit cooperation. Where the interests of the two sides collide, the United States and its allies need to defend their equities more vigorously and back up commitments with clear priorities, comprehensive strategies, and clarity of purpose.

As part of that effort, the United States should recognize that while China and Russia oppose the liberal international order, they present different challenges: Russia is a declining, revanchist power; China is a long-term, geostrategic competitor. The United States must develop strategies to contend with each. It should leverage the fact that it retains a broad network of allies that can set the rules of the road in areas of emerging competition like mobile Internet standards and artificial intelligence.[80]

The second principle is related to the first: involvement, not integration. In dealing with China and Russia, America and its allies should seek their occasional participation rather than attempt to integrate them into the liberal order over the near to medium

term. Beijing and Moscow will not embrace the liberal order any-
time soon. Instead of abandoning the goal of integration, the
United States and its allies should postpone it. The defenders of
the liberal order should involve China and Russia where possible
and encourage their cooperation in areas where both sides would
benefit from constructive approaches, including arms control and
nonproliferation, global financial stability, climate change, the Arctic, and counterterrorism. Involvement is not as satisfying as integration, and progress will be halting. But it is far wiser to wage
long-term competition with pragmatic strategies instead of false
hopes.

The third principle encompasses open channels with states
and outreach to societies. It is a dangerous myth that engaging
in dialogue is a concession to adversaries. The United States and
the Soviet Union maintained diplomatic relations throughout the
Cold War. Keeping channels open with Beijing and Moscow today
will enable Washington to present its interests more forcefully,
take stock of their intentions, and prevent accidents and miscalculations. Regimes can change, interests can shift, tensions can yield
to trust, and surprises lurk around corners. Few analysts predicted
the depth and pace of change from Brezhnev to Gorbachev in Russia or from Mao Zedong to Deng Xiaoping in China. The United
States need not assume it can change the domestic trajectory of
these regimes in order to lay the groundwork for more positive relations when and if they do. That is why outreach to societies in
Russia, China, and other authoritarian regimes is so important.
Building relationships with human rights activists, civil society
leaders, businesses, and educators is a mark of strength and a
shared investment in the prospects of a different future.

*Finally, strengthen institutional performance, creating a compelling
narrative that will mobilize popular support.* Sustaining an open, liberal international order will require Western and non-Western
democracies to show tangible wins for their citizens. For that to
happen, political leaders need to strengthen the institutional performance of democracies and adapt multilateral institutions to the
changing environment. A strong performance record can be used
to mobilize popular backing and create a narrative around the liberal order that captures the public imagination.

This final lesson courses through all the others. It recognizes that human beings are storytelling creatures: we use narratives to impose order on our lives, extract meaning, build relationships, and construct identities that are rooted in specific communities and places. Stories are felt with the heart before they are interpreted in the head. They can motivate grand acts of heroism or unspeakable acts of barbarism. Whether for good or for ill, people define themselves in and through stories. This insight is often lost in today's debates. Geopolitical competition can take many forms. One of the most neglected is the competition over narratives: Whose story fires the imagination of more people in more countries? The liberal order is as much a narrative about the origins and destiny of human freedom as it is a reflection of America's geopolitical interests. When power shifts, so do the narratives that capture the attention of the world. The two are one and inseparable.

Populist reactionaries and authoritarian powers today tell a story of grievance, victimhood, wounded pride, and rightful pride of place. They trade on people's fears of liberty and embrace what the historian Timothy Snyder calls the "politics of eternity," which puts the nation "at the center of a cyclical story of victimhood."[81] In Russia this narrative assumes a conservative cast: Moscow is the bulwark of traditional values and culture in a degenerate world of cosmopolitans and progressive elites. The journalist Roger Cohen captures this mentality in his description of Russia as the "preeminent counterrevolutionary power."[82] Russia's narrative today is not about moving forward toward a new future but about moving backward toward an imaginary past when Russia was the imperial czar and the empire was whole.[83] It is a vision based on fear, not hope, and it depends for its sustenance on people's unwillingness, in Vaclav Havel's phrase, to commit to "living within the truth."[84] This story may sound unappealing to Western ears, but more and more disgruntled citizens in the West find themselves drawn to it. They fear pluralism and seek comfort in a vision that promises safe harbor from the vicissitudes of the modern world.

Right now, the liberal story needs retelling. The current narrative is listless, forgettable, and supine in the face of reactionaries who are, in the phrase of the poet W. B. Yeats, "full of passionate intensity."[85] Too often the defenders of liberal order appeal to the head, not the heart. They tell a story of inevitable progress without recognizing the inevitable twists and turns and tragedies along the way. In addition to new domestic and international compacts, the United States and its allies require a new narrative compact. The German philosopher Friedrich Nietzsche observed, "If we have our own *why* of life, we shall get along with almost any *how*."[86] Defenders of the liberal order need a more compelling *why* before they can propose new methods for *how*. In the Cold War the United States and its allies depended on fear of the Communist menace to enlist public support for the liberal project. Fear is a powerful motivator, but once unleashed in the public domain it can spiral in dangerous directions and prove impossible to control. Hope is more elusive to summon but far more enduring in its appeal.

FDR was a master practitioner of hope. In his third inaugural address, in 1941, he cast his sights back to find inspiration and guidance for the present. He noted that for President Lincoln "the task of the people was to preserve that Nation from disruption from within. In this day the task of the people is to save that Nation and its institutions from disruption from without."[87]

Today, the danger comes from both directions. New technologies and old methods combine to aid the adversaries of liberal order as they challenge America and its allies from within and from without. The United States faces a choice not unlike that of Americans in the postwar period. Lincoln questioned whether Americans intend to be the authors of a new order or the finishers of the old. FDR offers a timeless answer to that question: "In the face of great perils never before encountered, our strong purpose is to protect and to perpetuate the integrity of democracy. For this we muster the spirit of America, and the faith of America."[88] We must summon that same faith and spirit now.

CHAPTER EIGHT

America's Way Forward

O N MAY 8, 1953, President Eisenhower convened his top advisors in secret in the Solarium room of the White House. After deliberating behind closed doors, they reached an agreement to conduct a series of high-level seminars to be held at the National War College. If anyone asked, the participants were to say it was the "First National War College Round-Table Seminar on 'Cold War and US Foreign Policy, 1953–1963.' "[1] In truth, Eisenhower's advisors would gather to reassess American strategy toward the Soviet Union. They called it Project Solarium.

Ever the master planner, President Eisenhower had as his goal devising a new approach that depended less on unilateral military force and bloated defense budgets and relied more on confronting the political and economic dimensions of the Soviet threat. Ike believed that sustained military mobilization would risk creating a garrison state at home, stifle the economy, and betray American values.[2] As he warned in his State of the Union address earlier that year, "Our problem is to achieve adequate military strength within the limits of endurable strain upon our economy. To amass military power without regard to our economic capacity would be to defend ourselves against one kind of disaster by inviting another."[3]

Ike knew that the Soviet threat tested American power and resolve on multiple fronts, so for the seminars he divided his most
senior advisors into three teams to examine alternative strategies.
Under the direction of George Kennan, the author of the Long
Telegram that defined the Soviet threat for generations of Cold
War planners, Team A focused on political and economic measures
that relied on multilateral cooperation and the industrial strength
of the West to contain Soviet aggression. Led by Major General
James McCormack, Team B looked at more assertive approaches,
which included forming "a continuous line around the Soviet bloc
beyond which the US will not permit Soviet or satellite military
forces to advance without general war."[4] Team C, led by Vice
Admiral Richard Conolly, was charged with developing a rollback
strategy that included creating "the maximum disruption and
popular resistance throughout the Soviet Bloc."[5] The three teams
deliberated over six weeks and presented their findings to the National Security Council on July 16, 1953.

Eisenhower's Basic National Security Policy, adopted in October 1953, embraced many of Team A's recommendations and incorporated elements of Teams B and C. America's new integrated
policy recognized that the competition with the Soviets was multifaceted and required investments not only in military power but
also in diplomatic, political, and economic measures; cooperative
action with allies; and collective defense.

The new policy put deterrence at the heart of US strategy. It
reaffirmed Kennan's original conception of long-term, vigilant
containment of the Soviet Union. Eisenhower's policy made clear
that a "strong, healthy and expanding US economy is essential
to the security and stability of the free world" and that "the support of defense expenditures should not seriously impair the basic
soundness of the US economy by undermining incentives or by
inflation."[6] It included a role for covert action and set the stage
for a rebalancing of the US military based on national priorities
and a renewed focus on education, infrastructure, and science and
technology.

Today, as America confronts decline, US strategy needs another reboot along the lines of a Project Solarium 2.0.[7] Just as
President Eisenhower used this deliberative process to break out of

the straitjacket of Cold War orthodoxy, America's leaders now must reclaim a willingness to question received verities, test assumptions, and rebalance national priorities.

If a future president were to charter a Solarium Project 2.0, what strategies would Teams A, B, and C recommend to America as a way forward in a post-dominant world? While policy makers and analysts have proposed Solarium as a model for national security planning or for combating specific threats, such as cyber, here I build on these recommendations by applying Solarium's three teams to the three principal schools of thought in US grand strategy today. My model adds a Team D to correspond to persistent traditions and sectoral interests in US foreign policy and domestic politics. As the debates among these four schools show, grand strategy is not a simple dichotomy between global leadership and retreat. Rich variations exist within each school, and their policy prescriptions are not valid for all times and places. By evaluating these four schools of thought in the context of the broad policy choices and trade-offs identified in this book, readers will gain a fuller appreciation of the prospects for American power in this post-dominant world.

Restraint

Imagine sitting in on the first meeting of a Project Solarium 2.0. A future US president charges the participants with articulating guiding principles for American grand strategy in the twenty-first century. What do the four teams advise?

Proponents of Team A advocate American restraint.[8] This conception of statecraft begins by underlining America's assets: its favorable geography and natural resource base, its ocean moats in the Atlantic and Pacific, its friendly neighbors to the north and south, its formidable military, and its possession of a credible nuclear deterrent. It emphasizes that America's strength abroad comes from its strength at home, including the strength of its scientific know-how, prosperous economy, and productive capacity.

Looking ahead, Team A restrainers argue that a declining America should not pursue the same grand strategy going forward that it did during the early years of the Cold War, when its GDP hovered around 45 to 50 percent of the world's total and its principal adversaries lay in ruins or were licking their wounds from war.[9] Team A cautions against foreign adventures that sap resources and pin down American power in regions of peripheral interest. While there are differences among restrainers about whether American dominance is a prudent and feasible goal, most warn that the costs of primacy are unsustainable and that nationalism and asymmetric strategies make land wars in the Middle East and Asia a debilitating proposition.[10] Restrainers contend that there are few, if any, challengers for hegemony in Europe. China may be intent on achieving hegemony in Asia, or it may want to carve out a sphere of influence and constrain US power internationally. Since the jury is still out on that question, in Team A's view the sensible approach urges caution and considers a warning: aggressively hostile policies will guarantee conflicts, not prevent them.

As for America's allies, Team A argues that they pay too little in burden sharing. They are rich, relatively secure, and capable of defending themselves. Therefore America should reduce its force structure overseas, limit its alliance commitments, and resolve to intervene only when the balance of power breaks down in regions of critical interest to the United States, with a particular focus on the Eurasian heartland. Instead of launching preventive strikes to stop nuclear proliferation or cyberattacks, restraint-minded Team A advocates a management approach that seeks to constrain rivals from going nuclear or launching cyber intrusions into America's democracy and way of life.

Team A points to history as the testing ground and guide. The Russo–Japanese war of 1905, the multiple wars between India and Pakistan, and the war in Ukraine since 2014 show that America can stay aloof militarily at little cost and not get pulled into foreign quarrels.[11] When the balance breaks down and America's interests demand its involvement, as was the case in World Wars I and II, Team A argues that it is far better to let others do the fighting, exhaust themselves, and create the space for a decisive American intervention. To accomplish this task the United States needs rapid reaction or "over-the-horizon" forces, not large armies and more aircraft carriers. Team A's restrainers seek to reposition militarily from forward basing in Europe, the Middle East, and Asia, contending that the presence of US troops in these regions failed to deter aggression or prevent wars from breaking out in the Balkans, Russia's invasion of Ukraine, and the turmoil that plagues the greater Middle East today.[12]

In short, Team A counsels restraint because it is less costly, more prudent, and far more likely to conserve America's diminishing power than an aggressive strategy that expends US limited power in pursuit of unwinnable objectives.

Deep Engagement

Team B advocates deep engagement for America, an approach sometimes called liberal internationalism.[13] Proponents of deep engagement start with a basic premise: America's security and prosperity at home depend on the security and prosperity of its allies and partners abroad. To keep America safe, Team B argues, US leaders need to make the case for robust alliances, forward deployments, and credible security guarantees as well as for the investments required to realize these initiatives. Instead of keeping US troops at home, advocates of deep engagement favor deploying US forces forward in Europe and Asia to maintain fragile balances of power, prevent arms races, deter great-power landgrabs, counter potential cyberattacks, and avoid technological surprise by would-be aggressors.

In a globalized world, Team B's argument for deep engagement abroad is that the United States cannot hide behind ocean moats and friendly neighbors. American power and purpose are necessary to keep open the sea lanes that facilitate global trade and protect the lines of communication that accelerate global commerce and travel. Team B warns that by pulling back from active global leadership America risks ceding the ground to authoritarian rivals and sowing the seeds for greater instability down the road.

Team B's advocates of deep engagement also claim history as a guide, arguing that the United States conducted a series of experiments in the twentieth century to test the proposition of retrenchment. The result was World War II, the Korean War, and the first Persian Gulf War. Team B contends that if America pulls back, its allies will not step forward in the absence of principled US leadership. The more likely outcome is that allies hedge their bets, seek accommodation with adversaries, or pursue military buildups that threaten regional stability. The history of deep engagement, Team B's advocates claim, offers America a more reassuring path forward: its track record coincides with the decades of relative peace, prosperity, and democratic growth that followed the end of World War II.

In theory Team B argues that restraint promises more benefits than deep engagement and at less cost; in practice Team B says that Team A's restraint is a flawed strategy. Knowing when and how to intervene is difficult in the best of circumstances; it is infinitely harder in times of crisis, when the rapid introduction of American forces can destabilize already volatile situations.[14] Team B observes that America's allies not only facilitate the projection of US military power through basing access and overflight rights but also defray the cost of US troops and installations, add strength through military manpower, and afford international legitimacy. While it's true that the United States foots a considerable bill for its global responsibilities, advocates of deep engagement point out that the price tag is manageable compared with what America spent during the Cold War. It is far wiser to invest modestly now in America's alliances than to incur the towering cost of major war in the next decades.

Primacy

Team C advocates American primacy. This approach is sometimes associated with unipolarity, which refers more to the way in which power can be distributed in the international system than to how it is wielded and to what ends. Team C's proponents of primacy argue that the surest path to peace and stability is the assertive use of American military might.[15]

As one comparative study of grand strategy notes, advocates of primacy differ from restrainers and liberal internationalists in their understanding of the principal threats in world politics, preferred conceptions of order, and definition of national interests.[16] In contrast to Team A's restrainers, who focus on stability among the great powers, and Team B's liberal internationalists, who focus on institutions, Team C's advocates of primacy focus on peer competitors. Team A's restrainers seek to uphold the status quo and construe vital interests narrowly. Team B's liberal internationalists seek to deepen economic interdependence and construe vital interests transnationally. Team C's primacists aim to extend American dominance and construe vital interests broadly.

Team A's restrainers, Team B's liberal internationalists, and Team C's primacists all seek the expansion of democracies globally, but they differ on the means of achieving this goal. Restrainers favor promoting democracy by example, while deep engagers prefer to support the growth of democracy through international institutions, economic interdependence, and transnational networks. By contrast, Team C's primacists are more inclined to pursue democratic enlargement through the deployment of US troops to hot zones around the world. In the aftermath of 9/11, advocates of primacy urged the United States to build up its military, command the global commons of air, land, sea, space, and cyber, and intervene preventively to deal with the threat of rogue regimes and nuclear proliferation. Primacists are ready to lean on allies but are equally ready to conduct military operations without them.

Team C argues that the global system tends toward instability in the absence of a global leader. In this view, history is a succession of one hegemon after another, from Portugal in the fifteenth century, to Spain in the sixteenth, the Netherlands in the early seventeenth, Britain in the nineteenth, and the United States in the post–World War II period. Since stability in the international system is a public good, and public goods are, by definition, available to all and excluded from none, there is an incentive to free ride. The only way out of this conundrum, Team C's thinking goes, is for American power to provide the public goods for which it claims the most benefit.

Applied to the challenges America faces today, Team C primacists identify China as the principal threat to the United States and call for more competitive strategies to balance, contain, and ultimately thwart its rise. This strategy requires the muscular use of American power, including military buildups in and around the South China Sea, robust freedom-of-navigation operations, and offensive actions with allies to counter cyber intrusions and avoid technological surprise. It recognizes that China is a threat not simply to America's allies in the Asia-Pacific but to democracies everywhere. Beijing interferes in democratic elections. It uses predatory investments in infrastructure to enfeeble vulnerable states along its periphery. It steals intellectual property and pursues strategic acquisitions of foreign companies to gain access to sensitive technologies. It oppresses its population and seeks to control them through high-tech surveillance systems.

In short, China is a geopolitical and ideological foe of the highest order with regard to America's primacy. The goal for Team C is not to coexist with China, as Teams A and B recommend, but to contain and roll back its advance. China is not a responsible stakeholder; it is a dangerous threat to international peace and security. Primed for competition, Team C seeks to restore unrivaled American dominance.

Isolationism

Finally, a Project Solarium 2.0 might include a Team D on isolationism and autonomy.[17] While isolationism is not a realistic policy option for America today, it is a persistent force in the US foreign policy tradition. Isolationism has a complicated history in the United States. As the historian Walter McDougall observes, isolationism did not appear in modern political discourse until the beginning of the twentieth century, and even then it was often employed as a disparaging term against critics.[18] Today, it is important to distinguish isolationism from restraint. Whereas Team D's isolationists seek to pull back US forces, cut loose US allies, and retreat behind higher tariff barriers and border walls, Team A's restrainers aim to reposition US forces, rebalance tasks and burdens among US allies, and recognize the importance of continued economic and commercial engagement. As scholars have demonstrated, great powers that practice restraint and retrenchment "rarely renounced most—let alone all—of their foreign policy commitments."[19] Restraint is not about relinquishing power; it is about repositioning power at home and abroad to adapt to changing political, economic, and security conditions.

When Eisenhower became president the politics of the time and the experience of World War II seared into the minds of US policy makers the dangers of America retreating within its borders. Eisenhower established control of his party and fended off prominent voices calling for a more inward-looking approach. Today's political parties are more polarized than those of earlier years, and their leaders cannot take for granted that a reservoir of public support exists for active, sustained global leadership. The foreign policy of Team D's isolationists argues that the preservation of liberty requires America to lead by the force of its example. Foreign entanglements threaten liberty by producing garrison states at home and provoking enemies abroad.

The Pros and Cons of the Four Teams

After assessing Teams A, B, C, and D, a future American president should recognize the opportunities and risks of each. Teams B and C argue for more commitments to be extended overseas to advance America's global reach, more use of force to protect US interests, and more trip wires to be defended.

Restraint, called for by Team A, is prudent during a period of relative decline, and it sensibly manages America's finances. But it neglects a crucial advantage that America enjoys over its principal adversaries: a global network of allies and partners. Because spheres of influence are not stable, America's forward military presence in Europe and Asia constitutes a vital insurance policy against old threats and emerging dangers.

The deep engagement of Team B recognizes the importance of allies, but its ambitions need to be tempered by the realities of American decline and the need for significant burden sharing with allies in order to alleviate the financial strain.

Team C's advocates of primacy are right to identify China and Russia as major competitors and to see the principal geopolitical fault line running between democracies and autocracies. By leading with the military first and recognizing no practical limits to US resources, however, primacy runs the risk of weakening American power instead of enhancing it. Primacy ignores the very real risks of precipitating an unnecessary conflict. It's one thing to gird for a long-term competition; it's quite another to rush headlong into a confrontation.

Isolationists of Team D are right to cherish liberty at home, but they ignore the fact that the principal threat to liberty today comes from powerful autocracies intent on subverting democracies from within. Team D isolationists also discount the possibility that regional conflicts can spiral out of control, particularly in the case of tensions between nuclear-armed powers. Isolationism may seem to be a cost-effective strategy, but it runs the risk of depleting the US budget on the next big war because it did not assert diplomatic leadership to ward off aggressive challengers.

The Way Ahead

One might hope that America's future president would choose a balanced, flexible, and affordable strategy that embodies an important observation of the theologian Reinhold Niebuhr: in an imperfect world there are only "proximate solutions to insoluble problems."[20] America needs immediate, consequential pathways for going forward as its power declines. Based on the lessons for statecraft in the preceding chapters, a future Project Solarium should embrace three proximate solutions: consolidate, adapt, and compete.

Start with consolidation of economic strength and productive capacity. America faces the twin perils of overstretch abroad and underreach at home. The right US approach needs to address both. The United States can gather its strength in the core by avoiding costly military interventions in the periphery. President Eisenhower's concerns about strategic solvency should guide America's leaders today in setting national priorities, cautioning them against taking on overly ambitious commitments that exceed the country's resources. Protecting a resilient core will require building up America's domestic economic strength and innovative potential, understanding that a nation's productive capacity underpins its military capacity over the long term.

As part of its emphasis on consolidation, the United States should undertake a multiyear, national innovation initiative to boost investments in R&D, science and technology, education, and infrastructure. It should redouble its efforts to find a bipartisan solution to immigration, which is essential to maintaining a vibrant, youthful population that drives economic growth and technological advances. And America should focus on rooting out the corruption of its political leadership and institutions at home, recognizing that competent, functioning institutions in service of ordinary Americans are crucial for projecting US power and influence in the world. An effective strategy against political corruption would attack the hydra on multiple fronts, reinforce norms of behavior for good governance, change the culture around money, and work with allies to close the space for kleptocrats to operate.

Consolidation begins at home, but it doesn't end there. America's leaders should avoid the lure of preventive war as the first and only solution for dealing with rising challengers. Foreign policy doesn't lend itself to silver-bullet certainty (see chapter 5). The United States confronts a dangerous mix of threats, including the potential of authoritarian states to pursue a nuclear weapons capability or proliferate weapons of mass destruction to other rogue states and nonstate actors. In such cases, preventive military attacks may be tempting to a declining great power, but this option entails risks: it relies on sound intelligence about the precise location of targets, which is more an art than a science and subject to myriad constraints and uncertainties; it presumes that military strikes can eliminate nuclear know-how, not just nuclear weapons capabilities; it sets the stage for costly interventions that may drain a great power's finances and trigger unintended consequences that are not subject to its control; and it runs the risk of worsening the very problem it aims to solve. Preventive military attacks against a would-be nuclear power may eliminate its short-term capabilities, but they will not extinguish its desire for nuclear weapons. If anything, preventive strikes will harden the adversary's resolve to develop such weapons and shore up public support behind the regime that seeks them.

Instead of turning to preventive military attacks the United States should leverage preventive engagement strategies as its enduring tool of first resort. These strategies are most effective when implemented in concert with allies and through international organizations. It is easy to exaggerate the benefits of military action and downplay the costs. Hard-nosed diplomacy combined with multilateral sanctions, backed by the credible threat of force, is a more potent strategic approach.

Consolidation is not about turning inward; it's about shoring up the foundations of power so that a nation can extend outward sustainably. That is why the United States should bolster democratic governance by playing to its strengths, including leading by example at home and expanding investments in education and exchange programs, public diplomacy, and new communications tools for people living in authoritarian societies.[21] The United States should work more closely with like-minded allies and partners to strengthen democracy and the rule of law in places as diverse as Tunisia, Nigeria, Georgia, and Ukraine. Regional organizations, such as the Economic Community of West African States and ASEAN, can play meaningful roles in stabilizing fragile democracies.[22] Consolidation also requires new methods for incorporating the perspectives and capacities of nonstate actors. Above all, it demands greater investments of time, energy, and resources in building public support for active, sustained US leadership in the world. Telling the story of democracy in a way that captures the imagination of people at home and across the globe is essential to securing America's interests over the long term.

Next, America should adapt. The United States is losing ground by not seizing the initiative in a changing world. Arati Prabhakar's leadership of DARPA points to the urgency of cultivating an innovator's mind-set, which is essential to the task of adaptation in a post-dominant world. Seizing the initiative requires inculcating practices and policies that encourage the development of long-term vision in the US government. Promising initiatives would include investments in rebuilding America's capacity for strategic assessment, such as a nonpartisan, standing office in the White House that conducts strategic planning, improves historical judgment and analysis, identifies the second- and third-order effects of different policy options, and assures continuity during transitions from one administration to the next.[23] Fostering an innovator's mind-set would also entail strengthening partnerships between federal, state, and local governments, industry, philanthropies, and academia to reimagine America's innovation ecosystem; and longer-term strategies for managing risks through affordable approaches, such as exploring the benefits, costs, metrics, and requirements of a unified national security budget to promote more holistic and forward-looking investments in diplomacy, development, and defense.[24]

Future success will require strategic anticipation and policy planning. FDR and Churchill started planning for the postwar world long before victory was achieved in Europe; President Truman and Secretary Acheson laid the institutional foundations for what is now called the liberal international order; and George Kennan, the former US diplomat and director of the State Department's policy planning staff, recognized the threat of the Soviet Union and articulated the intellectual framework for containment during the Cold War. Today, US political leaders need to adapt the postwar institutions to new realities, including a reformed World Trade Organization and flexible multilateral arrangements that address the challenges of state capitalism and set international rules of the road for emerging technologies in the digital era.

Adaptation will require changes to US fiscal policies and to the country's national security priorities. America should reengineer the level of debt and deficit spending in the interests of generating long-term economic productivity. It should rebalance its national security toolkit to favor preventive diplomacy and development over the military-first foreign policies that have dominated administrations of both parties for decades. Robust diplomacy is the sharpest and most cost-effective tool in a great power's arsenal. It's long past time for the United States to supply its diplomats and development professionals with the resources they need to advance US interests and values. America should also adapt its forward posture by modernizing the structures and capabilities of its alliances to changing threats on the horizon, building connections among allies in the Western Hemisphere, Europe, and Asia, and recalibrating the roles and responsibilities of America's forces and those of local partners on the front lines.

The imperative of seizing the initiative and playing the long game in an era of decline should not distract from the need to play the short game well.[25] If leaders of declining powers falter in setting or executing near-term priorities, they can weaken domestic and international support for their long-term strategy.

Finally, the United States should compete responsibly. The right approach would begin by understanding the strong connections between foreign and economic policy. Smart investments in science and technology, vocational training and apprenticeships, infrastructure projects, clean energy, and targeted development programs in rural areas and underserved communities will strengthen the US middle class, alleviate inequality, and boost social mobility for the next generation.[26] Many local communities in America are pioneering new approaches and devising innovative ways to adapt to changing economic realities.[27] These efforts will not only make the United States more dynamic and entrepreneurial at home but also build a stronger foundation for American power in the world. Similarly, the United States could restructure global trade and investment arrangements to alleviate domestic inequality and promote climate resilience for US farmers and coastal communities.[28] America could lead a new effort to reach agreement with other major economies on addressing a range of practices that distort markets, such as the lack of enforcement of intellectual property rights, and that adversely impact the American middle class, such as international tax avoidance.[29] These and other measures show the benefits of devising policies that cut across the domestic and international levels of analysis in an era of heightened geopolitical competition.

Planning smartly today, as President Eisenhower did yesterday, would recognize that the post–Cold War settlement based on a prostrate Russia and an inwardly focused China is no longer sustainable. Russia and China pose different challenges, and yet both threaten the liberal order. Therefore the United States should accept responsibility for leading a robust, multifaceted, and long-term alliance against rival authoritarian powers.

The rise of China occurred, in part, as a result of US choices and assumptions that are now increasingly called into question.[30] By defining the goals of its engagement with China and acknowledging the successes and limits of past strategies, America can approach China's rise today with greater clarity and sense of purpose. To manage this challenge, the United States should remember the lessons of the Cold War without repeating its mistakes or drifting into needless confrontation. US political leaders should apply a fundamental principle of Kennan's strategic thinking: America and its allies need to play the long game well. As discussed above, if leaders act on the conviction that decline is inevitable, they will adopt policies that are potentially damaging in comparison to those undertaken if they had acted on the conviction that decline is reversible. Acceptance or rejection of decline has implications for US–China policy. America need not tempt war or engage in costly, inefficient arms races to protect its interests and values in a competitive environment. Instead, it should nurture its economic fundamentals, perceive its strengths and weaknesses clearly, link arms with its allies, set the rules of the road for international relations, and deftly exploit the inefficiencies in rival models of authoritarian governance.

To return to a question this book asked at the outset: Is this American generation one that builds or one that manages or one that neglects? Americans can once again become a generation of builders. The United States can regain its edge, but leadership cannot be assumed or taken for granted. It will require hard choices, difficult trade-offs, and compromise. To recognize this fact is not unpatriotic. It is not defeatist. It is a necessity if America is to seize the initiative and build a nation that is competitive on the world stage.

Durbar, in New Delhi, is a large area north of the old city that the British used to mark the coronation of new monarchs and emperors. The Proclamation Durbar of 1877 celebrated the ascension of Queen Victoria. The British spared no expense and summoned the riches of empire to salute the new empress. Roads were paved. Railways were constructed. Waterlines were repaired and refurbished. And statues of the queen were built. The British repeated this exercise to proclaim the coronations of King Edward VII in 1903 and King George V in 1911. Many years later, after India had won its independence, the authorities gathered the statues of the British monarchs and emperors and empresses and put them on plinths in Durbar at Coronation Park.

On a diplomatic trip to New Delhi as the head of a US peace-keeping delegation, my father went with a tour guide to the Delhi Durbar. They sat in the shade of one of those statues, looking at a desolate wasteland of faded monarchs and crumbling ruins. As the sun drifted into an amber haze, the tour guide recalled the tale of Ozymandias, rendered immortal in the lines of the British poet Percy Bysshe Shelley:

I met a traveller from an antique land,
Who said—"Two vast and trunkless legs of stone
Stand in the desert. . . . Near them, on the sand,
Half sunk a shattered visage lies, whose frown,
And wrinkled lip, and sneer of cold command,
Tell that its sculptor well those passions read
Which yet survive, stamped on these lifeless things,
The hand that mocked them, and the heart that fed;
And on the pedestal, these words appear:
My name is Ozymandias, King of Kings;
Look on my Works, ye Mighty, and despair!
Nothing beside remains. Round the decay
Of that colossal Wreck, boundless and bare
The lone and level sands stretch far away."[31]

For a time, the United States was "King of Kings." Whether the fate of Ozymandias befalls the American hegemon is yet to be decided. The United States could build statues of its might and tell the world to look on its works and despair. Round the decay, a young boy or girl from another continent may one day sit in the ruins of America's empire and read "Ozymandias" and wonder why. Or the United States can take a different path. Instead of erecting statues celebrating the past, it could build bridges into a promising future. It could adapt to a world in which America's power is contested, but its purpose and values long endure. When the lone and level sands stretch far away, what remains?

We know the choices. Now is the time for America to go forward with resolve.

Notes

Introduction

1. See, e.g., Fareed Zakaria, *The Post-American World: Release 2.0* (New York: W. W. Norton, 2011); Barry Posen, *Restraint: A New Foundation for U.S. Grand Strategy* (Ithaca: Cornell University Press, 2015); David M. Edelstein, *Over the Horizon: Time, Uncertainty, and the Rise of Great Powers* (Ithaca: Cornell University Press, 2017); Graham Allison, *Destined for War: Can America and China Escape Thucydides's Trap?* (New York: Houghton Mifflin Harcourt, 2017); Kori Schake, *Safe Passage: The Transition from British to American Hegemony* (Cambridge: Harvard University Press, 2017); Amitav Acharya, *The End of American World Order* (Cambridge: Polity Press, 2018); Joshua R. Itzkowitz Shifrinson, *Rising Titans, Falling Giants: How Great Powers Exploit Power Shifts* (Ithaca: Cornell University Press, 2018); Paul K. MacDonald and Joseph M. Parent, *Twilight of the Titans: Great Power Decline and Retrenchment* (Ithaca: Cornell University Press, 2018); Robert Kagan, *The Jungle Grows Back: America and Our Imperiled World* (New York: Knopf, 2018); Stephen M. Walt, *The Hell of Good Intentions: America's Foreign Policy Elite and the Decline of U.S. Primacy* (New York: Farrar, Straus and Giroux, 2018); John J. Mearsheimer, *The Great Delusion: Liberal Dreams and International Realities* (New Haven: Yale University Press, 2018); William J. Burns, *The Back Channel: A Memoir of Diplomacy and the Case for Its Renewal* (New York: Random House, 2019); Parag Khanna, *The Future Is Asian* (New York: Simon & Schuster, 2019); Stacie E. Goddard, *When Right Makes Might: Rising Powers and World Order* (Ithaca: Cornell University Press, 2019).
2. On domestic challenges in the United States, see Howard S. Friedman, *The Measure of a Nation: How to Regain America's Competitive Edge and Boost Our Global Standing* (New York: Prometheus, 2012); J. D. Vance, *Hillbilly Elegy: A Memoir of a Family and Culture in Crisis* (New York: Harper, 2016); Nancy Isenberg, *White Trash: The 400-Year Untold History*

of Class in America (New York: Penguin, 2017); Steven Levitsky and Daniel Ziblatt, *How Democracies Die* (New York: Broadway Books, 2019).

3. On the concepts of relative and absolute decline, see Aaron L. Friedberg, *Britain and the Experience of Relative Decline, 1895–1905* (Princeton: Princeton University Press, 2010); Joseph S. Nye Jr., *Is the American Century Over?* (New York: Polity, 2015).

4. See, e.g., Daniel J. Sargent, *A Superpower Transformed: The Remaking of American Foreign Relations in the 1970s* (Oxford: Oxford University Press, 2015).

5. Samuel W. Rushay Jr., "Harry Truman's History Lessons," *Prologue Magazine* 41, no. 1 (2009).

6. Drawing historical analogies and applying lessons learned require great care, attention to context, awareness of one's biases and methodological assumptions, appreciation of differences and similarities between past cases and the present, and recognition of knowns and unknowns. See, e.g., Richard E. Neustadt and Ernest May, *Thinking in Time: The Uses of History for Decision Makers* (New York: Simon & Schuster, 1986); Yuen Foong Khong, *Analogies at War: Korea, Munich, Dien Bien Phu, and the Vietnam Decisions of 1965* (Princeton: Princeton University Press, 1992); Margaret MacMillan, *Dangerous Games: The Uses and Abuses of History* (New York: Random House, 2009); Paul F. Lauren, Gordon A. Craig, and Alexander L. George, *Force and Statecraft: Diplomatic Challenges of Our Time* (Oxford: Oxford University Press, 2013), 147–62.

7. The historical cases in this book are selected not for the purposes of theory testing but for the purposes of my research objective: to illustrate the key choices faced by great powers in decline, explore how leaders of great powers respond to decline, and distill critical warnings, lessons learned, and practical guidance for America's leaders today. See, e.g., Alexander L. George and Andrew Bennett, *Case Studies and Theory Development in the Social Sciences* (Cambridge: MIT Press, 2005).

8. Paul Kennedy, *The Rise and Fall of the Great Powers* (New York: Random House, 1987).

9. See, e.g., ibid.; Josef Joffe, *The Myth of America's Decline: Politics, Economics, and a Half Century of False Prophecies* (New York: Liveright, 2013).

10. The author wishes to acknowledge Ashley Tellis of the Carnegie Endowment for International Peace for his distinction between the secular, transient, and contingent realities of decline.

11. See, e.g., MacDonald and Parent, *Twilight of the Titans.*

12. Acharya, *The End of American World Order,* 26.

Chapter One. A Post-dominant World

1. Ibn Khaldun, *The Muqaddimah: An Introduction to History* (Princeton: Princeton University Press, 2015).

2. MacDonald and Parent, *Twilight of the Titans,* 45.

3. Ibid.
4. Michael Beckley, *Unrivaled: Why America Will Remain the World's Sole Superpower* (Ithaca: Cornell University Press, 2018).
5. Ibid.
6. Ibid., 33.
7. Ibid., 5.
8. Joffe, *The Myth of America's Decline*.
9. Joshua Shifrinson, "Should the United States Fear China's Rise?," *Washington Quarterly* 41, no. 4 (2019): 67.
10. Author's calculations of per capita GDP at current dollars, based on World Bank data. On the merits of shifts in relative ratios versus the size and significance of aggregate capabilities, see Joshua R. Itzkowitz Shifrinson and Michael Beckley, "Correspondence: Debating China's Rise and U.S. Decline," *International Security* 37, no. 3 (2012/13): 172–77.
11. Author's calculations from World Bank data, accessed August 2019.
12. "GDP Based on PPP, Share of World," World Economic Outlook, *International Monetary Fund*, October 2018. See also Arvind Subramanian, *Eclipse: Living in the Shadow of China's Economic Dominance* (Washington, DC: Peterson Institute for International Economics, 2011).
13. Long-term projections of China's economic growth need to confront fundamental uncertainties, including China's ability to adapt, improve its business environment, strengthen rule of law, combat corruption, and implement structural reforms. See China Power Team, "Is China Leading in Global Innovation?," *China Power*, May 28, 2019.
14. Martin Wolf, "The Future Might Not Belong to China," *Financial Times*, January 1, 2019.
15. Yukon Huang, "What Western Observers Get Wrong in Assessing China," *Global Times*, October, 18, 2017.
16. Steve Johnson, "The Great Haul of China, Illustrated," *Financial Times*, November 19, 2019.
17. Subramanian, *Eclipse*.
18. Martin Wolf, "US–China Rivalry Will Shape the 21st Century," *Financial Times*, April 10, 2018; Dennis Normile, "China Narrows U.S. Lead in R&D Spending," *Science*, October 19, 2018.
19. Randy Showstack, "China May Soon Surpass the United States in R&D Funding," *Earth and Space Science News*, February 20, 2018.
20. Ehsan Masood, "How China Is Redrawing the Map of World Science," *Nature*, May 1, 2019.
21. China Power Team, "Is China Leading in Global Innovation?" While the quantity of Chinese patent applications has surpassed that in the United States, their quality lags behind.
22. On China's share of triadic patents, see Organization for Economic Cooperation and Development, "Triadic Patent Families," 2018; Shifrinson, "Should the United States Fear China's Rise?," 67. Assessments of China's

innovative potential based on patent filings need to account for the reality of Chinese theft of intellectual property, the degree to which US companies treat their intellectual property as a trade secret rather than as a patent, and the extent to which multinational companies file patents in countries other than where the research occurred.

23. "Rise of the Global Start-up City: The New Map of Entrepreneurship and Venture Capital," *Center for American Entrepreneurship*, October 5, 2018; Rebecca Fannin, "China Rises to 38% of Global Venture Spending in 2018, Nears US Levels," *Forbes*, January 14, 2019. After several years of rapid growth China's venture capital market experienced a slowdown in the first half of 2019, largely as a result of trade tensions with the United States and concerns about the valuations of Chinese start-ups.

24. Nan Tian, Aude Fleurant, Alexandra, Kuimova, Pieter D. Wezeman, and Siemon T. Wezeman, "Trends in World Military Expenditure, 2018," SIPRI Fact Sheet, April 2019, 2.

25. Chris Dougherty, "Why America Needs a New Way of War," *Center for a New American Security*, June 12, 2019.

26. Andrew F. Krepinevich, "The Eroding Balance of Terror: The Decline of Deterrence," *Foreign Affairs*, January/February 2019.

27. On the costs of weapons procurement, see Shawn Snow, "Report: Day-to-day Operation Costs Eat Up Half of the Defense Budget," *Military Times*, January 13, 2017; Robert O. Work and Shawn Brimley, "20YY Preparing for War in the Robotic Age," *Center for a New American Security*, January 2014; Joseph M. Parent and Paul K. MacDonald, "The Wisdom of Retrenchment," *Foreign Affairs*, November/December 2011.

28. Gordon Lubold and Dustin Volz, "Chinese Hackers Breach U.S. Navy Contractors," *Wall Street Journal*, December 14, 2018; Cade Metz and Raymond Zhong, "The Race Is on to Protect Data from the Next Leap in Computers. And China Has the Lead," *New York Times*, December 3, 2018; Abraham Newman, "China Is Reportedly Hacking the Computer Motherboards. The Economic Fallout Could Be Huge," *Washington Post*, October 4, 2018.

29. Andrea Gilli and Mauro Gilli, "Why China Has Not Caught Up Yet: Military-Technological Superiority and the Limits of Imitation, Reverse Engineering, and Cyber Espionage," *International Security* 43, issue 3 (2019): 141–89; Michael C. Horowitz, Shahryar Pasandideh, Andrea Gilli, and Mauro Gilli, "Correspondence: Military-Technological Imitation and Rising Powers," *International Security* 44, issue 2 (2019): 185–92; Stephen G. Brooks and William C. Wohlforth, "The Once and Future Superpower," *Foreign Affairs*, May/June 2016.

30. See, e.g., Dougherty, "Why America Needs a New Way of War"; Elsa Kania, "Learning Without Fighting: New Developments in PLA Artificial Intelligence War-Gaming," *China Brief*, April 9, 2019.

31. Tian, Fleurant, Kuimova, Wezeman, and Wezeman, "Trends in World Military Expenditure, 2018," 3; Todd Sandler and Justin George, "Military Expenditure Trends for 1960–2014 and What they Reveal," *Global Policy* 7, issue 2 (2016): 1–11.

32. "Xi Jinping Wants China's Armed Forces to Be 'World Class' by 2050," *The Economist*, June 27, 2019.

33. "Military and Security Developments Involving the People's Republic of China 2019," Department of Defense, Annual Report to Congress, May, 2, 2019. See also David M. Finkelstein, "Everything You Need to Know About the Chinese Military If You Don't Read Chinese," *U.S. Naval Institute*, June 2019.

34. James Mulvenon, "China's 'Goldwater-Nichols'? The Long-Awaited PLA Reorganization Has Finally Arrived," *China Leadership Monitor*, Hoover Institution, issue 49 (2016): 1–6; "Military Reform: Army Dreamers," *The Economist*, June 29–July 5, 2019. On the PLA's military innovation, see Elsa Kania, "The Chinese Military Reforms and Transforms in the 'New Era,' " *Jamestown Foundation*, August 14, 2019.

35. "The Long View: How Will the Global Economic Order Change by 2050?," *PricewaterhouseCoopers*, February 2017.

36. On India's rising share of global GDP growth, see Alex Tanzi, "A 3-Point Jump for India? Country's Share of Global GDP Growth Expected to Rise," *Hindustan Times*, October 29, 2018; Samir Saran, "As a Rising Power, What Is India's Vision for the World?," *World Economic Forum*, August 14, 2018; Wolf, "The Future Might Not Belong to China."

37. "Global Trends 2025: A Transformed World," *National Intelligence Council*; Acharya, *The End of American World Order*, vi.

38. Lawrence H. Summers, "Prophecies of American Decline Will Prove to Be Self-denying Once Again," *Herzliya Conference*, February 6, 2011. See also Samuel P. Huntington, "The U.S.—Decline or Renewal?," *Foreign Affairs*, Winter 1988/89.

39. David A. Baldwin, "Power Analysis and World Politics: New Trends versus Old Tendencies," *World Politics* 31, no. 2 (1979): 161–94.

40. Shifrinson and Beckley, "Correspondence: Debating China's Rise and U.S. Decline."

41. See, e.g., Ashley J. Tellis, Janice Bially, Christopher Layne, Melissa McPherson, and Jerry M. Sollinger, *Measuring National Power in the Postindustrial Age* (Santa Monica: RAND Corporation, 2000), xiii.

42. Jeremi Suri, "State Finance and National Power: Great Britain, China, and the United States in Historical Perspective," quoted in Jeremi Suri and Benjamin Valentino, eds., *Sustainable Security* (New York: Oxford University Press, 2016), 116.

43. See, e.g., William C. Wohlforth, "Realism and the End of the Cold War," *International Security* 19, no. 3 (Winter 1994–95): 91–129.

44. See, e.g., Angus Deaton, *The Great Escape: Health, Wealth, and the Origins of Inequality* (Princeton: Princeton University Press, 2015); Jim Edwards, "500 Years Ago, China Destroyed Its World-Dominating Navy Because Its Political Elite Was Afraid of Free Trade," *Independent*, March 5, 2017.

45. On the implications of perceiving decline as reversible or irreversible in the context of the Cold War, and on the role of time in revealing gaps between commitments and resources, see Wohlforth, "Realism and the End of the Cold War."

46. On the role of time in decision making and the rise of great powers, see Edelstein, *Over the Horizon*.

47. Baldwin, "Power Analysis and World Politics," 163.

48. See, e.g., John L. Gaddis, "International Relations Theory and the End of the Cold War," *International Security* 17, no. 3 (1992–93): 5–58; Erik Gartzke, "War Is in the Error Term," *International Organization* 53, issue 3 (1999): 567–87; Lawrence Freedman, *Strategy: A History* (Oxford: Oxford University Press, 2013).

49. On seeing diplomacy through the lenses of science and art, see David Milne, *Worldmaking: The Art and Science of American Diplomacy* (New York: Farrar, Straus and Giroux, 2015).

50. John G. Ruggie, "International Regimes, Transactions, and Change: Embedded Liberalism in the Postwar Economic Order," *International Organization* 36, issue 2 (1982): 379–415; Henry Kissinger, *World Order* (New York: Random House, 2014). On defining, measuring, and comparing different concepts of order, see Shiping Tang, "Order: A Conceptual Analysis," *Chinese Political Science Review* 1, issue 1 (2016): 30–46.

51. David Lake, "Escape from the State of Nature," *International Security* 32, no. 1 (2007): 54.

52. Geir Lundestad, "Empire by Invitation? The United States and Western Europe, 1945–1952," *Journal of Peace Research* 23, issue 3 (1986): 263–77.

53. Geir Lundestad, *"Empire" by Integration: The United States and European Integration, 1945–1997* (Oxford: Oxford University Press, 1998), 2.

54. Zbigniew Brzezinski, *Game Plan: How to Conduct the U.S.–Soviet Contest*, quoted in ibid., 3.

55. See, e.g., G. John Ikenberry, *After Victory: Institutions, Strategic Restraint and the Rebuilding of Order after Major Wars* (Princeton: Princeton University Press, 2001); Daniel Deudney and G. John Ikenberry, "The Myth of the Autocratic Revival," *Foreign Affairs*, January/February 2009. On the durability of international order and the role of "structural power" in maintaining the rules, institutions, and norms that comprise it, see Nicholas Kitchen and Michael Cox, "Power, Structural Power, and American Decline," *Cambridge Review of International Affairs* 32, issue 6 (2019): 734–52.

56. Hal Brands, "The Unexceptional Superpower: American Grand Strategy in the Age of Trump," *Survival* 59 (2017): 7–40.

57. On the core bargains of the post–World War II liberal order, see Ikenberry, *After Victory*; Richard Haass, "How a World Order Ends," *Foreign Affairs*, January/February 2019. See also Michael J. Mazarr, Miranda Priebe, Andrew Radin, and Astrid Stuth Cevallos, *Understanding the Current International Order* (Santa Monica: RAND Corporation, 2016), 23–26.

58. Daniel H. Nexon, "On American Hegemony, Part I," *Lawyers, Guns & Money*, July 27, 2018; Alexander D. Barder, "International Hierarchy," International Studies Compendium Project, Theory Section, *Oxford Research Encyclopedia of International Studies* (Oxford: Oxford University Press, 2017); Daniel H. Nexon and Iver B. Neumann, "Hegemonic-order Theory: A Field-theoretic Account," *European Journal of International Relations* 24, issue 3 (2018): 662–86.

59. Fareed Zakaria, "The Self-Destruction of American Power," *Foreign Affairs*, July/August 2019; Daniel W. Drezner, "This Time Is Different," *Foreign Affairs*, May/June 2019; Robert Jervis, "International Primacy: Is the Game Worth the Candle?," *International Security* 17, no. 4 (1993): 52–67.

60. Julie Ray, "World's Approval of U.S. Leadership Drops to New Low," *Gallup*, January 18, 2018; Julie Ray, "Image of U.S. Leadership Now Poorer than China's," *Gallup*, February 28, 2019.

61. Ray, "Image of U.S. Leadership Now Poorer than China's."

62. For global views of US power as a threat, see "Publics Around the World Increasingly See Climate Change, Cyberattacks and American Power as Threats," *Pew Research Center*, February 7, 2019; Jacob Poushter and Christine Huang, "Climate Change Still Seen as the Top Global Threat, but Cyberattacks a Rising Concern," *Pew Research Center*, February 10, 2019. More than 40 percent of Germans think that the United States is less reliable than China. For more on German perceptions of the United States under Trump, see Civey, "Wer ist der verlässlichere Partner für Deutschland: China oder die USA?," *Atlantik-Brücke*, December 2018, 8. According to one Allensbach survey, more Germans view the United States under Trump (56 percent) as a greater threat than North Korea (45 percent) or Russia (41 percent). See Matthias Kamann, "Die USA machen den Deutschen am meisten Angst," Allensbach-Studie, *Welt*, February 13, 2019.

63. Larry Diamond, "Democracy Demotion," *Foreign Affairs*, July/August 2019.

64. On the dynamics of "multi-power proxy interaction," see Heather A. Conley, "Transatlantic Relations: The Long Holiday from History Is Over," *College of Europe Policy Brief*, September 2019. See also Joshua Kurlantzick, *State Capitalism: How the Return of Statism Is Transforming the World* (Oxford: Oxford University Press, 2016); John Gapper, "Huawei Is Too Great a Security Gamble for 5G Networks," *Financial Times*, January

30, 2019; Markus Brunnermeier, Rush Doshi, and Harold James, "Beijing's Bismarckian Ghosts: How Great Powers Compete Economically," *The Washington Quarterly* 41, issue 3 (2018): 161–76.

65. See, e.g., Nye, *Is the American Century Over?*; William O. Walker, *The Rise and Decline of the American Century* (Ithaca: Cornell University Press, 2018).

66. See, e.g., Richard N. Haass, *Foreign Policy Begins at Home: The Case for Putting America's House in Order* (New York: Basic Books, 2014).

Chapter Two. Core or Periphery?

1. Barbara Salazar Torreon and Sofia Plagakis, "Instances of Use of United States Armed Forces Abroad, 1798–2019," *Congressional Research Service*, July 17, 2019.

2. Scholars have used the core–periphery model in different ways and for different purposes. My usage parallels that of Charles Kupchan in *Vulnerability of Empire* (Ithaca: Cornell University Press, 1996). Other works that employ variations of the core–periphery model include Immanuel Wallerstein, *The Modern World-System I: Capitalist Agriculture and the Origins of the European World-Economy in the Sixteenth Century* (Berkeley: University of California Press, 2011); Christopher Chase-Dunn, Yukio Kawano, and Benjamin D. Brewer, "Trade Globalization since 1795: Waves of Integration in the World-System," *American Sociological Review* 65, no. 1 (2000): 77–95; Thomas P. M. Barnett, *The Pentagon's New Map: War and Peace in the Twenty-First Century* (New York: Penguin Group, 2004); Salvatore J. Babones, "The Country-Level Income Structure of the World Economy," *Journal of World-Systems Research* 11, issue 1 (2005): 29–55. See also Posen, *Restraint*; Mearsheimer, *The Great Delusion*; Walt, *The Hell of Good Intentions*.

3. See, e.g., Ben Judah, *Fragile Empire: How Russia Fell In and Out of Love with Vladimir Putin* (New Haven: Yale University Press, 2014); Masha Gessen, *The Future Is History: How Totalitarianism Reclaimed Russia* (New York: Random House, 2017).

4. See, e.g., Robert Legvold, "Russian Foreign Policy During Periods of Great State Transformation," in Robert Legvold, ed., *Russian Foreign Policy in the 21st Century & The Shadow of the Past* (New York: Columbia University Press, 2007); Dmitry Trenin, *Russia* (New York: Polity, 2019).

5. Nicholas Eberstadt, "With Great Demographics Comes Great Power," *Foreign Affairs*, July/August 2019.

6. Huang, "What Western Observers Get Wrong in Assessing China."

7. See, e.g., Khanna, *The Future Is Asian*; Kurt M. Campbell and Jake Sullivan, "Competition without Catastrophe," *Foreign Affairs*, August 1, 2019.

8. Kupchan, *Vulnerability of Empire*.

9. "The Soviet Invasion of Afghanistan: Five Years Later: An Intelligence Assessment," Directorate of Intelligence, *CIA Historical Review Program*, 1999.

10. It is also worth noting the differences. For example, the Soviets took un-sustainable casualties, particularly after the United States introduced Stinger missiles into the conflict. Today, by contrast, the Afghan National Army has taken the lion's share of the casualties. The extreme brutality of the Soviet occupation also contrasts with the US approach.

11. John Pike, "Soviet Objectives in Afghanistan," *Global Security*. See also Nicholas J. Spykman, *America's Strategy in World Politics: The United States and the Balance of Power* (New York: Harcourt, 1942).

12. Tom Blanton and Svetlana Savranskaya, eds., "The Soviet Invasion of Af-ghanistan, 1979: Not Trump's Terrorists, Nor Zbig's Warm Water Ports," *National Security Archive*, Briefing Book #657, January 29, 2019.

13. Andrew Bennett, *Condemned to Repetition? The Rise, Fall, and Reprise of So-viet Russian Military Interventionism, 1973–1996* (Cambridge: MIT Press, 1999), 167–94.

14. Ibid.

15. Svetlana Savranskaya, ed., "Volume II: Afghanistan: Lessons from the Last War," *National Security Archive*, October 9, 2011.

16. Ibid.

17. Bennett, *Condemned to Repetition?*, 216–18.

18. "Domestic Costs to the Soviet Regime of Involvement in Afghanistan," Directorate of Intelligence, *Central Intelligence Agency*, October 25, 1984.

19. Leon Aron, "The Mystery of Soviet Collapse," *Journal of Democracy* 17, no. 2 (2006): 21–35.

20. Nicole Alie and Peter Gizewski, "Strategic Shock: The Collapse of the So-viet Union: 1989," *Center for Operational Research and Analysis*, August 2010.

21. Fred Coleman, *The Decline and Fall of the Soviet Empire: Forty Years that Shook the World, from Stalin to Yeltsin* (New York: St. Martin's Press, 1996), 209.

22. Stephen F. Cohen, *Soviet Fates and Lost Alternatives: From Stalinism to the New Cold War* (New York: Columbia University Press, 2009), 141.

23. Chris Miller, *The Struggle to Save the Soviet Economy: Mikhail Gorbachev and the Collapse of the USSR* (Chapel Hill: University of North Carolina Press, 2016).

24. Dan Berschinski, "Veterans' Day Special: An Afghan War Casualty Looks Back and Wonders Why," *Foreign Policy*, November 10, 2017.

25. According to the State Department "President Trump Was Clear That Military Power Alone Will Not End the War." See "Fact Sheet: U.S. Re-lations with Afghanistan," Bureau of South and Central Asian Affairs, US Department of State, July 26, 2018.

26. Robert Kaplan, "Time to Get Out of Afghanistan," *New York Times*, Janu-ary 1, 2019.

27. Jock Covey, Michael Dziedzic, and Leonard R. Hawley, eds., *The Quest for Viable Peace: International Intervention and Strategies for Conflict Transforma-tion* (Washington, DC: United States Institute of Peace, 2005), 42–43.

28. See, e.g., Charles Maier, *Among Empires: American Ascendancy and Its Predecessors* (Cambridge: Harvard University Press, 2007).

29. Stephen G. Brooks, *Producing Security: Multinational Corporations, Globalization, and the Changing Calculus of Conflict* (Princeton: Princeton University Press, 2005), 68–70.

30. David M. Edelstein, *Occupational Hazards: Success and Failure in Military Occupation* (Ithaca: Cornell University Press, 2011).

31. See, e.g., Parent and MacDonald, "The Wisdom of Retrenchment"; Kupchan, *Vulnerability of Empire*; Posen, *Restraint*; John J. Mearsheimer and Stephen M. Walt, "The Case for Offshore Balancing," *Foreign Affairs*, July/August 2016; Walt, *The Hell of Good Intentions*; Mearsheimer, *The Great Delusion*; Eugene Gholz, Daryl G. Press, and Harvey M. Sapolsky, "Come Home, America: The Strategy of Restraint in the Face of Temptation," *International Security* 21, issue 4 (1997): 5–48.

32. Celeste Wallander, "NATO's Enemies Within," *Foreign Affairs*, July/August 2018; Charles A. Kupchan, "The Battle Line for Western Values Runs Through Poland," *New York Times*, January 10, 2018; Agata Gostyńska-Jakubowska, "New Approaches to Upholding Democratic Values in Poland," *Carnegie Endowment for International Peace*, October 5, 2018; Richard Youngs, "After the Hungary Vote, EU Needs a Broader Approach to Halt Illiberal Slide," *Carnegie Endowment for International Peace*, September 13, 2018.

33. Walter Lippmann, *U.S. Foreign Policy: Shield of the Republic* (Boston: Little, Brown, 1943), 9.

34. See, e.g., Samuel P. Huntington, "Coping with the Lippmann Gap," *Foreign Affairs*, 1987/1988; Richard K. Betts, "A Disciplined Defense," *Foreign Affairs*, November/December 2007.

35. Michael J. Mazarr, "The Risks of Ignoring Strategic Insolvency," *Washington Quarterly* (Fall 2012), 13; Friedberg, *Weary Titan*, 189.

36. See, e.g., William J. Burns, "10 Parting Thoughts for America's Diplomats," *Foreign Policy*, October 23, 2014; Jon Finer and Robert Malley, "Trump Is Right to Seek an End to America's Wars," *New York Times*, January 8, 2019.

37. Rick Atkinson, "The Long, Blinding Road to War," *Washington Post*, March 7, 2004.

38. Gideon Rose, *How Wars End: Why We Always Fight the Last Battle* (New York: Simon & Schuster, 2011).

39. Gregory Feifer, *The Great Gamble: The Soviet War in Afghanistan* (New York: Harper Perennial, 2009), 290.

40. Leonard R. Hawley, "Interagency Planning for Crisis Intervention" (Unpublished paper, 2016), 1.

41. Daniel Byman, "Mr. Obama, Don't Draw That Line," *New York Times*, May 4, 2013.

42. The evidence on credibility in international relations is mixed. Some contend that past actions and reputations for resolve are decisive; others argue that the current balance of will and capabilities is what matters. On

the former, see Mark J. C. Crescenzi, Jacob Kathman, Katja B. Kleinberg, and Reed M. Wood, "Reliability, Reputation, and Alliance Formation," Paper prepared for the 2009 Annual Meeting of the American Political Science Association, Toronto, Canada; Alex Weisiger and Keren Yarhi-Milo, "Revisiting Reputation: How Past Actions Matter in International Politics," *International Organization* 69, no. 2 (2015): 481, 486. On the latter, see Daryl G. Press, *Calculating Credibility: How Leaders Assess Military Threats* (Ithaca: Cornell University Press, 2007). On backing down and the likelihood of enduring further challenges, see Paul Huth, Christopher Gelpi, and D. Scott Bennet, "The Escalation of Great Power Militarized Dispute: Testing Rational Deterrence Theory and Structural Realism," *American Political Science Review* 87, no. 3 (1993): 618.

43. Daniel Byman and Matthew Waxman, *The Dynamics of Coercion: American Foreign Policy and the Limits of Military Might* (Cambridge: Cambridge University Press, 2002); Hal Brands, Eric Edelman, and Thomas G. Mahnken, "Credibility Matters: Strengthening American Deterrence in an Age of Geopolitical Turmoil," *Center for Strategic and Budgetary Assessments*, May 9, 2018. Hal Brands and Peter D. Feaver, "What Are America's Alliances Good For?," *Parameters* 47, no. 2 (2017): 15–30.

44. MacDonald and Parent, *Twilight of the Titans*, 15. See also Craig S. Cohen, ed., "Capacity and Resolve: Foreign Assessment of U.S. Power," *Center for Strategic and International Studies*, June 2011.

45. See, e.g., Thomas J. Wright, *All Measures Short of War: The Contest for the 21st Century and the Future of American Power* (New Haven: Yale University Press, 2017).

46. To say nothing of the sacrifices of NATO and coalition troops or the many thousands of Afghans—military, police, and civilian—injured or killed over the course of this war. See "Afghanistan: Protection of Civilians in Armed Conflict Annual Report 2017," *United Nations Assistance Mission in Afghanistan*, February 15, 2018.

47. Rosella Cappella Zielinski, "U.S. Wars Abroad Increase Inequality at Home," *Foreign Affairs*, October 5, 2018.

Chapter Three. Butter or Guns?

1. "Innovation at DARPA," *DARPA*, July 2016.

2. Renee D. Wegrzyn, "Setting a Safe Course for Gene Editing Research," Presentation at the 2017 Department of Energy Joint Genome Institute User Meeting, March 22, 2017.

3. Ibid.

4. Renee D. Wegrzyn, "Engineering Gene Safety," *The Long Now Foundation*, October 30, 2017.

5. Walter Isaacson, *The Innovators: How a Group of Hackers, Geniuses, and Geeks Created the Digital Revolution* (New York: Simon & Schuster, 2015).

6. On balancing ends and means in grand strategy, see John L. Gaddis, *On Grand Strategy* (New York: Random House, 2018). See also Paul Poast, "Beyond the 'Sinew of War': The Political Economy of Security as a Subfield," *Annual Review of Political Science* 22 (2019): 225.

7. Poast, "Beyond the 'Sinew of War,' " 225.

8. Kennedy, *The Rise and Fall of the Great Powers*, xvi.

9. Ibid.; Poast, "Beyond the 'Sinew of War' "; Michael R. Brawley, *Political Economy and Grand Strategy: A Neoclassical Realist View* (London: Routledge, 2009); Stephen. G. Brooks and William Wohlforth, *America Abroad: The United States' Global Role in the 21st Century* (Oxford: Oxford University Press, 2016).

10. "April 16, 1953: Chance for Peace," *UVA Miller Center*, accessed August 2019.

11. Poast, "Beyond the 'Sinew of War,' " 225.

12. "Dwight D. Eisenhower and Science & Technology," Dwight D. Eisenhower Memorial Commission, November 2008. During the administration of President Lyndon B. Johnson, his staff pushed for redefining DARPA's mission, then referred to as ARPA. As the authors Matthew Lyon and Katie Hafner note, "The staff of ARPA saw an opportunity to redefine the agency as a group that would take on the really advanced 'far-out' research." See Lyon and Hafner, *Where Wizards Stay Up Late: The Origins of the Internet* (New York: Simon & Schuster, 1998), 22.

13. On the argument that defense spending supports the middle class, see Hal Brands, "Progressives Should Learn to Love the Pentagon Budget," *Bloomberg*, March 17, 2019. On local perceptions of the defense budget in Ohio, see Salman Ahmed et al., "U.S. Foreign Policy for the Middle Class: Perspectives from Ohio," *Carnegie Endowment for International Peace*, December 10, 2018.

14. The author wishes to acknowledge the insights of Paul MacDonald of Wellesley College. See Errol Anthony Henderson, "Military Spending and Poverty," *Journal of Politics* 60, issue 2 (1998): 503–20; John D. Abell, "Military Spending and Income Inequality," *Journal of Peace Research* 31, issue 1 (1994): 35–43.

15. Daniel Drezner, "Military Primacy Doesn't Pay (Nearly as Much as You Think)," *International Security* 38, issue 1 (2013): 52–79. As Paul Stares of the Council on Foreign Relations notes, "By some calculations, a dollar spent on defense makes less of a contribution to the economy than other types of government spending." See Paul Stares, *Preventive Engagement: How America Can Avoid War, Stay Strong, and Keep the Peace* (New York: Columbia University Press, 2017), 15; David A. Shlapak, "Towards a More Modest American Strategy," *Survival* 57, no. 2 (2015): 59–78.

16. Robert Pollin and Heidi Garrett-Peltier, "The U.S. Employment Effects of Military and Domestic Spending Priorities," *Political Economy Research Institute*, University of Massachusetts, Amherst, December 2011; Uk Heo

and Robert J. Eger III, "Paying for Security: The Security–Prosperity Dilemma in the United States," *Journal of Conflict Resolution* 49, issue 5 (2005): 792–817.

17. "Federal Policies and Innovation," *Congressional Budget Office*, November 2014; Fareed Zakaria, "American Innovation Is in Trouble," *Washington Post*, January 1, 2015; Margaret O'Mara, "Silicon Valley Can't Escape the Business of War," *New York Times*, October 26, 2018; Anthony J. Blinken, "Trump Is Ceding Global Leadership to China," *New York Times*, November 8, 2017.

18. James N. Miller and Michael O'Hanlon, "Quality over Quantity: U.S. Military Strategy and Spending in the Trump Years," *Brookings Institution*, January 2019; Eric Edelman and Gary Roughead, co-chairs, "Providing for the Common Defense: The Assessment and Recommendations of the National Defense Strategy Commission," November 14, 2018, vi–vii; Susanna V. Blume, "What's Wrong with the Defense Department's 2019 Budget Request and What Congress Can Do to Fix It," *War on the Rocks*, May 15, 2018.

19. "People, product and process" is common shorthand for innovation among the business community.

20. Tellis et al., *Measuring National Power in the Postindustrial Age*, 47.

21. Robert Litan, "Start-up Slowdown," *Foreign Affairs*, January/February 2015.

22. Sally French, "China Has 9 of the World's 20 Biggest Tech Companies," *MarketWatch*, May 31, 2018.

23. Edward Luce, *It's Time to Start Thinking: America in the Age of Descent* (New York: Atlantic Monthly Press, 2012); Drew DeSilver, "U.S. Students' Academic Achievement Still Lags That of Their Peers in Many Other Countries," *Pew Research Center*, February 15, 2017. See also Michael S. Teitelbaum, *Falling Behind? Boom, Bust, and the Global Race for Scientific Talent* (Princeton: Princeton University Press, 2014).

24. "Rapid Rise of China's STEM Workforce Charted by National Science Board Report," *American Institute of Physics*, January 31, 2018; Jonathan Gruber and Simon Johnson, "To Counter China, Out-Invent It," *Foreign Affairs*, September 12, 2019.

25. Field Cady and Oren Etzioni, "China May Overtake US in AI Research," *Medium*, March 13, 2019.

26. "Tsinghua University May Soon Top the World League in Science Research," *The Economist*, November 17, 2018. The share of top paper awards in prominent conferences is a helpful indicator, but it is also subject to various measurement biases, such as self-citation and difficulties in ascertaining the origins of publications.

27. "Failure to Act: Closing the Infrastructure Investment Gap for America's Economic Future," *American Society of Civil Engineers*, 2016.

28. Brian Harding, "China's Digital Silk Road and Southeast Asia," *Center for Strategic and International Studies*, February 15, 2019. China extends its

influence through the Belt and Road Initiative, but its model of debt-trap diplomacy and lack of transparency have encountered resistance in several countries. See James Schwemlein, "What Pakistan and Malaysia Could Teach Both China and the U.S. About the Belt and Road Initiative," *South China Morning Post*, November 5, 2018.

29. Ibid.

30. Mariana Mazzucato, "The Innovative State," *Foreign Affairs*, January/February 2015. See also Mariana Mazzucato, *The Entrepreneurial State: Debunking Public vs. Private Sector Myths* (London: Anthem Press, 2013). On the role of the "national security state" in driving technological innovation in the United States, see Linda Weiss, *America Inc.? Innovation and Enterprise in the National Security State* (Ithaca: Cornell University Press, 2014).

31. Peter Dizikes, "Jump-starting the Economy with Science," *MIT News*, April 17, 2019.

32. Jonathan Gruber and Simon Johnson, *Jump-starting America: How Breakthrough Science Can Revive Economic Growth and the American Dream* (New York: Public Affairs, 2019), 119.

33. See, e.g., Miller and O'Hanlon, "Quality over Quantity."

34. See, e.g., Edelman and Roughead, "Providing for the Common Defense"; Dougherty, "Why America Needs a New Way of War."

35. Based on author calculations of Function 150 (International Affairs) and Function 050 (National Defense) spending for Fiscal Year 2019.

36. U.S. Global Leadership Coalition, "China Is Outpacing and Outspending US in Diplomacy and Development," *Global Trade*, August 30, 2018.

37. Eric Katz, "Trump's Budget Will Require 10 Percent Spending Cuts at Non-Defense Agencies," *Government Executive*, February 27, 2017; Dan De Luce, "State Department, USAID Face Drastic Budget Cut," *Foreign Policy*, February 12, 2018.

38. Zach Silberman, "The Military Understands Smart Power," *U.S. Global Leadership Coalition*, March 8, 2013.

39. Lawrence J. Korb, "Assessing the Debates: Development, Diplomacy, and Defense as a Policy Framework," *Center for American Progress*, March 20, 2009, 1.

40. David Stevenson, "Militarization and Diplomacy in Europe before 1914," *International Security* 22, no. 1 (1997): 125–61.

41. James F. Jeffrey, "To Save the State Department, Rex Tillerson May Have to Break It," *Foreign Policy*, March 3, 2017.

42. Richard K. Betts, "U.S. National Security Strategy: Lenses and Landmarks," Paper presented for the launch conference of the Princeton Project "Toward a New National Security Strategy," November 2004, 9.

43. Ibid., 31.

44. Amber Marcellino, "CBO's Projections of Spending for the 2018–2028 Period," *Congressional Budget Office*, April 17, 2018.

45. "The 2019 Annual Report of the Board of Trustees of the Federal Old-Age and Survivors Insurance and Federal Disability Insurance Trust Funds," *Board of Trustees, Federal Old-Age and Survivors Insurance and Federal Disability Insurance Trust Funds*, Washington, DC, April 25, 2019; Jeanne Sahadi, "Social Security Must Reduce Benefits in 2034 if Reforms Aren't Made," *CNN*, June 5, 2018.

46. "Budget Basics: Medicare," *Peter G. Peterson Foundation*, April 30, 2019.

47. Michael D. Tanner, "America's Entitlement Crisis Just Keeps Growing," *National Review*, June 13, 2018.

48. Jason Furman and Lawrence H. Summers, "Who's Afraid of Budget Deficits? How Washington Should End Its Debt Obsession," *Foreign Affairs*, January 27, 2019.

49. "The 2019 Long-Term Budget Outlook," *Congressional Budget Office*, June 2019.

50. Gillian Tett, "Investors Start to Fret about Ballooning US Public Debt," *Financial Times*, November 8, 2018; Fareed Zakaria, "Are We at 'Peak America'?," *Washington Post*, November 29, 2018.

51. Dan Keeler, "How the Ballooning Federal Debt Threatens U.S. Defense," *Brookings Institution*, June 27, 2018.

52. Michael Pettis, "Why U.S. Debt Must Continue to Rise," *Carnegie Endowment for International Peace*, February 7, 2019.

53. Andy W. Marshall, "Long-Term Competition with the Soviets: A Framework for Strategic Analysis" (Santa Monica: RAND Corporation, 1972). In the present context, see Thomas Wright, "Trump's Mystifying Victory Lap at the UN," *The Atlantic*, September 26, 2018. Wess Mitchell notes that Habsburg financial imbalances left it exposed to powers that could pursue sizable arms buildups and draw out the costs of war. See A. Wess Mitchell, *The Grand Strategy of the Habsburg Empire* (Princeton: Princeton University Press, 2018), 326.

54. Michael Mastanduno, "System Maker and Privilege Taker: US Power and the International Political Economy," *World Politics* 61, no. 1 (2009): 121–54. On the structural advantages of American hegemony, see Carla Norrlof, *America's Global Advantage: U.S. Hegemony and International Cooperation* (Cambridge: Cambridge University Press, 2010).

55. Mastanduno, "System Maker and Privilege Taker."

56. Daniel Drezner, "Why I'm Starting to Worry about the US Dollar," *Washington Post*, November 16, 2018.

57. Ibid.

58. On America's financial staying power, the author wishes to acknowledge the insights of Mark Copelovitch, professor of political science and public affairs at the University of Wisconsin.

59. See, e.g., Subramanian, *Eclipse*, 8–9; Abraham Newman, "The Wrong Way to Punish Iran," *New York Times*, November 1, 2018; Ian Talley and Isabel Coles, "U.S. Warns Iraq It Risks Losing Access to Key Bank Account if Troops Told to Leave," *Wall Street Journal*, January 11, 2020.

60. Drezner, "Why I'm Starting to Worry about the US Dollar." See also Edward Luce, "Donald Trump Is Jeopardizing the Dollar's Supremacy," *Financial Times*, May 30, 2018; Jeffrey D. Sachs, "Trump's Politics Will Displace the Dollar," *Project Syndicate*, September 3, 2018.

61. On the relationship between debt and growth, see Manmohan Kumar and Jaejoon Woo, *Public Debt and Growth*, Working Paper 10/174, *International Monetary Fund*, Washington, DC, 2010.

62. Michael Pettis, "Why U.S. Debt Must Continue to Rise," *Carnegie Endowment for International Peace*, February 7, 2019.

63. Furman and Summers, "Who's Afraid of Budget Deficits?"

64. "Mullen: Debt Is Top National Security Threat," *CNN*, August 27, 2010.

65. Miller and O'Hanlon, "Quality over Quantity."

66. See, e.g., Steven Erlanger and Katrin Bennhold, "Rift Between Trump and Europe Is Now Open and Angry," *New York Times*, February 17, 2019.

67. On corporate tax reform and "expensing," see Furman and Summers, "Who's Afraid of Budget Deficits?"

68. Carlo M. Cipolla, *The Economic Decline of Empires* (London: Methuen, 1970), 15.

69. Suri, "State Finance and National Power.

70. Earl J. Hamilton, "Revisions in Economic History: VIII.—The Decline of Spain," *Economic History Review* 8, no. 2 (May, 1938): 169.

71. See, e.g., Jan Glete, *War and the State in Early Modern Europe: Spain, the Dutch Republic, and Sweden as Fiscal-Military States, 1500–1660* (London: Routledge, 2001).

72. Ruth Mackay, *'Lazy, Improvident People': Myth and Reality in the Writing of Spanish History* (Ithaca: Cornell University Press, 2006), 237.

73. Cipolla, *The Economic Decline of Empires*; Kennedy, *The Rise and Fall of the Great Powers*.

74. Cipolla, *The Economic Decline of Empires*, 123.

75. Ibid., 134.

76. Ibid., 161.

77. Kennedy, *The Rise and Fall of the Great Powers*, 48.

78. Ibid., 54.

79. Cipolla, *The Economic Decline of Empires*, 185.

80. Ibid.

81. Rafael Torres Sánchez, *Constructing a Fiscal-Military State in Eighteenth-Century Spain* (Basingstoke: Palgrave Macmillan, 2015), 3–4.

82. Aaron Graham, "Review of Rafael Torres Sánchez, 'Constructing a fiscal-military state in eighteenth century Spain,'" *Economic History Review* (2016): 387–88.

83. Sánchez, *Constructing a Fiscal-Military State in Eighteenth-Century Spain*, 77.

84. Neustadt and May, *Thinking in Time*, 12.

85. Hal Brands, "The Lost Art of Long-term Competition," *The Washington Quarterly* 41, issue 4 (2018): 41; Edelstein, *Over the Horizon*.

86. Hal Brands and William Inboden, "Wisdom through Tears: Statecraft and the Uses of History," *Survival* 41, issue 7 (2018): 916–46.

87. Niccolò Machiavelli, *The Prince* (Chicago: University of Chicago Press, 1998). See also Gaddis, *On Grand Strategy*; Steven B. Smith, "Lecture 11—New Modes and Orders: Machiavelli, The Prince (chaps. 13–26)," Yale University.

88. John L. Gaddis, *Surprise, Security and the American Experience* (Cambridge: Harvard University Press, 2005).

89. Casimir Yost, "Grand Strategy and Strategic Surprise," *Institute for the Study of Diplomacy*, Georgetown University, iii.

90. Patrick Doherty, "A New U.S. Grand Strategy," *Foreign Policy*, January 9, 2013.

91. On the crucial link between economic and security policy in the early Cold War, see Melvyn P. Leffler, *A Preponderance of Power: National Security, the Truman Administration, and the Cold War* (Stanford: Stanford University Press, 1993). On the connections between US foreign and economic policy today, see Ahmed et al. "U.S. Foreign Policy for the Middle Class"; Heather Hurlburt, "Security Policy Is Economic Policy," *Journal of Democracy*, no. 48 (2018).

92. See, e.g., Doherty, "A New U.S. Grand Strategy"; Sarah Chayes, *Thieves of State: Why Corruption Threatens Global Security* (New York: W. W. Norton, 2015).

93. Lindsey Ford, "The 'Lippmann Gap' in Asia: Four Challenges to a Credible U.S. Strategy," *War on the Rocks*, December 3, 2018; Ketian Zhang, "Cautious Bully: Reputation, Resolve, and Beijing's Use of Coercion in the South China Sea," *International Security* 44, issue 1 (2019): 117–59; Hal Brands, "How to Wage Political Warfare," *National Interest*, December 16, 2017.

94. Brunnermeier, Doshi, and James, "Beijing's Bismarckian Ghosts," 166.

95. David Ignatius, "The U.S. Needs to Learn How to Win Wars without Fighting," *Washington Post*, November 29, 2018.

96. Glenn Thrush and Coral Davenport, "Donald Trump Budget Slashes Funds for E.P.A. and State Department," *New York Times*, March 15, 2017.

97. On the requirements for military modernization, see Miller and O'Hanlon, "Quality over Quantity"; Mara Karlin, "Recommendations for Future National Defense Strategy," *Brookings Institution*, December 2017; Susanna Blume, "What's Wrong with the Defense Department's

2019 Budget Request—and What Congress Can Do to Fix It," *War on the Rocks,* May 15, 2018; Christian Brose, "The New Revolution in Military Affairs," *Foreign Affairs,* May/June 2019.

98. James Manyika, Jaana Remes, Jan Mischke, and Mekala Krishnan, "The Productivity Puzzle: A Closer Look at the United States," *McKinsey Global Institute,* March 2017, 3. See also Robert J. Gordon, *The Rise and Fall of American Growth* (Princeton: Princeton University Press, 2017).

99. Measuring productivity beyond the superficially obvious is difficult. See, e.g., Lawrence H. Summers, "The Age of Secular Stagnation," *Foreign Affairs,* March/April 2016; Paul Krugman, "Monetary Policy in a Liquidity Trap," *New York Times,* April 11, 2013; Ben S. Bernanke, "Why Are Interest Rates So Low, Part 3: The Global Savings Glut," *Brookings Institution,* April 1, 2015; Robert M. Solow, "We'd Better Watch Out," *New York Times Book Review,* June 12, 1987; Martin Wolf, "The Long Wait for a Productivity Resurgence," *Financial Times,* June 12, 2018; "The Next Capitalist Revolution," *The Economist,* November 17–23, 2018.

100. Melissa Flagg, "Running Joyfully into the Endless Frontier of Science," *Medium,* January 31, 2018.

101. The author wishes to acknowledge the insights of Melissa Flagg, former US deputy assistant secretary of defense for research at the Department of Defense.

102. Mary Catherine O'Connor, "A Conversation with Arati Prabhakar, former DARPA director, on how to improve our R&D ecosystem," *Medium,* August 3, 2018.

103. Bret Stephens, "Our Real Immigration Problem," *New York Times,* June 21, 2018.

104. Ruchir Sharma, "The Demographics of Stagnation: Why People Matter for Economic Growth," *Foreign Affairs,* March/April 2016.

105. Nicholas Eberstadt, "With Great Demographics Comes Great Power," *Foreign Affairs,* July/August 2019.

106. On the rate at which immigrants start businesses compared to native-born Americans, see Dane Stangler and Jason Wiens, "The Economic Case for Welcoming Immigrant Entrepreneurs," *Kauffman Foundation,* September 8, 2015. On whether illegal immigrants are more likely to commit a crime than ordinary citizens, see Alex Nowrashteh, "Illegal Immigrants and Crime—Assessing the Evidence," *CATO,* March 4, 2019; Christopher Ingraham, "Two Charts Demolish the Notion That Immigrants Here Illegally Commit More Crime," *Washington Post,* June 19, 2018.

107. "Charlemagne: Waiting for Godot," *The Economist,* October 13, 2018.

Chapter Four. Allies or Autonomy?

1. Richard Nixon, "Address to the Nation Announcing an Agreement on Ending the War in Vietnam," January 23, 1973.

2. Barbara W. Tuchman, *The Guns of August* (New York: Ballantine Books, 1994), 381.

3. Franklin D. Roosevelt, "Fourth Inaugural Address," January 20, 1945.

4. On NATO as being "obsolete," see Cyra Master, "Trump Tells German Paper: NATO Is 'Obsolete,' " *The Hill*, January 15, 2017. On NATO as an anchor of liberal order, see Richard Conner, "Angela Merkel Warns of Global Political Disintegration at Munich Security Conference," *DW*, February 16, 2019; Paul D. Miller, "This Is How the Liberal Order Dies," *Atlantic Council*, July 12, 2018. On critiques of NATO as a protection racket and why those critiques are misplaced, see Michael McFaul, "Mr. Trump, NATO Is an Alliance, Not a Protection Racket," *Washington Post*, July 25, 2016. On NATO as a "security community," see Michael C. Williams and Iver B. Neumann, "From Alliance to Security Community: NATO, Russia, and the Power of Identity," *Millennium* 29, no. 2 (2000): 357–87; Emanuel Adler and Michael Barnett, eds., *Security Communities* (Cambridge: Cambridge University Press, 1998).

5. Thucydides quoted in Robert B. Strassler, ed., *The Landmark Thucydides: A Comprehensive Guide to the Peloponnesian War* (New York: Simon & Schuster, 1996), 16.

6. Gaddis, *On Grand Strategy*, 38–58.

7. Thucydides quoted in Strassler, ed., *The Landmark Thucydides*, 352.

8. Rick Berger, " 'Cost Plus 50' and Bringing U.S. Troops Home: A Look at the Numbers," *War on the Rocks*, March 15, 2019.

9. While not formally an alliance, military cooperation between Russia and China is growing. In the summer of 2019 Russia and China conducted a joint air patrol over the Sea of Japan, causing South Korea to scramble its fighter jets and fire warning shots. See "Russia and South Korea Spar over Airspace 'Intrusion,' " *BBC News*, July 24, 2019.

10. See, e.g., Stephen D. Krasner, ed., *International Regimes* (Ithaca: Cornell University Press, 1983); Robert Keohane, *Cooperation and Discord in the World Political Economy* (Princeton: Princeton University Press, 1984); Robert Powell, "Anarchy in International Relations Theory: The Neorealist–Neoliberal Debate," *International Organization* 48 (1994): 313–44; Ikenberry, *After Victory*.

11. Stephen M. Walt, "Why Alliances Endure or Collapse," *Survival* 39, no. 1 (1997): 157–58.

12. See, e.g., Mira Rapp-Hooper, *Shields of the Republic: The Triumph and Peril of America's Alliances* (Cambridge: Harvard University Press, 2020).

13. See, e.g., Kenneth N. Waltz, *Theory of International Politics* (New York: McGraw-Hill, 1979); Walt, "Why Alliances Endure or Collapse"; John J. Mearsheimer, *The Tragedy of Great Power Politics* (New York: W. W. Norton, 2001); Randall L. Schweller, "Bandwagoning for Profit: Bringing the Revisionist State Back In," *International Security* 19, no. 1 (1994): 72–107.

14. Richard Fontaine, "Trump Gets NATO Backwards," *The Atlantic*, November 15, 2018.

15. John S. Duffield, "NATO's Functions after the Cold War," *Political Science Quarterly* 109, no. 5 (1994–95): 763–87.

16. George Washington, "Farewell Address," September 19, 1796.

17. Thomas Jefferson, "First Inaugural Address," March 4, 1801.

18. Charles N. Edel, *Nation Builder: John Quincy Adams and the Grand Strategy of the Republic* (Cambridge: Harvard University Press, 2014), 300.

19. David Fromkin, "Entangling Alliances," *Foreign Affairs*, July 1970.

20. G. John Ikenberry, "Power and Liberal Order: America's Postwar World Order in Transition," *International Relations of the Asia-Pacific* 5, issue 2 (2005): 133–52.

21. On the "three temptations" of geography, technology, and ideology, see Jakub J. Grygiel and A. Wess Mitchell, *The Unquiet Frontier: Rising Rivals, Vulnerable Allies, and the Crisis of American Power* (Princeton: Princeton University Press, 2016), 17–28.

22. See, e.g., Peter Beinart, "America Needs an Entirely New Foreign Policy for the Trump Age," *The Atlantic*, September 16, 2018. On restraint, see Posen, *Restraint*. On offshore balancing, see Mearsheimer and Walt, "The Case for Offshore Balancing."

23. Charles Edel and Hal Brands, "The Disharmony of the Spheres," *Commentary*, December 2017.

24. In the Asia-Pacific context, see Michael J. Green, *Grand Strategy and American Power in the Asia-Pacific since 1783* (New York: Columbia University Press, 2017). In the European context, see Melvyn P. Leffler, *Safeguarding Democratic Capitalism: U.S. Foreign Policy and National Security, 1920–2015* (Princeton: Princeton University Press, 2017).

25. Robert Kagan, "Trump's America Does Not Care," *Washington Post*, June 14, 2018.

26. Julian E. Barnes and Helene Cooper, "Trump Discussed Pulling U.S. from NATO, Aides Say, Amid New Concerns over Russia," *New York Times*, January 14, 2019.

27. Jane Cai, "Why Donald Trump's Threatened Trade War with China Could Also Hurt South Korea, Japan and Taiwan," *South China Morning Post*, June 27, 2018; Ryan Hass, "On U.S.–China Trade, America Is Off Track," *Brookings Institution*, June 24, 2019.

28. "Japan Is Worried about Its Alliance with America," *The Economist*, September 6, 2018.

29. Eric Schmitt, "Pentagon and Seoul Surprised by Trump Pledge to Halt Military Exercises," *New York Times*, June 12, 2018.

30. Daniel R. Coats, "Statement for the Record: Worldwide Threat Assessment of the U.S. Intelligence Community," *Senate Select Committee on Intelligence*, January 29, 2019.

31. These and other benefits are developed in Brands and Feaver, "What Are America's Alliances Good For?," 15–30.

32. Michael J. Lostumbo et al., "Overseas Basing of U.S. Military Forces: An Assessment of Relative Costs and Strategic Benefits," *RAND National Defense Research Institute*, 2013.

33. Stephen G. Brooks, G. John Ikenberry, and William C. Wohlforth, "Lean Forward: In Defense of American Engagement," *Foreign Affairs*, January/February 2013.

34. Brett A. Leeds, "Do Alliances Deter Aggression? The Influence of Military Alliances on the Initiative of Militarized Interstate Disputes," *American Journal of Political Science* 47, no. 3 (July 2003): 427–39.

35. See, e.g., Francis J. Gavin, "Strategies of Inhibition: U.S. Grand Strategy, the Nuclear Revolution, and Non-proliferation," *International Security* 40, no. 1 (2015): 9–46; Jeremy Pressman, *Warring Friends: Alliance Restraint in International Politics* (Ithaca: Cornell University Press, 2008).

36. Nigel Thalakada, *Unipolarity and the Evolution of America's Cold War Alliances* (New York: Palgrave Macmillan 2012); Hal Brands, "Fools Rush Out? The Flawed Logic of Offshore Balancing," *Washington Quarterly* 38, no. 2 (2015): 7–28.

37. Stephen G. Brooks, G. John Ikenberry, and William Wohlforth, "Don't Come Home, America: The Case against Retrenchment," *International Security* 37, no. 3 (2012/13): 7–51; Francis Gavin, *Gold, Dollars, and Power: The Politics of International Monetary Relations, 1958–1971* (Chapel Hill: University of North Carolina Press, 2004). On the economic benefits of America's security guarantees, see Norrlof, *America's Global Advantage*.

38. Nexon, "On American Hegemony, Part I." See also Abraham Newman and Daniel H. Nexon, "Trump Says American Allies Should Spend More on Defense. Here's Why He's Wrong," *Vox*, February 16, 2017.

39. Ashley J. Tellis, "Seeking Alliances and Partnerships: The Long Road to Confederationism in U.S. Grand Strategy," quoted in Ashley J. Tellis, Abraham M. Denmark, and Greg Chaffin, eds., *Strategic Asia 2014–15: U.S. Alliances and Partnerships at the Center of Global Power* (Washington, DC: National Bureau of Asian Research, 2014).

40. Martha Finnemore, "Legitimacy, Hypocrisy, and the Social Structure of Unipolarity: Why Being a Unipole Isn't All It's Cracked Up to Be," *World Politics* 61, no. 1 (2009): 58–85; Brands and Feaver, "What Are America's Alliances Good For?," 26–27; Joseph M. Grieco et al., "Let's Get a Second Opinion: International Institutions and American Public Support for War," *International Studies Quarterly* 55, no. 2 (2011): 563–83.

41. Glenn H. Snyder, "The Security Dilemma in Alliance Politics," *World Politics* 36, no. 4 (July 1984): 461–95.
42. Ibid.
43. Michael Beckley, "The Myth of Entangling Alliances: Reassessing the Security Risks of U.S. Defense Pacts," *International Security* 39, no. 4 (2015): 7–48; Tongfi Kim, "Why Alliances Entangle but Seldom Entrap," *Security Studies* 20, issue 3 (2011): 350–77.
44. David M. Edelstein and Joshua R. Itzkowitz Shifrinson, "It's a Trap! Security Commitments and the Risks of Entrapment," quoted in Ben Friedman and Trevor Thrall, eds., *The Case for Restraint in U.S. Foreign Policy* (New York: Routledge, 2018).
45. Marc Trachtenberg, *A Constructed Peace: The Making of the European Settlement, 1945–1963* (Princeton: Princeton University Press, 1999), 153.
46. Zack Beauchamp, "How Trump Is Killing America's alliances," *Vox*, June 12, 2018.
47. Mark Trachtenberg, "The Structure of Great Power Politics, 1963–1975," in Melvyn P. Leffler and Odd Arne Westad, eds., *The Cambridge History of the Cold War II: Crises and Détente* (Cambridge: University Press, 2010), 482–502.
48. See, e.g., Henry Kissinger, *Diplomacy* (New York: Simon & Schuster, 1994), 601–2.
49. According to a RAND study, "As currently postured, NATO cannot successfully defend the territory of its most exposed members. Across multiple games using a wide range of expert participants in and out of uniform playing both sides, the longest it has taken Russian forces to reach the outskirts of the Estonian and/or Latvian capitals of Tallinn and Riga, respectively, is 60 hours. Such a rapid defeat would leave NATO with a limited number of options." David A. Shlapak and Michael Johnson, *Reinforcing Deterrence on NATO's Eastern Flank: Wargaming the Defense of the Baltics* (Santa Monica: RAND Corporation, 2016). See also Josh Shifrinson, "Time to Consolidate NATO," *Washington Quarterly* (2017): 109–23; Scott Boston, Michael Johnson, Nathan Beauchamp-Mustafaga, and Yvonne. K. Crane, *Assessing the Conventional Force Imbalance in Europe: Implications for Countering Russian Local Superiority* (Santa Monica: RAND Corporation, 2018).
50. Ibid.
51. In an interview with David Sanger and Maggie Haberman of the *New York Times*, President Trump said of America's allies, "With massive wealth. Massive wealth. We're talking about countries that are doing very well. Then yes, I would be absolutely prepared to tell those countries, 'Congratulations, you will be defending yourself.'" See "Transcript: Donald Trump on NATO, Turkey's Coup Attempt and the World," *New York Times*, July 21, 2016.

52. Glenn H. Snyder, "Mearsheimer's World-Offensive Realism and the Struggle for Security: A Review Essay," *International Security* 27, no. 1 (2002): 165–66.

53. Jeffrey F. Taliaferro, "Security Seeking under Anarchy: Defensive Realism Revisited," *International Security* 25 (2000–2001): 145–47.

54. See, e.g., Kupchan, *Vulnerability of Empire*.

55. Paul Schroeder, "Historical Reality vs. Neo-Realist Theory," *International Security* 19, no. 1 (1994): 108–48.

56. István Diószegi, *Hungarians in the Ballhausplatz: Studies on the Austro-Hungarian Common Foreign Policy*, 1983, quoted in Alan Sked, *The Decline and Fall of the Habsburg Empire, 1815–1918* (New York: Longman 1994), 1.

57. I draw especially on Wess Mitchell's history of Habsburg grand strategy for this case study. See Mitchell, *The Grand Strategy of the Habsburg Empire*, 9.

58. Charles W. Ingrao, *The Habsburg Monarchy, 1618–1815* (Cambridge: Cambridge University Press, 2000), 2.

59. Mitchell, *The Grand Strategy of the Habsburg Empire*, 21–51.

60. On the Habsburg Monarchy's use of time as a strategic asset, see ibid.

61. Ibid., 82–117.

62. Pieter M. Judson, *The Habsburg Empire: A New History* (Cambridge: Belknap Press of Harvard University Press, 2016), 24–26.

63. Mitchell, *The Grand Strategy of the Habsburg Empire*, 174.

64. Ibid., 173–85. See also Judson, *The Habsburg Empire*, 26–29.

65. Franz A. J. Szabo, *The Seven Years War in Europe* (London: Routledge, 2007). The competitive dynamics and tensions between allies are covered in Marco Cesa, *Allies Yet Rivals: International Politics in 18th Century Europe* (Stanford: Stanford University Press, 2010).

66. Mitchell, *The Grand Strategy of the Hapsburg Empire*, 151–52.

67. Kaunitz, quoted in ibid., 151.

68. The author wishes to acknowledge the insights of Jakub Grygiel of Catholic University of America.

69. Brad L. LeVeck and Neil Narang, "How International Reputation Matters: Revisiting Alliance Violations in Context," *International Interactions* 43, issue 5 (2017): 797–821; Beauchamp, "How Trump Is Killing America's Alliances."

70. Brands and Feaver, "What Are America's Alliances Good For?," 28–29; Robert J. Art, *A Grand Strategy for America* (Ithaca: Cornell University Press, 2003), 201–2.

71. On the decline of US allies, see Brands, "Dealing with Allies in Decline"; Yascha Mounk and Roberto Stefan Foa define the liberal democratic alliance to include "the West's Cold War alliance against the Soviet Union—in North America, western Europe, Australasia, and postwar Japan," and argue that "now, for the first time in over a hundred years, its share of

global GDP has fallen below half." See Mounk and Foa, "The End of the Democratic Century."

72. Todd Harrison and Seamus P. Daniels, "Bad Idea: Demanding Allies Spend Two Percent of GDP on Defense," *Defense 360*, December 21, 2018; Azita Raji, "Salvaging Trump's Legacy in Europe: Fixing NATO Burden-Sharing," *War on the Rocks*, February 26, 2018.

73. Anthony H. Cordesman, "NATO: Going from the 2% Non-Solution to Meaningful Planning," *Center for Strategic and International Studies*, June 28, 2019, 19–21.

74. Ibid. See also Jeffrey Rathke, "NATO: Measuring Result, Not Dollars, in Transatlantic Security," *Center for Strategic and International Studies*, July 9, 2018.

75. Yost, "Grand Strategy and Strategic Surprise."

76. The author wishes to acknowledge the insights of the former US under-secretary of defense Frank Kendall on the need for reallocating roles and burden-sharing among allies.

77. Lostumbo et al., "Overseas Basing of U.S. Military Forces." On options for achieving greater efficiencies in the US force structure, see Susanna Blume, "How the United States Can Get More Strategic Bang for Its Force Structure Buck," *War on the Rocks*, February 1, 2018. On the debate about forward deployments, see Hal Brands, Peter D. Feaver, John J. Mearsheimer, and Stephen Walt, "Should America Retrench?," *Foreign Affairs*, November/December 2016.

78. Rick Berger and Mackenzie Eaglen, " 'Hard Choices' and Strategic Insolvency: Where the National Defense Strategy Falls Short," *War on the Rocks*, May, 16, 2019.

79. Dina Smeltz, Ivo Daalder, Karl Friedhoff, Craig Kafura, and Lily Wojtowicz, "America Engaged: 2018 Chicago Council Survey," *Chicago Council on Global Affairs*, 2018.

80. Julie Smith, "Getting Out and About: Talking with Americans Beyond Washington about Their Place in the World," *Texas National Security Review* 1, Issue 3, May 2018.

81. "2018 Midterm Voters: Issues and Political Values," *Pew Research Center*, October 4, 2018.

82. On democracies and alliance choice, see Michael W. Simon and Erik Gartzke, "Political System Similarity and the Choice of Allies: Do Democracies Flock Together or Do Opposites Attract?," *Journal of Conflict Resolution* 40, no. 4 (1996): 617–35. On the advantages of democracies in warfighting, see Dan Reiter and Allan C. Stam, *Democracies at War* (Princeton: Princeton University Press, 2002). For a critical perspective on democracy and war, see Michael C. Desch, "Democracy and Victory: Why Regime Type Hardly Matters," *International Security* 27, no. 2 (2002): 5–47.

83. Anthony J. Blinken and Robert Kagan, "America First Is Making the World Worse. Here's a Better Approach," *Washington Post*, January 1, 2019.

84. Celeste A. Wallander, "NATO's Enemies Within: How Democratic Decline Could Destroy the Alliance," *Foreign Affairs*, July/August 2018.

Chapter Five. Persuasion or Coercion?

1. Don Oberdorfer and Robert Carlin, *The Two Koreas: A Contemporary History* (New York: Basic Books, 2014), 247.

2. Leon V. Sigal, *Disarming Strangers: Nuclear Diplomacy with North Korea* (Princeton: Princeton University Press, 1998), 155.

3. Ibid., 277.

4. Joel S. Wit, Daniel B. Poneman, and Robert L. Gallucci, *Going Critical: The First North Korean Nuclear Crisis* (Washington, DC: Brookings, 2004), 327.

5. Jarrett Blanc, "Here's Why World Leaders Are Laughing at Trump," *Politico Magazine*, September 25, 2018.

6. Stares, *Preventive Engagement*, 2.

7. On employing sanctions as a deterrent strategy, see Edward Fishman, "Even Smarter Sanctions," *Foreign Affairs*, November/December 2017. On the distinctions between immediate and general deterrence and direct and extended deterrence, see Michael J. Mazarr, "Understanding Deterrence," *RAND Corporation*, 2018. On debates surrounding the conditions for successful deterrence and the role of alliances in deterring the onset of crisis and the escalation of disputes, see Paul Huth and Bruce Russett, "What Makes Deterrence Work? Cases from 1900–1980," *World Politics* 36, issue 4 (1984): 496–526; Jesse C. Johnson and Brett Ashley Leeds, "Defense Pacts: A Prescription for Peace," *Foreign Policy Analysis* 7, issue 1 (2011): 45–65; Michael R. Kenwick and John A. Vasquez, "Defense Pacts and Deterrence: Caveat Emptor," *Journal of Politics* 49, no. 1 (2017): 329–34.

8. See, e.g., Dale C. Copeland, *Economic Interdependence and War* (Princeton: Princeton University Press, 2015); Henry Farrell and Abraham L. Newman, "Weaponized Interdependence: How Global Economic Networks Shape State Coercion," *International Security* 44, issue 1 (2019): 42–79.

9. Levy places these differences in four categories: time, source of danger, fear of likely consequences, and incentives to strike first. See Jack S. Levy, "Declining Power and the Preventive Motivation for War," *World Politics* 40, no. 1 (1987): 82–107.

10. The key point is that power is filtered through perceptions and expectations. See ibid., 91.

11. On the three images and different levels of analysis, see Kenneth N. Waltz, *Man, The State, and War: A Theoretical Analysis* (New York: Columbia University Press, 2001).

12. Paul W. Schroeder, "World War I as Galloping Gertie: A Reply to Joachim Remak," quoted in Levy, "Declining Power and the Preventive Motivation for War," 82–107.

13. Ibid., 87.

14. Allison, *Destined for War.*

15. Schake, *Safe Passage.*

16. See, e.g., William Burr and Jeffrey T. Richelson, "Whether to 'Strangle the Baby in the Cradle': The United States and the Chinese Nuclear Program, 1960–64," *International Security* 25, issue 3 (2000–2001): 54–99; J. S. Levy and J. R. Gochal, "Democracy and Preventive War: Israel and the 1956 Sinai Campaign," *Security Studies* 11, issue 2 (2001): 1–49; Sean M. Lynn-Jones, "Détente and Deterrence: Anglo-German Relations, 1911–1914," *International Security* 11, no. 2 (1986): 121–50.

17. Francis Fukuyama, *America at the Crossroads: Democracy, Power, and the Neoconservative Legacy* (New Haven: Yale University Press, 2006); Keir A. Lieber and Daryl G. Press, "Why States Won't Give Nuclear Weapons to Terrorists," *International Security* 38, no. 1 (2013): 80–104.

18. Fukuyama, *America at the Crossroads,* 84–87; Francis Fukuyama, "After Neoconservatism," *New York Times Magazine,* February 19, 2006.

19. Robert Kagan, *Of Paradise and Power: America and Europe in the New World Order* (New York: Random House, 2004).

20. Evan Montgomery explores the conditions under which leading powers accommodate or oppose rising regional powers. See Montgomery, *In the Hegemon's Shadow: Leading States and the Rise of Regional Powers* (Ithaca: Cornell University Press, 2016).

21. See Charles Doran, *Systems in Crisis: New Imperatives of High Politics at Century's End* (Cambridge: Cambridge University Press, 2008); George Modeleski, *Long Cycles in World Politics* (New York: Palgrave Macmillan, 1987); Robert Gilpin, *War and Change in World Politics* (Cambridge: Cambridge University Press, 1983). The phrase "acute relative decline" comes from MacDonald and Parent, *Twilight of the Titans.*

22. Kennedy, *The Rise and Fall of the Great Powers,* 228.

23. Manufacturing output numbers are cited in ibid., 200, 228.

24. Friedberg, *Weary Titan,* 25.

25. Steel production numbers are cited in Kennedy, *The Rise and Fall of the Great Powers,* 200.

26. Friedberg, *Weary Titan,* 92.

27. Perkins, *The Great Rapprochement,* 158.

28. See, e.g., Norrin M. Ripsman and Jack S. Levy, "Wishful Thinking or Buying Time? The Logic of British Appeasement in the 1930s," *International Security* 33 (2008): 148–81.

29. Bradford Perkins, *The Great Rapprochement: England and the United States, 1895–1914* (New York: Atheneum, 1968), 18–19.

30. Schake, *Safe Passage,* 12.

31. Ibid.

32. See, e.g., Perkins, *The Great Rapprochement;* Charles A. Kupchan, Emanuel Adler, Jean-Marc Coicaud, and Yuen Foong Khong, *Power in Transition:*

The Peaceful Change of International Order (Tokyo: United Nations University Press, 2001).

33. Perkins, *The Great Rapprochement*, 141.

34. Ibid., 150.

35. Ibid., 56–57.

36. Kupchan et al., *Power in Transition*.

37. Charles S. Campbell, *Anglo-American Understanding, 1898–1903* (Santa Barbara: Greenwood Press, 1957), 299.

38. Schake, *Safe Passage*, 6; Charles A. Kupchan, *How Enemies Become Friends: The Sources of Stable Peace* (Princeton: Princeton University Press, 2012), 8.

39. See, e.g., D. Cameron Watt, *Succeeding John Bull: America in Britain's Place 1900–1975* (Cambridge: Cambridge University Press, 2008).

40. See, e.g., Friedberg, *Weary Titan*.

41. Kupchan et al., *Power in Transition*, 45.

42. Fareed Zakaria, *From Wealth to Power: The Unusual Origins of America's World Role* (Princeton: Princeton University Press, 1999), 5.

43. Campbell, *Anglo-American Understanding*, 23. As early as 1903 Russian designs on the Persian Gulf, Central Asia, and East Asia preoccupied British leaders. See ibid., 326.

44. Friedberg, *Weary Titan*, 179–80.

45. Perkins, *The Great Rapprochement*, 158.

46. On the cultural commonalities between the United States and Britain, the author wishes to acknowledge the insights of the historian and former US diplomat John Campbell.

47. See, e.g., Daniel M. Kliman, *Fateful Transitions: How Democracies Manage Rising Powers, from the Eve of World War I to China's Ascendance* (Philadelphia: University of Pennsylvania Press, 2015).

48. Schake, *Safe Passage*, 2.

49. Ibid., 271.

50. Kupchan, *How Enemies Become Friends*, 73–112.

51. See, e.g., Dale C. Copeland, *The Origins of Major War* (Ithaca: Cornell University Press, 2001).

52. Robert Jervis, *Perception and Misperception in International Politics* (Princeton: Princeton University Press, 1976).

53. See, e.g., Kupchan, *Vulnerability of Empire*.

54. Gaddis, "International Relations Theory and the End of the Cold War," 5.

55. Ibid., 18.

56. Scott A. Silverstone, *From Hitler's Germany to Saddam's Iraq: The Enduring False Promise of Preventive War* (New York: Rowman & Littlefield, 2018), 22.

57. Jonathan Kirshner, "Rationalist Explanations for War," *Security Studies* 10, issue 1 (2000): 143–50.

58. Charles Glasner notes that there can be a rational, as opposed to a purely cognitive, basis for the security dilemma. See Charles L. Glaser, "The Security Dilemma Revisited," *World Politics* 50, no. 1 (1997): 171–201.

59. See, e.g., Gaddis, "International Relations Theory and the End of the Cold War," 55–58; Hal Brands and Charles Edel, *The Lessons of Tragedy: Statecraft and World Order* (New Haven: Yale University Press, 2019).

60. Brent Durbin, "Bureaucratic Politics Approach," *Encyclopedia Britannica*, accessed August 2019.

61. A. F. K. Organski and Jacek Kugler, *The War Ledger* (Chicago: University of Chicago Press, 1980).

62. Jack S. Levy, "Power Transition Theory and the Rise of China," quoted in Robert S. Ross and Zhu Feng, eds., *China's Ascent: Power, Security, and the Future of International Politics* (Ithaca: Cornell University Press, 2008), 23–24.

63. Sun Tzu, *The Art of War* (London: Luzac, 1910), 24.

64. MacDonald and Parent, *Twilight of the Titans*, 14–15.

65. See, e.g., Edelstein, *Over the Horizon*; Shifrinson, *Rising Titans, Falling Giants*.

66. Goddard, *When Right Makes Might*.

67. The author wishes to acknowledge the insights of the former US deputy secretary of state William J. Burns on the opportunity to shape the environment within which China's rise takes place.

68. Ikenberry, *After Victory*.

69. See, e.g., Randall L. Schweller, "The Problem of International Order Revisited: A Review Essay," *International Security* 26, no. 1 (2001): 179; Ikenberry, *After Victory*; G. John Ikenberry, "Institutions, Strategic Restraint, and the Persistence of American Postwar Order," *International Security* 23, no. 3 (1998/1999): 43–78.

Chapter Six. People Power or Pinstripe Rule?

1. All passages from Nizam al-Mulk's text are quoted in Sarah Chayes, *Thieves of State: Why Corruption Threatens Global Security* (New York: W. W. Norton, 2015). Sarah's reflections on the mirror for princes literature and Nizam al-Mulk's text are developed in Sarah Chayes, *Thieves of State*, 8–15.

2. Ibid., 5.

3. Zephyr Teachout, *Corruption in America: From Benjamin Franklin's Snuff Box to Citizens United* (Cambridge: Harvard University Press, 2016), 19.

4. Mancur Olson, *The Rise and Decline of Nations: Economic Growth, Stagflation, and Social Rigidities* (New Haven: Yale University Press, 1984).

5. See, e.g., "Corruption Perceptions Index 2018," *Transparency International*; Beckley, *Unrivaled*, 68.

6. Daron Acemoğlu and James A. Robinson, *Why Nations Fail* (New York: Crown, 2012).

7. Sarah Chayes, "Kleptocracy in America," *Foreign Affairs*, September/October 2017.

8. Leslie Holmes, *Corruption: A Very Short Introduction* (Oxford: Oxford University Press, 2015), 6–7.

9. Sarah Chayes, "Corruption and State Fragility," *Fragility Study Group*, Policy Brief, no. 1, September 2016.

10. "How Do You Define Corruption?," *Transparency International*. Arnold Heidenheimer distinguishes between three models of corruption. See Arnold J. Heidenheimer and Michael Johnston, eds., *Political Corruption: Concepts and Contexts* (New York: Routledge, 2002), 7–10.

11. Ibid., 17.

12. Martin Gilens and Benjamin I. Page, "Testing Theories of American Politics: Elites, Interest Groups, and Average Citizens," *Perspectives on Politics* 12, no. 3 (2014): 564–81.

13. Sean Illing, "What America Can Learn from the Fall of the Roman Republic," *Vox*, January 5, 2019.

14. See, e.g., Samuel Huntington, *Political Order in Changing Societies* (New Haven: Yale University Press, 1996); Francis Fukuyama, "America in Decay," *Foreign Affairs*, September/October 2014.

15. Nancy MacLean, *Democracy in Chains: The Deep History of the Radical Right's Stealth Plan for America* (New York: Random House, 2017), xx.

16. Jane Mayer, *Dark Money* (New York: Random House, 2017), 6.

17. Ibid., xvii–xviii.

18. Fukuyama, "America in Decay."

19. Bill Allison and Sarah Harkins, "Fixed Fortunes: Biggest Corporate Interests Spend Billions, Get Trillions," *Sunlight Foundation*, November 17, 2014.

20. Fukuyama, "America in Decay"; Morris P. Fiorina, *Disconnect: The Breakdown of Representation in American Politics* (Norman: University of Oklahoma Press, 2011); Elmer E. Schattschneider, *The Semi-sovereign People: A Realist's View of Democracy in America* (Boston: Wadsworth, 1975).

21. Franklin Foer, "Russian-style Kleptocracy Is Infiltrating America," *The Atlantic*, March 2019.

22. See, e.g., ibid.

23. Daniel H. Nexon, "Toward a Neo-Progressive Foreign Policy," *Foreign Affairs*, September 4, 2018.

24. Raymond Lonergan, *Mr. Justice Brandeis, Great American* (New York: Columbia, 1941), 42.

25. Citizens United, Appellant v. Federal Election Commission, 558 U.S., 1, 33 (2010).

26. Ellen L. Wentraub, "Taking on Citizens United," *New York Times*, March 30, 2016.

27. Scott Casleton, "It's Time for Liberals to Get Over Citizens United," *Vox*, May 7, 2018.

28. Citizens United, Appellant v. Federal Election Commission, 558 U.S., 1, 41 (2010).
29. Josh Gerstein, "Supreme Court Overturns Bob McDonnell's Corruption Convictions," *Politico*, June 27, 2016.
30. McDonnell v. United States 579 U.S., 1, 28 (2016).
31. Fred Wertheimer, "Symposium: McDonnell Decision Substantially Weakens the Government's Ability to Prevent Corruption and Protect Citizens," *SCOTUSblog*, June 28, 2016.
32. Maggie Koerth, "How Money Affects Elections," *FiveThirtyEight*, September 10, 2018.
33. "New Voting Restrictions in America," *Brennan Center for Justice*.
34. Sarah Chayes, "A Hidden Cost of Corruption: Environmental Devastation," *Washington Post*, June 16, 2017.
35. Martin Gilens and Benjamin I. Page, "Testing Theories of American Politics: Elites, Interest Groups, and Average Citizens," *Perspectives on Politics* 12, no. 3 (2014): 564–81.
36. Levitsky and Ziblatt, *How Democracies Die*, 23–24.
37. David Frum, "America's Slide Toward Autocracy," *The Atlantic*, October 2018. See also David Frum, *Trumpocracy: The Corruption of the American Republic* (New York: HarperCollins, 2018).
38. See, e.g., Jane Mayer, "The Making of the Fox News White House," *New Yorker*, March 11, 2019.
39. See, e.g., Virginia H. Askan and Daniel Goffman, *The Early Modern Ottomans: Remapping the Empire* (Cambridge: Cambridge University Press, 2007); Christine Woodhead, "Consolidating the Empire: New Views on Ottoman History, 1453–1839," *English Historical Review* 123, no. 503 (2008): 973–87.
40. Woodhead, "Consolidating the Empire."
41. See, e.g., Cemal Kafadar, "The Question of Ottoman Decline," *Harvard Middle East and Islamic Review* 4 (1997–98): 30–75.
42. Karen Barkey, *Bandits and Bureaucrats: The Ottoman Route to State Centralization* (Ithaca: Cornell University Press, 1994), 2.
43. Kafadar, "The Question of Ottoman Decline," 38.
44. Francis Fukuyama, *The Origins of Political Order: From Prehuman Times to the French Revolution* (New York: Farrar, Straus, Giroux, 2012), 219.
45. Kafadar, "The Question of Ottoman Decline," 38.
46. Fukuyama, *The Origins of Political Order*, 218.
47. Kafadar, "The Question of Ottoman Decline," 38.
48. Alan Palmer, *The Decline and Fall of the Ottoman Empire* (New York: Barnes and Noble Books, 1992), 6.
49. Fukuyama, *The Origins of Political Order*, 223.
50. Ibid., 225.
51. Norman Itzkowitz, *Ottoman Empire and Islamic Tradition* (Chicago: University of Chicago Press, 1980), 89–90.

52. Ibid., 91–92.

53. Woodhead, "Consolidating the Empire," 976.

54. Ibid.; Linda T. Darling, *Revenue-raising and Legitimacy: Tax Collection and Finance Administration in the Ottoman Empire, 1560–1600* (Leiden: E. J. Brill, 1996). See also Suraiya N. Faroqhi, *The Cambridge History of Turkey*. Vol. III: *The Later Ottoman Empire, 1603–1839* (Cambridge: Cambridge University Press, 2006).

55. Woodhead, "Consolidating the Empire," 976; Dina Rizk Khoury, *State and Provincial Society in the Ottoman Empire: Mosul, 1540–1834* (Cambridge: Cambridge University Press, 1997).

56. Kafadar, "The Question of Ottoman Decline," 34.

57. Sarah Chayes, "Fighting the Hydra: Lessons from Worldwide Protests Against Corruption," *Carnegie Endowment for International Peace*, April 12, 2018.

58. Chayes, "Kleptocracy in America."

59. Rachel L. Kleinfeld, *A Savage Order: How the World's Deadliest Countries Can Forge a Path to Security* (New York: Random House, 2018).

60. Chayes, "Kleptocracy in America."

61. Martha C. Nussbaum, *Creating Capabilities: The Human Development Approach* (Cambridge: Harvard University Press, 2013); Amartya Sen, *Development as Freedom* (New York: Random House, 2000).

62. John Tzetzes, *Book of Histories (Chiliades)*, trans. Francis R. Walton, 2, 129–30, quoted in Chris Rorres, "The Lever: Quotations," *Archimedes*, accessed October 2019.

63. Nexon, "Toward a Neo-Progressive Foreign Policy."

64. Ibid.

65. Langston Hughes, "Let America Be America Again," poets.org.

Chapter Seven. Open or Closed?

1. This phrase is attributed to the former US senator from Missouri Carl Schurz. See Carl Schurz, Remarks in the Senate, February 29, 1872, quoted in "Respectfully Quoted: A Dictionary of Quotations. 1989," *Bartleby.com*.

2. John F. Kerry, *Every Day Is Extra* (New York: Simon & Schuster, 2018), 371.

3. Steven Pinker, *The Better Angels of Our Nature: Why Violence Has Declined* (New York: Penguin Group, 2011); Pasquale Cirillo and Nassim Nicholas Taleb, "On the Statistical Properties and Tail Risk of Violent Conflicts," *Physica A* 452 (2016): 29–45; Steven Pinker, "Fooled by Belligerence: Comments on Nassim Taleb's 'The Long Peace Is a Statistical Illusion,' " accessed August 2019; Bear F. Braumoeller, "Is War Disappearing?," Paper presented at the 109th Annual Convention of the American Political Science Association, Chicago, August 28–September 1, 2013; Zack Beauchamp, "This Fascinating Academic Debate Has

Huge Implications for the Future of World Peace," *Vox*, May 21, 2015. On the long peace during the Cold War, see John L. Gaddis, "The Long Peace: Elements of Stability in the Postwar International System," *International Security* 10 (1986): 99–142.

4. Robert Kagan, "Superpowers Don't Get to Retire: What Our Tired Country Still Owes the World," *New Republic*, May 26, 2014; Kagan, *The Jungle Grows Back*.

5. David Armitage, *The Declaration of Independence: A Global History* (Cambridge: Harvard University Press, 2007). See also Charles Edel, "How the Declaration of Independence Became a Beacon to the World," *Washington Post*, July 3, 2019.

6. Ibid., 3.

7. "Declaration of Independence: A Transcription," *National Archives*, July 4, 1776.

8. Danielle Allen, "The Declaration of Independence: Lessons for Citizenship in Challenging Times," Public Talk at Claremont McKenna College, February 8, 2018. See also Danielle Allen, *Our Declaration: A Reading of the Declaration of Independence in Defense of Equality* (New York: W. W. Norton, 2015).

9. Abraham Lincoln, "The Gettysburg Address," Bliss Copy, November 19, 1863.

10. Abraham Lincoln, "Second Inaugural Address," March 4, 1865.

11. Gaddis, *On Grand Strategy*, 232.

12. "President Woodrow Wilson's Fourteen Points," Avalon Project, Yale Law School, January 8, 1918.

13. Erez Manela, *The Wilsonian Moment: Self-Determination and the International Origins of Anticolonial Nationalism* (Oxford: Oxford University Press, 2007).

14. John J. Mearsheimer, "The False Promise of International Institutions," *International Security* 19, no. 3 (Winter 1994/1995): 5–49.

15. Woodrow Wilson, "Address in Support of the League of Nations." On the limits of Wilson's approach, see Mearsheimer, "The False Promise of International Institutions"; Hal Brands and Charles Edel, "How Woodrow Wilson Lost the Peace," *American Interest*, January 30, 2019.

16. "Atlantic Charter, Date: 1941," *Digital History*, accessed August 2019.

17. Robert Dallek, *Franklin Roosevelt and American Foreign Policy, 1932–1945* (Oxford: Oxford University Press, 1995), 282.

18. "Confidential: Press Conference #762, Executive Offices of the President, August 19, 1941," *Press Conferences of President Franklin D. Roosevelt, 1933–1945*, Franklin D. Roosevelt Presidential Library and Museum, accessed August 2019. Robert Dallek details this press briefing and the Atlantic Conference in Dallek, *Franklin Roosevelt and American Foreign Policy*, 283–84.

19. Ibid.

20. Jessica T. Matthews, "What Trump Is Throwing Out the Window," *New York Review of Books*, February 9, 2017; Fareed Zakaria, "FDR Started the Long Peace. Under Trump, It May Be Coming to an End," *Washington Post*, January 26, 2017.

21. G. John Ikenberry, "The Illusion of Geopolitics," *Foreign Affairs*, May/June 2014.

22. Warren F. Kimball, *Forged in War: Roosevelt, Churchill, and the Second World War* (New York: William Morrow, 1997), 198.

23. Ikenberry, *After Victory*. On America's moral vision for world order, see Kissinger, *World Order*, 256–79.

24. Patrick Porter, "A World Imagined: Nostalgia and Liberal Order," Policy Analysis No. 843, *CATO Institute*, June 5, 2018; Paul Staniland, "Misreading the 'Liberal Order': Why We Need New Thinking in American Foreign Policy," *Lawfare*, July 29, 2018.

25. On the realist origins of the postwar order, the author wishes to acknowledge Paul Staniland of the University of Chicago. See also Staniland, "Misreading the 'Liberal Order.' " On the connections between Indochina and European integration, see Mark Atwood Lawrence, *Assuming the Burden: Europe and the American Commitment to War in Vietnam* (Berkeley: University of California, 2005). On interference in elections, see Dov H. Levin, "When the Great Power Gets a Vote: The Effects of Great Power Electoral Interventions on Election Results," *International Studies Quarterly* 60, issue 2 (2016): 189–202; Elisabeth Malkin, "An Apology for a Guatemalan Coup, 57 Years Later," *New York Times*, October 20, 2011.

26. On the assumptions that underpinned the extension of liberal order in the 1990s, the author wishes to acknowledge Salman Ahmed of the Carnegie Endowment for International Peace.

27. See, e.g., George H. W. Bush and Brent Scowcroft, *A World Transformed* (New York: Random House, 1999), 89; Robert Zoellick, "Whither China? From Membership to Responsibility," Remarks to the National Committee on U.S.–China Relations, New York City, September 21, 2005; William J. Clinton, "China and the National Interest," Remarks at the Voice of America, Washington, DC, October 24, 1997. See also Svetlana Savranskaya and Mary Sarotte, eds., "The Clinton–Yeltsin Relationship in Their Own Words," Briefing Book #640, *National Security Archive*, October 2, 2018.

28. In 1997 the scholar Jessica T. Matthews anticipated many of the challenges and opportunities of regionalism and the diffusion of power to nonstate actors. See Matthews, "Power Shift," *Foreign Affairs*, January/February 1997.

29. See, e.g., William J. Clinton, "Inaugural Address," Washington, DC, January 20, 1997; Tony Blair, "Doctrine of the International Community," Chicago Economic Club, April 22, 1999.

30. See, e.g., Kagan, *The Jungle Grows Back;* Thomas Wright, "The Return to Great Power Rivalry Was Inevitable," *The Atlantic,* September 12, 2018.

31. Paul Musgrave and Daniel H. Nexon, "American Liberalism and the Imperial Temptation," in Noel Parker, ed., *Empire and International Order* (London: Routledge, 2013), 131–48.

32. On integrating Russia into international institutions, see Stephen Sestanovich, "Could It Have Been Otherwise?," *American Interest,* April 14, 2015. On overpromising and underdelivering on aid to Russia, see James M. Goldgeier and Michael McFaul, *Power and Purpose: U.S. Policy Toward Russia After the Cold War* (Washington, DC: Brookings Institution Press, 2003), 356.

33. On "embedded liberalism," see Ruggie, "International Regimes, Transactions, and Change."

34. Sargent, *A Superpower Transformed,* 2.

35. Dani Rodrik, "Globalization's Wrong Turn," *Foreign Affairs,* July/August 2019.

36. See, e.g., Gary Clyde Hufbauer and Zhiyao Lu, "The Payoff to America from Globalization: A Fresh Look with a Focus on Costs to Workers," *Peterson Institute for International Economics,* May 2017.

37. Franklin D. Roosevelt, "December 29, 1940: Fireside Chat 16: On the 'Arsenal of Democracy,' " *Miller Center,* University of Virginia.

38. Andrew Glass, "Congress Passes Johnson Debt Default Act, April 13, 1934," *Politico,* April 13, 2018.

39. Lynne Olson, *Those Angry Days: Roosevelt, Lindbergh, and America's Fight Over World War II, 1939–1941* (New York: Random House, 2014), 222.

40. Ibid., 223.

41. Ibid., 225, 311.

42. Kennedy later changed his views and urged support for Britain and intervention on behalf of America's European allies. See Olson, *Those Angry Days,* 224, 286.

43. Lend-Lease Bill, H.R. 1776, 77th Cong. (1941).

44. Ibid., 55.

45. Ibid., 277.

46. The interventionist camp grappled with its own divisions. Some believed that US interests required vigorous aid to Britain short of joining the war. Others advocated for direct involvement. See Wayne S. Cole, *America First: The Battle Against Intervention 1940–41* (New York: Norton, 1953).

47. Nicholas Wapshott, *The Sphinx: Franklin Roosevelt, the Isolationists, and the Road to World War II* (New York: W. W. Norton), 249.

48. Olson, *Those Angry Days,* 278.

49. Ibid., 286.

50. On the diverse rationales and motivations of the noninterventionist camp, see Cole, *America First;* Justus D. Doenecke, *In Danger Undaunted:*

The Anti-Interventionist Movement of 1940–1941 (Stanford: Hoover Institution Press, 1990).

51. Olson, *Those Angry Days*, 236.
52. Krishnadev Calamur, "A Short History of 'America First,' " *The Atlantic*, January 21, 2017.
53. Charles Lindbergh, "Des Moines Speech," Des Moines, Iowa, September 11, 1941.
54. This section draws on Sarah Churchwell's account of the history of America First in Churchwell, "End of the American Dream? The Dark History of 'America First,' " *The Guardian*, April 21, 2018.
55. Donald J. Trump, "Remarks by President Trump to the 73rd Session of the United Nations General Assembly," New York, September 25, 2018.
56. Joseph Nye, "Globalism versus Globalization," *The Globalist*, April 15, 2002; Robert O. Keohane and Joseph S. Nye Jr., *Power and Interdependence* (New York: Pearson, 2011).
57. "Franklin D. Roosevelt, 1941 State of the Union Address 'The Four Freedoms' (6 January 1941)," *Voices of Democracy*, U.S. Oratory Project, accessed August 2019.
58. John F. Kerry, "Remarks on the Release of the 2015 Country Reports on Human Rights Practices," April 13, 2016.
59. Patrick Porter, "A World Imagined: Nostalgia and Liberal Order," Policy Analysis Number 843, *CATO Institute*, June 5, 2018. On the question of multiple liberal orders, see Alastair I. Johnston, "The Failures of the 'Failure of Engagement' with China," *Washington Quarterly* 42, issue 2 (2019): 99–114.
60. Graham Allison, "The Myth of the Liberal Order," *Foreign Affairs*, July/ August 2018.
61. Mearsheimer, *The Great Delusion*, viii.
62. Mira Rapp-Hooper and Rebecca F. Lissner, "The Liberal Order Is More Than a Myth," *Foreign Affairs*, July 31, 2018.
63. Ibid.
64. Daniel H. Nexon, "On American Hegemony, Part II: Liberal Order, What Is the Concept Good For?," *Lawyers, Guns, and Money*, July 29, 2018.
65. Ibid.
66. On the permutations of sovereignty, see Stephen Krasner, *Sovereignty: Organized Hypocrisy* (Princeton: Princeton University Press, 1999). On the medieval roots of representative institutions in the West, see Brian Downing, *The Military Revolution and Political Change* (Princeton: Princeton University Press, 1992). On the peaceful succession of liberal powers, see Schake, *Safe Passage*.
67. The RAND political scientist Michael J. Mazarr notes that critiques of liberal order "typically conflate three different orders: the post-war institutional order, the components of that system that espouse liberal values,

and the U.S.-led global military order with its goal of U.S. primacy." See Mazarr, "The Real History of the Liberal Order," *Foreign Affairs*, August 7, 2018.

68. See, e.g., Jennifer Lind and William C. Wohlforth, "The Future of the Liberal Order Is Conservative," *Foreign Affairs*, March/April 2019.

69. John F. Kerry, "Saving Our Future," *New York Times*, September 23, 2018.

70. Jake Sullivan, Daniel Baer, and Jennifer Harris, "Trump Is Partly Right About Trade Deals. He's Wrong About How to Fix Them," *Politico Magazine*, March 15, 2018; Salman Ahmed et al., "U.S. Foreign Policy for the Middle Class: Perspectives from Ohio," *Carnegie Endowment for International Peace*, 2018.

71. Ibid.

72. Richard Youngs, "Upholding Democracy in a Post-Western Order," *Carnegie Endowment for International Peace*, February 2019.

73. The author wishes to acknowledge Amitav Acharya of American University. See Acharya, *The End of American World Order*.

74. Youngs, "Upholding Democracy in the Post-Western Order."

75. On proposals for targeting democracy assistance, see Andrea Kendall-Taylor, Testimony Before the House Permanent Select Committee on Intelligence, Hearing on "Autocracy's Advance and Democracy's Decline: National Security Implications of the Rise of Authoritarianism Around the World," February 26, 2019; Thomas Carothers and Frances Z. Brown, "Can U.S. Democracy Promotion Survive Trump?," *Carnegie Endowment for International Peace*, October 1, 2018.

76. Stephen J. Stedman, "Spoiler Problems in Peace Processes," *International Security* 22, no. 2 (1997): 5–53.

77. Or, as Robert Kagan asks, "how can autocrats enter the liberal international order without succumbing to the forces of liberalism?" Kagan, "The End of the End of History," *New Republic*, April 23, 2008.

78. See, e.g., Thomas Wright, "The Return to Great-Power Rivalry Was Inevitable," *The Atlantic*, September 12, 2018; Jake Sullivan, "More, Less, or Different," *Foreign Affairs*, January/February, 2019.

79. Robert Zoellick, "Whither China? From Membership to Responsibility," *National Committee on U.S.–China Relations*, September 21, 2005.

80. Brunnermeier, Doshi, and James, "Beijing's Bismarckian Ghosts."

81. On "the politics of eternity," see Timothy Snyder, *Road to Unfreedom: Russia, Europe, America* (New York: Random House, 2018), 8.

82. Roger Cohen, "Counterrevolutionary Russia," *New York Times*, June 25, 2015.

83. On the dangers of national majorities seeking wholeness in an age of globalization, see Arjun Appadurai, *Fear of Small Numbers: An Essay on the Geography of Anger* (Durham: Duke University Press, 1999).

84. Václav Havel, *The Power of the Powerless: Citizens Against the State in Central Eastern Europe* (New York: Routledge, 2016), 43.

85. W. B. Yeats, "The Second Coming."

86. Friedrich Nietzsche quoted in Walter Kaufmann, ed., *The Portable Nietzsche* (New York: Penguin Books, 1977), 468.

87. "Third Inaugural Address of Franklin D. Roosevelt," January 20, 1941, Avalon Project, Yale Law School.

88. Franklin D. Roosevelt, "Third Inaugural Address," January 20, 1941.

Chapter Eight. America's Way Forward

1. In telling the history of Project Solarium, I draw on Valerie L. Adams, *Eisenhower's Fine Group of Fellows: Crafting a National Security Policy to Uphold the Great Equation* (New York: Lexington Books, 2006), 47; Raymond Millen, "Eisenhower and U.S. Grand Strategy," *Parameters* 44 (2014): 35–47; Marvin Kalb, "American Foreign Policy: Obama Should Summon His Own Project Solarium," *Brookings*, July 18, 2013.

2. Aaron Friedberg, *In the Shadow of the Garrison State: America's Anti-Statism and Its Cold War Grand Strategy* (Princeton: Princeton University Press, 2000).

3. Dwight D. Eisenhower, "Annual Message to the Congress on the State of the Union, February 2, 1953," *Eisenhower Foundation*, accessed August 2019.

4. Millen, "Eisenhower and U.S. Grand Strategy," 38.

5. Ibid., 39.

6. "A Report to the National Security Council by the Executive Secretary on Basic National Security Policy," October 30, 1951, 23.

7. A number of policy makers and analysts have proposed Solarium as a model for national security planning and cyber security. See Michèle Flournoy, "Strategic Planning for National Security: A New Project Solarium," *Joint Forces Quarterly* 41 (2006): 80–86. For more on Solarium as a model for defending against cyber threats, see Peter Feaver and Will Inboden, "Washington Needs a New Solarium Project to Counter Cyberthreats," *Foreign Policy*, June 26, 2018; Steve Slick, "U.S. Intelligence Should Embrace Sasse Solarium Commission," *War on the Rocks*, August 16, 2018.

8. For arguments in favor of restraint, see Posen, *A New Foundation for U.S. Grand Strategy*; Jeremy Shapiro (moderator), Barry Posen, and Robert Kagan (panelists), "U.S. Grand Strategy: World Leader or Restrained Power?," *Brookings Institution*, October 14, 2014; Gholz, Press, and Sapolsky, "Come Home, America," 5–48. For arguments in favor of offshore balancing, see Mearsheimer and Walt, "The Case for Offshore Balancing." See also Walt, *The Hell of Good Intentions*; Mearsheimer, *The Great Delusion*. For a critique of offshore balancing, see Brands, "Fools Rush Out?" For debates around offshore balancing, see Brands, Feaver, Mearsheimer, and Walt, "Should America Retrench?"

9. Shapiro (moderator), Posen and Kagan (panelists), "U.S. Grand Strategy."

10. On the differences among restrainers on this point, see MacDonald and Parent, *Twilight of the Titans*, 198. See also Mearsheimer, *The Great Delusion*.

11. These and other historical examples are noted in Mearsheimer and Walt, "The Case for Offshore Balancing."

12. See, e.g., ibid.

13. For advocates of this approach, see Stephen G. Brooks and William C. Wohlforth, *America Abroad: Why the Sole Superpower Should Not Pull Back from the World* (Oxford: Oxford University Press, 2018); Brooks, Ikenberry, and Wohlforth, "Lean Forward"; G. John Ikenberry, *Liberal Leviathan: The Origins, Crisis and Transformation of the American World Order* (Princeton: Princeton University Press, 2012); Ikenberry, *After Victory*.

14. Brands, Feaver, Mearsheimer, and Walt, "Should America Retrench?"

15. On primacy, see Kagan, *Of Paradise and Power;* William Kristol and Robert Kagan, "Toward a Neo-Reaganite Foreign Policy," *Foreign Affairs,* July/August 1996; Robert Kagan and William Kristol, eds., *Present Dangers: Crisis and Opportunity in American Foreign and Defense Policy* (San Francisco: Encounter Books, 2000); Joshua Muravchik, *The Imperative of American Leadership: A Challenge to Neo-Isolationism* (Washington, DC: AEI Press, 1996). For assessments of primacy in comparative perspective, see Barry R. Posen and Andrew L. Ross, "Competing Visions for U.S. Grand Strategy," *International Security* 21, no. 3 (Winter 1996/97): 5–53; Michael E. Brown, Owen R. Coté Jr., Sean M. Lynn-Jones, Steven E. Miller, and Graham Allison, eds., *Primacy and Its Discontents* (Cambridge: MIT Press, 2009).

16. The political scientists Barry Posen and Andrew Ross elaborate on these distinctions in "Competing Visions for U.S. Grand Strategy."

17. See, e.g., Eric A. Nordlinger, *Isolationism Reconfigured* (Princeton: Princeton University Press, 1996).

18. Walter A. McDougall, *Promised Land, Crusader State: The American Encounter with the World Since 1776* (New York: Houghton Mifflin, 1997), 39–56.

19. MacDonald and Parent, *Twilight of the Titans*, 196. See also Stephen M. Walt, "Restraint Isn't Isolationism—and It Won't Endanger America," *Foreign Policy,* July 22, 2019.

20. Reinhold Niebuhr, *The Children of Light and the Children of Darkness: A Vindication of Democracy and a Critique of Its Traditional Defense* (Chicago: University of Chicago Press, 2011), 118.

21. Diamond, "Democracy Demotion."

22. Carothers and Brown, "Can U.S. Democracy Promotion Survive Trump?"

23. Casimir Yost argues that a "critical and necessary change is the addition of a permanent office in the White House responsible for strategic planning

and anticipation with special responsibility for providing continuity during changes of administrations. This means the office would not turn over or expire when an administration leaves office—though, of course, the incoming president would appoint its new director." See Yost, "Grand Strategy and Strategic Surprise," 4.

24. On reviving America's innovation ecosystem and economy through investments in science, see Gruber and Johnson, *Jump-starting America*. On the concept of a unified national security budget, see Task Force on a Unified Security Budget, "Rebalancing Our National Security," *Center for American Progress*, October 30, 2012; Catherine Dale, Nina M. Serafino, and Pat Towell, "A Unified National Security Budget? Issues for Congress," *Congressional Research Service*, March 14, 2013; Brett Rosenberg and Jake Sullivan, "The Case for a National Security Budget," *Foreign Affairs*, November 19, 2019.

25. The former US deputy secretary of state Bill Burns makes a compelling case for both in his memoir. See Burns, *The Back Channel*.

26. Jake Sullivan, "The New Old Democrats," *Democracy*, June 20, 2018.

27. See, e.g., James Fallows and Deborah Fallows, *Our Towns: A 100,000-Mile Journey into the Heart of America* (New York: Pantheon, 2018).

28. Jennifer Harris, "Making Trade Address Inequality," *Democracy*, no. 48. (2018); Adrian Henry Macey, "How Trade Policies Can Support Global Efforts to Curb Climate Change," *The Conversation*, July, 27, 2017; Heather Hurlburt, "Back to Basics: The Core Goals a 'Progressive' Foreign Policy Must Address," *Texas National Security Review*, December 4, 2018.

29. Harris, "Making Trade Address Inequality."

30. See, e.g., Tellis, "Seeking Alliances and Partnerships"; Ashley J. Tellis, "The Geopolitics of the TTIP and TPP," quoted in Sanjaya Baru and Suvi Dogra, eds., *Power Shifts and New Blocs in the Global Trading System* (London: Routledge, 2015), 93–120; Kurt M. Campbell and Ely Ratner, "The China Reckoning," *Foreign Affairs*, March/April 2018; Campbell and Sullivan, "Competition Without Catastrophe"; Johnston, "The Failures of the 'Failure of Engagement' with China."

31. Percy Bysshe Shelley, "Ozymandias," *Poetry Foundation*.

Index

247